*Key History
for GCSE*

# Key Themes of the Twentieth Century

*Philip Sauvain*

Stanley Thornes (Publishers) Ltd

First published in 1996 by:
Stanley Thornes (Publishers) Ltd
Ellenborough House
Wellington Street
CHELTENHAM  GL50 1YW
England

96 97 98 99 00 / 10 9 8 7 6 5 4 3 2 1

A catalogue record for this book is available from the British
Library.

ISBN 0-7487-2549-0

Printed and bound in Hong Kong

## Acknowledgements

The author and publishers are grateful to the following
for permission to reproduce illustrations and photographs
in this book.

Courtesy AEEU (photo Derek Davies) 46t; Makovsky
Death in the Snow, 1905/Museum of the Revolution,
Moscow/Bridgeman Art Library, London 52; AKG,
London 85/© DACS 1996 73, 77; Bundesarchiv, Koblenz
78t, 82t, 84, 89tr, 142t; Camera Press 145tr, 166b,
186t, 189t; Centre for the Study of Cartoons and
Caricature, University of Kent/Solo Syndication 110b,
119, 144, 149tr, 150b,© Telegraph plc London 1980
172cl; Jean-Loup Charmet 10t, 68br; J. Launois/Black
Star/Colorific! 134b; Corbis 100; ET Archive 9r, 12t, 135;
Mary Evans Picture Library 19tr; Fotomas 8, 89; German
Embassy Photo Library 155t; Granger Collection 91;
Hulton-Deutsch Collection 49, 159; Imperial War
Museum 125, 127, 128, 129, 130, 137b, 139; David
King 59tr, 63, 64, 65, 66, 67t, 122, 156; National
Archives Trust Fund Bond, Washington 124b; Novosti
57; Photri 121, 132, 149; Popperfoto 99t, 148, 152t,
157, 188, 190; Punch 103, 106t, 113t, 118b, 134t,
136, 137t, 141tr & cr; Rex Features 156, 160, 164t,
165, 167b, 170, 172, 174, 178, 183, 191; Richard
Sauvain 126t; School of Slavonic and East European
Studies 151; Solo Syndication 155b; Frank Spooner
Pictures 164b, 176; Topham Picturepoint 169, 182,
186b; Visual Arts Library 68bl, 95.

Other illustrations and photographs were supplied by the
author.

Every effort has been made to contact copyright holders
and we apologise if any have been overlooked.

# Contents

# 1 Changing Britain: 1900-14

## The first welfare state

▶ **How far was the Welfare State established by 1914?**
**How far had the system of Government in Britain changed by 1914?**

### Democracy and poverty

For all its apparent prosperity and success (Source **A**). Britain in 1900 was not yet a true democracy and its wealth was very unevenly shared. Only one adult in every three had a vote, and half the people (the women) weren't allowed to vote at all. A further third of all men did not qualify as voters because they were not classed as householders or because they paid less than £10 a year in rent. Not only did women lack the right to vote, they were unfairly treated by employers and by the law (page 8). Many were also poor. Despite the country's great wealth, millions of people lived in conditions of desperate poverty (Source **B**).

**Source B**   The causes of poverty in 1900

| Old age | Out of work |
|---|---|
| No retirement pensions | No unemployment benefit |
| Illness | Low wages |
| No sickness benefit | Very low rates of pay |
| Large families | Disability |
| No maternity allowance, child benefit or family income support | No disability benefit or compensation for injuries |
| One-parent families | Orphans |
| No widows' or one-parent benefits | No orphans' benefit |

**Source A**   By 1900, London, the capital of a vast empire, was the most important industrial, trading, business and finance centre in the world - and its largest city

In 1910, the Liberal politician, David Lloyd George, told a meeting:

'Four spectres haunt the Poor – Old Age, Accident, Sickness and Unemployment. We are going to get rid of them. We are going to drive hunger from the home.'

State aid for the poor was limited, although the old, the sick and the handicapped could live in the local workhouse, a grim building paid for out of local rates. The unemployed could also apply for help from the locally-elected Guardians of the Poor. They got cash or food in return for work, such as breaking stones or repairing roads. Aid was only given to those in desperate need and even then was not enough. Many people turned to the charities for help, such as the Salvation Army.

### The first Welfare State

What was to be done? The population of the cities was growing fast. Some people feared a revolution, the growth of socialism, or the spread of a deadly epidemic from the slums. Others thought it immoral that so many should be so poor. Hopes were high, then, when a Liberal Government, promising reform, was elected in 1906 with a massive majority. A new Prime Minister, Herbert Asquith, and his Chancellor of the Exchequer, David Lloyd George, began to lay the

A scene on the Thames Embankment – grim contrast in the social scale. This picture vividly represents how our beautiful Embankment is given up to people at the extreme ends of the social scale. The Embankment is a favourite way by which business men dash to and from the City in the mornings and evenings. The seats on the pavement, on the other hand, are crowded with some of the dirtiest specimens of our lowest classes.

**Source C** Picture and caption from *The Sphere* magazine, 26 August 1905

foundations of the modern Welfare State. Supported by the newly-formed Labour Party, the Liberals brought in laws to help children in 1906–8, old age pensions in 1908, job centres (called labour exchanges) in 1909, and a health and unemployment insurance scheme in 1911.

## Old Age Pensions

The question of Old Age Pensions was debated in Parliament in July 1908 (Sources **D** and **E**). From 1 January 1909, old people were paid a tiny, weekly pension of 5s (25p) a week if they were British, over 70 years of age, resident in the UK, not already in receipt of poor relief and had an existing income of less than £21 a year.

**Source D** Lady Asquith interviewed on BBC television in about 1960

My father [Herbert Asquith] introduced old age pensions, 5 shillings a week only [on 7 May 1908]. It sounds a meagre amount now but it aroused the most furious opposition. Lord Lansdowne said it would undermine the thrift and self-respect of the working classes of this country. Lord Rosebery, a Liberal, warned that it might deal a mortal blow to the Empire. Can you believe that such days and such men existed? There in the House of Lords, these cosy old peers living fatly on an unearned income. What about their self-respect and moral fibre?

**Source E** Will Crooks, a Labour MP, in Parliament, 9 July 1908

Here in a country rich beyond description there are people poverty-stricken beyond description. If it be necessary to have a strong Army and Navy to protect the wealth of the nation, do not let us forget that it is the veterans of industry who have created that wealth. Let us bring decency and comfort to our aged men and women.

Quoted in *Contemporary Sources and Opinions in Modern British History*, edited by Lloyd Evans and Philip J. Pledger, Frederick Warne, 1967

**Source F** From *Lark Rise to Candleford*, by Flora Thompson

When the Old Age Pensions began, life was transformed for such aged cottagers. They were relieved of anxiety. They were suddenly rich. Independent for life! At first when they went down to the Post Office to draw it, tears of gratitude would run down the cheeks of some, and they would say as they picked up their money, 'God bless that Lord George'.

**Q**uestions

1 Make a list of the arguments which were, or could have been, used to justify the granting of old age pensions in 1908–9. What arguments were used against?

2 Look at Source **C**. Did the artist have the same attitude to London's poor as the caption writer?

3 What are the advantages and disadvantages of using a picture like this as historical evidence?

## Improving living conditions for children

One way of dealing with poverty was to feed the children. In 1906 the School Meals Act gave education authorities the power to provide school meals for pupils who were

'unable, by lack of food, to take advantage of the education provided for them.'

Bradford's schoolchildren enjoyed

'solid, tasty, two-course dinners consisting of broths, pies, vegetables, and puddings, with occasionally meat or fish.'

A similar reform set up the school medical service in 1907. Regular health inspections in schools helped doctors treat skin and hair diseases, such as scabies and impetigo. The Children's Charter (1908) stopped children under 16 buying cigarettes and using pubs. Juvenile courts were set up and child offenders sent to Borstal institutions instead of prison.

## Opposition to social reform

Many people complained about the cost of these reforms. Others disliked the idea of the State helping people who should (they thought) be helping themselves. They said it was not the job of the State to educate and feed working class children, pay old people a pension, or help insure workers against sickness and unemployment.

The opposition was particularly angered by Lloyd George's 'People's Budget' in 1909 (Source **G**). As Chancellor of the Exchequer, he proposed to pay for social reforms by taxing the rich (Source **H**).

The Tories were furious. The unelected House of Lords, the majority of whom were rich and Conservative, vetoed (voted against) the 'People's Budget' in November 1909, saying the people should decide the matter at the polls. This was intolerable to the House of Commons. So after the election two months later, the new Liberal government, supported by Labour, decided to abolish the veto anyway. The

**Source H** Tax proposals in the People's Budget 1909

- Income tax raised to 1s 2d (6p) in every pound for people with more than £2000 a year.
- Income tax of 1s 4½d (7p) in the pound for those with more than £5000 a year [over 50 times the income of the average worker].
- Death duties doubled. [These were taxes on property and wealth handed on when someone died.]
- Special tax on people who owned land.

King agreed to create enough new peers to outvote the Conservatives, provided the people agreed. The second election brought no change, so the Lords gave in. The Parliament Bill of 1911 took away their veto. From this time on, the elected House of Commons ruled Britain, not the unelected House of Lords.

## Health and unemployment insurance

In March 1911, Lloyd George announced plans for a State scheme for compulsory health and unemployment insurance. The health proposals were bitterly opposed by doctors who said it would not pay them fairly for their work (Source **I**). But it proved a boon to the poorest workers who could not afford to go to a doctor. For many years afterwards, workers off sick said they 'were on the Lloyd George.'

The unemployment insurance scheme applied at first to under three million people in trades where workers were often laid off, such as the building industry. They were paid 7 shillings (35p) a week for up to fifteen weeks provided they could work, were not on strike, had worked for over six months in the last five years, and had paid sufficient contributions into the fund. By 1920, the scheme had been extended to cover 12 million workers.

**Source G** May 1909. Newspaper posters show what the Press thought of the 'People's Budget'.

Source J Protest meeting in Trafalgar Square

**Source I** National Insurance Act: Health proposals 1911

- Covered 15 million workers earning less than £160 a year.
- Cost 9d (4p) a week: workers paid 4d, employers 3d, Government 2d.
- Did not apply to: the self-employed, wives, farmworkers, domestic servants, women workers (until 1920).
- Benefits: free medical treatment and medicines, sickness benefit when absent from work, disablement benefit if away for more than six months.

## Political protest

During this period of social reform, the power of the trade unions was growing fast. Until 1900, MPs were not paid, so only the well-to-do entered the House of Commons. Then, in 1900, the Labour Representation Committee (LRC) was formed and paid trade union MPs a small wage out of funds provided mainly by the unions making a small charge, or levy, on each of their members. Two MPs were elected in 1900 and 30 in 1906 when the LRC changed its name to the Labour Party. In 1910, however, a judge ruled that the levy was illegal. This is why the Liberal Government

brought in two new laws. The first, in 1911, paid all MPs an official salary for the first time. The second, in 1913, made it lawful for a trade union to charge a political levy provided members could opt out if they wished.

Despite this, there were many bitter strikes, as trade unions fought to improve their pay and working conditions. Coal miners in South Wales confronted police and troops. In 1914, the railwaymen joined with other transport workers and the miners to form the Triple Alliance, so that joint action could be taken in disputes affecting their unions. By working together they could paralyse the country and bring it to a standstill.

1 Write a paragraph in your own words, saying how the Liberal Government helped children, the elderly, the ill, and the unemployed between 1906 and 1914.

2 How useful are the newspaper posters (Source **G**) as evidence of different attitudes to the Liberal reforms? How do they differ?

3 Design a poster *either* attacking the Liberal Party's social reforms *or* telling workers about the National Insurance proposals.

Questions

## The Suffragettes

▶ *How did the position of women in Britain change in the early years of the century?*

### Discrimination against women

Although working class men could sit in Parliament, women, no matter how rich or talented, could not. This was just one form of discrimination against women at that time. Husbands could get a divorce more easily than their wives. They were more likely to be given custody of the children. Few women went to university or became lawyers, businesswomen, doctors or dentists. Most jobs were for young women, although older women could work in a factory or as a servant. Where women did the same work as men, they were almost always paid less. Employers, like everyone else, assumed that when a woman married, she would leave her job to look after her husband.

### Fighting for women's rights

Some women were no longer prepared to put up with these disadvantages. They wanted equal pay for equal work and the same opportunities and same rights as a man. Above all, they wanted suffrage – the right to vote. Only then could they elect MPs who would support changes in the law to end discrimination. Those in favour of gradual change were suffragists. Those who wanted action now were suffragettes – members of the Women's Social and Political Union (WSPU) founded by Emmeline Pankhurst in 1903. Their opponents formed the National League for Opposing Women's Suffrage (Source **A**). You can see some of the arguments used by both sides in these sources.

**Source A**   Poster issued in 1912 by the National League for Opposing Women's Suffrage.

**Source C**   Frederick Ryland in 1896

Why should a person otherwise qualified be refused a vote simply on the ground of sex? Mrs.B's gardener or coachman will probably have a vote, while she is without one.

Extract from *The Girl's Own Paper*, 16 May 1896

**Source D**   Sir Edward Clarke (lawyer and former Conservative MP) in a speech in January 1913

Women are much less educated than men. Studying politics would make a woman a much worse mother and a much less pleasant wife.

**Source B**   Letter to *The Times*, 20 January 1913

Women, it is said, must not vote because they cannot fight. As well say that men should not vote because they cannot bear children.

**Source E**   Herbert Asquith (Liberal Prime Minister 1908–16)

I do not think you will bring this change about until you have satisfied the country that the majority of women are in favour of it.

## The suffragette campaign

At first the suffragettes held meetings and made their protests in a noisy but peaceful fashion. But when Mrs Pankhurst's daughter, Christabel, and Annie Kenney, a cotton worker, were arrested at a public meeting in Manchester, they were sent to prison after refusing to pay a fine. Emmeline Pankhurst described the consequences (Source **F**).

The suffragettes put up posters, chained themselves to railings, broke windows and set fire to letter boxes. When they went to prison, they refused to eat. Prison authorities were afraid a suffragette might die in prison, so they forcibly fed the prisoners on hunger strike (Sources **H** and **I**).

**Source G** Protesting suffragettes expelled from Parliament.

**Source F** By Emmeline Pankhurst

It was the beginning of a campaign the like of which was never known in England. We interrupted a great many meetings. Always we were violently thrown out and insulted. Often we were painfully bruised and hurt.

Extract from *My Own Story*, by Emmeline Pankhurst, Eveleigh Nash, 1914.

**Source H** Mary Leigh, a suffragette, was forcibly fed in prison

The sensation is most painful, the drums of the ears seem to be bursting and there is a horrible pain in the throat and breast. I have to lie on the bed, pinned down by two wardresses, one doctor stands on a chair holding the funnel end at arm's length, and the other doctor forces the other end up the nostrils. The one holding the funnel end pours the liquid down.

Quoted in *Shoulder to Shoulder*, by Midge Mackenzie, Penguin

**Source I** Suffragette poster issued by the WSPU

Many MPs supported the suffragettes but some Liberals, including Asquith, were afraid that more Conservative women than Liberals would qualify as voters, since they were more likely to own property. The delay in granting the vote further infuriated the suffragettes. Telephone wires were cut and buildings set on fire. There were many more arrests and the Prisoners' Temporary Discharge for Ill Health Act – or 'Cat and Mouse Act' – was passed. Prisoners on hunger strike were released when very ill and sent back to prison when they got better. Emmeline Pankhurst went to prison twelve times in as many months and became very weak. In June 1913 Emily Wilding Davison died after being knocked down by a horse at the Derby, while making a protest for the suffragette movement. The Prime Minister was attacked as he played golf in Scotland. Valuable paintings were badly damaged. As a result, many supporters turned against the suffragettes (Source **J**). The campaign ended when war broke out in August 1914 (page 32).

**Source J** Lloyd George – after his house was badly damaged by suffragettes

Hasn't she the sense to see that the very worst way of campaigning for the franchise is to try to intimidate or blackmail a man into giving her what he would gladly give her otherwise?

Questions

1  Using the sources, list the arguments that people used **a)** to attack and **b)** to defend votes for women.

2  How could the suffragists and suffragettes prove to Asquith 'that the majority of women' wanted the right to vote?

3  Look at Sources **A** and **I**. Which do you think is the more effective poster? Why?

4  Did the suffragettes help or hinder the votes for women campaign? Discuss this with your friends or write a paragraph explaining your answer.

## Overview: Long-term causes of the First World War

### Why did tension increase in Europe between 1900 and 1914?

### Colonial Rivalry

The German Kaiser wanted to expand his 'growing' empire (Source **B**). In 1905, when France and Britain discussed the future of Morocco (in North Africa), he went to Tangier to show that Germany had an interest there too. After French troops put down a rebellion in Morocco in 1911, the Kaiser nearly started the First World War there and then, when he sent the gunboat *Panther* to the Moroccan port of Agadir. The French had to give Germany part of the French Congo before Morocco became part of their empire.

### The Arms Race

Every major power except Britain had trained a huge army of conscripts (young men forced by law to become soldiers for a year or so), which could be mobilised (called-up) at a moment's notice. Guns, shells, bullets and other weapons had been stockpiled in case of war. Although Britain only had a small professional army, her Royal Navy was the most powerful in the world. Since it outgunned and outnumbered all other navies, Britain as an island must be safe – or was it? Many people worried when Germany began to build a navy as well. Why did she need warships as well as Europe's largest army? The Kaiser's reasons (Source **B**) were not convincing since the German Empire was small (see map on page 38). When the British built the super-battleship, *Dreadnought*, in 1906, Germany followed suit. In 1909, Britain had eight *Dreadnoughts* to Germany's seven. By 1914, Britain had 24 with 11 more to be completed. Germany had 15 with 6 more to be launched.

**Source A** France's President Loubet (right) meets Russia's Tsar Nicholas II (left) in 1902. The slogan below the two men suggests that peace is best achieved by preparing for war.

### Balkan Nationalism

Russia saw herself as protector of the Slavs – the peoples of Eastern Europe, such as the Serbs. When Austria took over Bosnia and Herzegovina, the home of many Serbs, in 1908, she ran the risk of war with Serbia and Russia alike. The Serbs and Russians had to climb down when Germany backed Austria – but would they climb down again in future if provoked? Meanwhile, a group of Serb nationalists who hated Austria formed the 'Black Hand' terrorist group to fight for a Greater Serbia.

**Source C** The Balkans in 1914

AUSTRO-HUNGARIAN EMPIRE
TRANSYLVANIA
RUSSIA
Belgrade
ROMANIA
BOSNIA
Sarajevo
SERBIA
DALMATIA
MONTENEGRO
BULGARIA
Bosphorus
ALBANIA
Dardanelles
GREECE
TURKEY

Turkish (Ottoman) Empire until 1913

BOSNIA Provinces of the Austro-Hungarian Empire

0    100    200
kilometres

**Source B** The Kaiser's reasons for building a navy

Germany is a young and growing empire. Her worldwide trade is rapidly expanding. Germany must have a powerful fleet to protect that commerce and her interests in even the most distant seas.

*Daily Telegraph* in 1908

## The Schlieffen Plan

Germany fearing an attack on two fronts - France from the west and Russia from the east - had finalised a war plan by 1905. General von Schlieffen estimated that Russia would need six weeks to mobilise her army. This left Germany time enough to knock France out of the war. Since the French frontier with Germany was strongly defended, von Schlieffen intended to strike first by sending his armies through neutral Holland into Belgium and northern France to outflank the main French armies. General von Moltke later weakened the Plan by taking a shortcut to France by crossing the more heavily-defended Belgian frontier instead of moving into Holland. There were two other drawbacks: (a) Germany would have to start the war since she couldn't allow France and Russia to mobilise first and (b) Britain had promised to defend Belgium's neutrality. Would she intervene in the event of war?

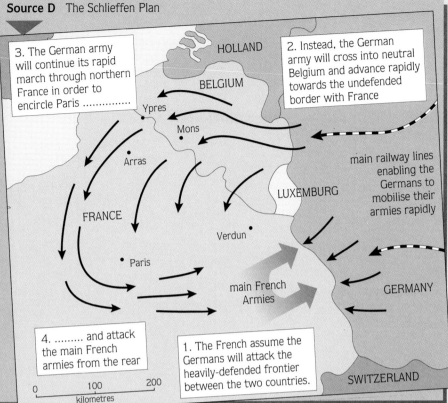

**Source D**   The Schlieffen Plan

3. The German army will continue its rapid march through northern France in order to encircle Paris ...............

2. Instead, the German army will cross into neutral Belgium and advance rapidly towards the undefended border with France

main railway lines enabling the Germans to mobilise their armies rapidly

4. ......... and attack the main French armies from the rear

1. The French assume the Germans will attack the heavily-defended frontier between the two countries.

## The Alliance System

The French had bitter memories of the Franco-Prussian War in 1870-71 when the Germans seized Alsace and Lorraine. The French wanted this territory back, so both countries looked for allies to help them in case of war. Germany formed the Triple Alliance with Italy and Austria-Hungary. Russia had an understanding (*Entente*) with France (Source **A**). If either country was attacked by Germany, the other would come to her aid. Since most wars begin with *both* sides claiming the other attacked first, the members of both alliances ran the risk of being dragged into a war against their will. At first, Britain remained aloof since she had been in dispute with both France and Russia over colonies. But alarmed by German war preparations, she settled her differences with France over Egypt (the *Entente Cordiale*) in 1904 and with Russia over Central Asia in 1907, to form the Triple Entente.

## German Militarism

Many German commanders thought the situation in Europe had worsened and that war was inevitable (Source **E**). Russia was already modernising (page 52) and might soon be a formidable enemy. Better to attack now rather than later.

**Source E**   Secret meeting between the Kaiser and his top commanders, 8 December 1912

The German Kaiser predicted that if the Austrians did not now face up to the Serbian menace, they would have considerable trouble from the Slav minorities within the Austro-Hungarian monarchy. The fleet must henceforth look on England as an enemy. Moltke [*the Army Chief*] regarded war as unavoidable, 'the sooner the better.' Tirpitz [*the Navy Chief*] wanted another eighteen months to get the navy ready for war.

Extract from Alan Palmer, *The Kaiser*, Weidenfeld and Nicolson, 1978

**1**   List the statements in Source **E** which show that Germany intended to go to war. Does this meeting prove that Germany started the First World War?

**2**   How did Germany's desire for colonies play a part in creating tension between the big powers before the First World War?

**3**   Colonial rivalry – the Arms Race – Balkan Nationalism – the Alliance System – the Schlieffen Plan – German Militarism. How were these factors long-term causes of the First World War?

*Questions*

## *Sarajevo*

### ▶ *Why did the assassination at Sarajevo lead to war in 1914?*

### Tension in the Balkans

After 1908 (page 10) tension increased in the Balkans. War broke out in 1912 when the Balkan countries seized most of the land held by Turkey in Europe and divided it between them. But Bulgaria was not satisfied with her share. She started a second war which led to Serbia becoming the leading power in the Balkans, to Austrian alarm. When the Archduke Franz Ferdinand, heir to the Austrian throne, visited the Bosnian capital Sarajevo on 28 June 1914, several members of the Serbian 'Black Hand' terrorist group (page 10) lay in wait for him as he and his wife drove through the city. A bomb was thrown at the Archduke's car, but he threw it back. Cancelling the visit, they began to leave when another assassin, Gavrilo Princip, shot them both dead with a pistol (Source **A**). The news shocked the world (Source **D**) but an Austrian official in Belgrade said the Serbs were delighted (Source **B**).

Serbia was held responsible, but the Austrian response to the outrage was delayed, despite the fact that the heir to the throne had been killed. If Austria declared war on Serbia, would Russia aid the Serbs or could the war be confined to the Balkans? If the former, would Germany come to Austria's aid? The Austrians had to find out. They got their answer on 5 July. The Kaiser met the Austrian ambassador near Berlin and told him to go ahead (Source **C**).

**Source A**
Assassination of the Archduke Ferdinand and his wife in Sarajevo

**Source B**   Serb reactions to the assassination

> The accounts of eyewitnesses say that people fell into one another's arms in delight, and remarks were heard, such as: 'It serves them right, we have been expecting this for a long time.'

So, on 23 July, the Austrians dealt with Serbia. They delivered an ultimatum they knew the Serbs would have to reject. The Austrian Foreign Minister deliberately phrased it so 'that it would be wholly impossible for Serbia to accept.' Even so, the Serbian reply was so reasonable that the Kaiser, who by now had got cold feet, said, 'Now there can be no object in going to war.' But the Austrians, seeking revenge, went ahead anyway. On 28 July, they declared war on Serbia. Russian mobilisation in support of Serbia followed on 29 July. The next day, 30 July, the Kaiser warned the Tsar to stop mobilising and on 31 July the Kaiser gave Russia a threatening ultimatum (Source **F**).

**Source C**

> It is now or never. Deal with the Serbs. Straight away. The Tsar is unlikely to intervene but if he does, Germany will stand at Austria's side.

**Source D**   Headlines in the *Daily Telegraph*, Monday, 29 June 1914: A reporter in Paris commented 'The consequences of the outrage may, it is feared here, be many and perilous.'

THE DAILY TELEGRAPH, MONDAY, JUNE 29, 1914.

# TRAGEDY OF THE AUSTRIAN THRONE.

## MURDER OF ARCHDUKE FRANZ FERDINAND AND HIS WIFE.

**Source E** Cartoon published in *Punch* after Austria issued its 23 July ultimatum to Serbia:
'THE POWER BEHIND. Austria (*at the ultimatum stage*). "I don't quite like his attitude. Somebody must be backing him"'

**THE POWER BEHIND.**
Austria (*at the ultimatum stage*). "I DON'T QUITE LIKE HIS ATTITUDE. SOMEBODY MUST BE BACKING HIM."

**Source F** The Kaiser's ultimatum to Russia

German mobilisation is bound to follow if Russia does not stop every measure of war against us and against Austria-Hungary within 12 hours.

Meanwhile the German Ambassador in Paris was also asked to talk to the French (Source **G**).

**Source G**

Please ask French Government whether it intends to remain neutral in a Russo-German war. Reply must be made in 18 hours.

On 1 August the German Ambassador in Paris reported back to Berlin (Source **H**).

**Source H**

Upon my repeated definite inquiry whether France would remain neutral in the event of a Russo-German war, the Prime Minister declared that France would do that which her interests dictated.

Behind the scenes, the Tsar, the Kaiser and the leading statesmen of Russia, Germany and Britain had been dithering, sending telegrams, hoping for some kind of agreement, fearful of starting a general war. But the generals had already taken over, each afraid of being caught unprepared for war. Germany mobilised her forces and declared war on Russia that same day (1 August). France immediately ordered a general mobilisation from midnight, while Italy, the third partner in the Triple Alliance, declared she would remain neutral.

On 3 August Germany declared war against France and on 4 August invaded Belgium. The British Ambassador told the German Chancellor, Bethmann Hollweg, that failure to withdraw from Belgium would mean war, since Britain had signed a treaty guaranteeing Belgian neutrality. The reply he got was one of amazement (Source **I**).

**Source I**

Just for a word – 'neutrality', a word which in wartime has so often been disregarded – just for a scrap of paper Great Britain is going to make war on a kindred nation who desires nothing better than to be friends with her.

British opinion was divided. Some wanted to keep out of the conflict altogether but the newspapers supported the government (Source **J**). When the Germans ignored the ultimatum, Britain declared war.

**Source J** From *The Times*, Sunday, 2 August

The Empire has no written undertakings which say it must intervene. But it has an obligation of honour. We have a vital interest in seeing that France is not overwhelmed by Germany.

Italy joined Britain and the *Entente Powers* in 1915, hoping to make sweeping gains at Austria's expense at the end of the war. Germany and Austria-Hungary were later joined by Turkey in November 1914 and Bulgaria in October 1915. They were called the *Central Powers* because of their position in Europe. Both Turkey and Bulgaria hoped to regain territories lost in the Balkans. Meanwhile, Japan declared war on Germany in August 1914 and China did so in August 1917. By that time the United States (page 34) had entered the conflict as well.

**Questions**

1  What was the point of the cartoon (Source **E**)? How did it sum up the situation in Europe on 23 July 1914?

2  Look at the sequence of events after the Archduke was murdered. Which were the decisive actions which led to the outbreak of war?

3  Was Germany entirely to blame for starting the war? Discuss this with your friends, each one representing the views of one of the main participants – Serbia, Austria, Germany, Russia, France, Britain.

# 3 War to end all wars

## Overview: The First World War 1914-18

### START OF THE WAR (page 16)

The German armies invade France through Belgium. They reach the fringes of Paris but are driven back at the battle of the River Marne. The Schlieffen Plan has failed.

### STALEMATE ON THE WESTERN FRONT (page 17)

Germany is determined to hold on to the ground she has won. Both sides dig an intricate system of trenches, protected by heavy guns, machine-guns, mines and barbed wire. Any attack across 'no man's land' between the two sets of trenches is met by devastating machine-gun fire and ends in heavy casualties and very little gain in territory. Neither side seems able to overcome the opposition. The war on the Western Front has reached stalemate.

### WAR IN THE BALKANS AND ITALY (page 25)

Any chance of an Allied breakthrough on the Serbian and Italian fronts vanishes when Bulgaria joins the Austro-Hungarian forces occupying much of Serbia and the Austrians invade northern Italy.

### WAR IN THE AIR (page 26)

German airships – Zeppelins – drop bombs on the Allies but do little damage and several are shot down in flames. Small aircraft spy on troop movements. Larger planes bomb England. The air raids have little effect on the course of the war but increase British hatred of the enemy.

### WAR AGAINST TURKEY (page 24)

Turkey declares war in October 1914 and stops Allied war supplies reaching Russia through the Dardanelles. The Allies respond with a 'sideshow' – by landing troops at Gallipoli in April 1915. Their attempt to capture the Dardanelles to help Russia ends in disaster. The survivors have to withdraw.

### WAR AT SEA (page 27)

The Germans hope to starve the British and French into submission. U-boats (submarines) patrol the Atlantic sinking Allied ships carrying food to Europe. Convoys of merchant ships protected by warships reduce the losses, but food is still rationed. The Royal Navy stops German warships leaving the North Sea. Only one major naval battle is fought. After the Battle of Jutland in 1916, the British Blockade of German ports causes great hardship. Germany is close to starvation.

### ENDING THE STALEMATE (page 24)

Both sides seek a way of ending the stalemate. Germany aims to knock Russia out of the war first. The Allies pin their hopes on new inventions, achieving a breakthrough on another Front or by means of a diversion or 'sideshow'. Both sides use different types of sea power to starve the other into submission.

### NEW WEAPONS (page 18)

The Germans use POISON GAS but it is difficult to control, affects friendly troops as well as the enemy and can be countered by soldiers wearing gas masks. Both sides have HUGE GUNS which bombard the enemy with shells but the men in the trenches are well protected. Shell holes provide cover in 'no man's land'. MACHINE-GUNS prove to be the deadliest of the new weapons. Their devastating fire-power annihilates troops advancing across 'no man's land'.

### THE RUSSIAN FRONT (page 24)

Russian armies invade East Prussia and are decisively defeated at the Battle of Tannenberg in August 1914. In 1915, the Germans concentrate their forces in the East, intent on knocking Russia out of the war. They drive the Russian armies back 500 km but, in 1916, Russian General Brusilov retaliates, inflicting a major defeat on the Austrians. By 1917, nearly 2 million Russian soldiers have died and there is widespread dissatisfaction with the war.

### SEEKING AN ALLY (page 27)

The British try to get the Americans to join the Allies. But they stay out of the war for nearly three years – even after a huge ocean liner, the *Lusitania*, is sunk by U-boats in May 1915 with the loss of 128 American lives.

## REVOLUTION IN RUSSIA (page 24)

In March 1917, the Tsar is forced to abdicate. The war continues but Russia's armies begin to disintegrate. After the Bolshevik Revolution in November, the Russians agree an armistice (ceasefire) in December 1917. German and Austrian forces from the Eastern Front are sent to reinforce the tired and depleted armies on the Western and Italian Fronts.

## THE USA JOINS THE WAR (page 34)

The United States enters the war, at last, in April 1917, after German U-boats sink American shipping in the Atlantic. The Allied armies will soon be reinforced by millions of fresh troops and much-needed military supplies.

## GERMAN SPRING OFFENSIVE 1918 (page 34)

Germany, worried that US involvement in the war will soon overwhelm her forces, decides to launch a fierce, all-out attack along the Somme on 21 March 1918 to finish the war as soon as possible. The German army, reinforced by troops from the Eastern Front, drives the Allies back to the Marne but the campaign is a failure when the Allies counter-attack and Germany's war-weary soldiers can no longer hold back the tide.

## THE FINAL PUSH (page 35)

A large number of tanks and aeroplanes support the British and French armies when they break through the German lines at the Battle of Amiens on 8 August 1918. General Ludendorff, the German commander, calls it the 'Black Day of the German Army. The war must be ended!' Six weeks later the American army plays a decisive part in the Meuse-Argonne offensive which ends German resistance for good.

## TRENCH WARFARE (page 16)

The Germans are on the defensive in 1915 but go on the attack in 1916. There are over a million French and German casualties when they try to capture the fortress town of Verdun. The British army suffers similar losses during the Battle of the Somme (July-November 1916) and at the Third Battle of Ypres (Passchendaele) in July-November 1917.

## INVENTION OF THE TANK (page 19)

British engineers invent the tank – an armour-plated, track-laying vehicle armed with a powerful gun and machine-guns. At last, the Allies have a weapon which can crush barbed wire underfoot, ride over trenches, fire shells and withstand and return machine-gun fire. It is first used in 1916, but early models are slow and unreliable.

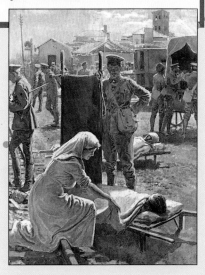

## ARMISTICE (page 35)

Meanwhile, there is chaos and unrest inside Germany and Austria-Hungary. The Allied naval blockade has left people desperately short of food. They are worn out after four years of war. One by one, Germany's allies desert her. In September and October, Bulgaria and Turkey surrender and Czechoslovakia and Hungary break away from Austria to form independent republics. Austria agrees an armistice on 3 November. The Kaiser abdicates six days later and Germany agrees an armistice on 11 November 1918. The war is over.

---

1 Tank – Zeppelin – aeroplane – *Dreadnought* battleship – machine-gun – U-boat – poison gas. Which three weapons do you think **a)** a German and **b)** an Allied leader would have chosen if asked to name the outstanding weapons of the war?

2 What two events in 1917 played a crucial part in ending the war?

3 List the main reasons why Germany lost the war.

Questions

# The Western Front

 **Why was the war not over by Christmas 1914?**
**What were conditions like in the trenches on the Western Front?**

## Mobilising the armies

When the Kaiser mobilised Germany's armed forces on 1 August 1914 (page 13), his commanders knew exactly what to do. Fully-trained reserve soldiers were called up and taken by railway to the front. Over 500 troop trains a day crossed the Rhine. Other countries mobilised as fast as they could. Britain was the only major power without a conscript army to call on. But hundreds of thousands of men soon volunteered (page 29). Throughout Europe, soldiers and civilians alike told each other; 'The war will be over by Christmas'.

## German invasion of Belgium and Northern France

The German armies swept into Belgium and Luxembourg but the Belgian army held up the German advance at Liege, giving time enough for a British Expeditionary Force (BEF) of 90,000 men to reach Flanders in support of the Belgian and French armies. The Kaiser called it a 'contemptible little army.' Although the BEF fought stubbornly, it was forced to retreat after struggling to hold Mons. The Schlieffen Plan had called for the encirclement of Paris (Source **D** on page 11). But the German First Army, led by General von Kluck, which should have passed to the west of Paris, advanced to the north-east instead. The French Sixth Army mounted a counter-attack from the south and drove the German armies back to the river Marne in September (Source **A**).

## Trench Warfare

Up to this point, the generals on both sides expected the war to be one of rapid movement – with the cavalry on horseback leading the way, supported by the infantry on foot. But the accuracy of the heavy guns and the overwhelming fire-power of the machine-guns soon put a stop to that. Survival meant taking

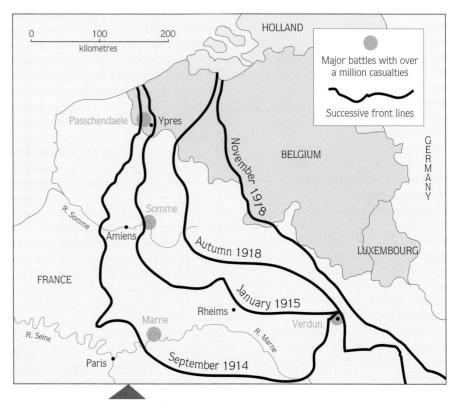

**Source A**  Map of the Western Front

**Source B**  Photograph of a British trench

**Source C** Captured German dug-out in 1916

cover and in the flattish landscape of northern France, this meant digging a trench. 'The armies went underground,' said a war correspondent. 'They were locked in trenches and wire from the North Sea to the Alps.'

The result was stalemate. The Germans, intent on holding the French and Belgian territory so far gained, built an elaborate system of trenches with deep, shell-proof dug-outs 10 to 30 metres below the ground to house the troops (Source **C**). Communicating trenches supplied them with ammunition and food. Water, electricity and telephone lines were installed and underground hospitals, kitchens, ammunition dumps and supply depots were built there as well. Despite this, a German sergeant later described an entirely different set of conditions he had experienced in the trenches on the Somme (Source **D**).

**Source D** By [ex-Sergeant] Otto Dix, a German artist

Lice, rats, barbed wire entanglements, fleas, grenades, bombs, caves, corpses, blood, drink, mice, cats, gases, cannons, filth, bullets, machine-guns, fire, steel. That's what war is! Nothing but the devil's work!

Quoted in *Otto Dix*, by Eva Karcher, Taschen, 1988

British trenches were more primitive than the German trenches (Sources **B** and **E**), although the officers and men tried to make them as comfortable as possible (Source **F**).

**Source E** Why the British trenches were miserable

Our trench warfare seemed to be based on the idea that we, the British, were not stopping in the trenches for long. Very soon we would be chasing Jerry across country. As a result, we lived a mean and impoverished sort of existence in lousy scratch holes.

Quoted in *The Bloody Game*, edited by Paul Fussell, Scribners, 1991

Candles and braziers glinted through the chinks
And curtain-flaps of dug-outs …
A flare went up; the shining whiteness spread
And flickered upward, showing nimble rats
And mounds of glimmering sand-bags, bleached with rain.

**Source F** Poem 'A Working Party' by Siegfried Sassoon

Most of those who wrote about the war came from comfortable homes. But many of the soldiers serving under them knew only rural poverty or city slums – as you saw earlier in Chapter One. A modern historian explains what effect this had in Source **G**.

**Source G** From *The Great War* (1979), by Correlli Barnett

To the majority of soldiers, actual living conditions in and behind the line on quiet sectors were little if any worse than in peacetime. Certainly many British working class soldiers enjoyed a better diet, better medical care and better welfare than they had as civilians.

For long periods, sectors of the front line were quiet. The main problems were boredom, coping with rats and lice, and enduring the weather. Rain drained into the trenches, of course, turning everything to mud and impeding progress when walking on slatted wooden boards from trench to trench. Biting winds, bitter cold and persistent damp gave rise to painful diseases, such as trench foot (swollen feet) and trench mouth (swollen gums). Many caught the infectious disease trench fever from the lice in their clothes.

No man's land between the trenches was usually barren of cover. Anyone raising his head was a target for a sniper. To deter the enemy, wiring parties erected and repaired massive barbed wire entanglements in front of the trenches. When the soldiers went 'over the top', they took with them equipment weighing 30 kilograms – food, ammunition, helmets, wire cutters, spades and hand grenades.

**Questions**

1 Why did the Schlieffen Plan fail? Why was the war not over by Christmas 1914? Mention the following in your answer: Belgian resistance, BEF, Battle of the Marne, von Kluck, stalemate, German trench system.

2 Explain how the British trenches were different from those of the Germans. What does this tell you about British and German strategies on the Western Front?

3 How do Sources **C** and **G** affect the picture of trench warfare given by Sources **B**, **D**, **E** and **F**? What would happen if only Sources **C** and **G** were used when writing an account of trench warfare in 1914–18?

## *Impact of new technology*

▶ **What impact did new technology have on the First World War?**

### Poison gas

As the war on the Western Front got bogged down in trench warfare, the latest weapons were used to try to break the deadlock. They soon influenced the tactics and strategy used to fight the war. The Germans were the first to use poison gas – on 22 April 1915, at Ypres. Thousands of British soldiers choked in the fumes and there were 5000 casualties (Source **A**). But poison gas was difficult to control. Gusts of wind could carry it back across your own lines and it impeded progress when you advanced (Source **B**).

**Source A**   Allied victims of a gas attack

**Source B**   By a senior German officer

M arch 22, 1918. Yesterday's attack would have completely succeeded had not the gas-cloud from our own guns lain too long on the ground. The infantry could not get forward through this poison barrier.

Extract from a memoir by Rudolf Binding printed in *I Was There!*, edited by Sir John Hammerton, The Waverley Book Company, 1938

Luckily, the greenish-yellow fumes of the chlorine gas could be seen, so there was often plenty of time to put on a gas mask. Soldiers in one unit were told: 'There are two kinds of men in gas attacks. The QUICK and the DEAD' (Source **C**).

**Source C**   By Wilfred Owen

G as! GAS! Quick boys! – An ecstasy of fumbling, Fitting the clumsy helmets just in time; But someone still was yelling out and stumbling And floundr'ing like a man in fire or lime.

The Allies retaliated by firing their own gas shells. Two years later, German scientists perfected a yet more terrible weapon. This was mustard gas. Gas masks could not stop it from blistering the skin.

### Heavy artillery

Both sides employed heavy guns and high explosives (Source **D**). On land they were used to maintain a constant bombardment of enemy positions before an attack. At one stage, the Germans had over 20,000 guns including *Big Bertha* in 1918. Mounted on a railway truck, it fired shells weighing nearly a tonne at Paris, 100 kilometres away. But if the soldiers sheltered in deep dugouts, as the Germans did on the Somme, they could survive (Source **D**). The British discovered this to their cost on 1 July 1916 (page 21).

**Source D**   By Wilfred Owen

W e'd found an old Boche [*German*] dug-out, and he knew, And gave us hell, for shell on frantic shell Hammered on top, but never quite burst through.

**Source E** The development of high explosives and new types of gun increased the firepower of warships as well as artillery on land

Since a heavy artillery barrage invariably preceded a major thrust by troops, it posted a warning to the enemy that an attack was imminent and allowed them time to take all necessary precautions. Another downside to an artillery barrage was the fact that it left no man's land pitted with huge craters. These made launching an attack even more difficult for the soldiers, especially when the craters were filled with water (Source **T** on page 23). On the other hand, they did provide cover when firing became intense.

## Machine-guns

Machine-guns were the most effective weapons of the war. They were easy to deploy and their withering fire cut down advancing troops like a gardener scything grass. The German Maxim machine-guns could fire up to 600 rounds of ammunition a minute and accounted for 90 per cent of Allied victims at the Battle of the Somme. Nonetheless, they were heavy and had to be operated from a fixed site instead of on the move. This made them highly vulnerable to return fire, once enemy gunners located their position. Knocking out machine-gun nests later became a top priority for tanks (Source **F** on page 35).

## Tanks

The tank (Source **F**) was easily the most original new invention of the war. It was invented by Ernest Swinton, an army officer and engineer, after seeing the stalemate on the Western Front. His idea was eagerly taken up by Winston Churchill. But he thought of them as landships carrying soldiers into battle rather than as the fighting machines they became – mobile machine-gun nests, slow, cumbersome and unreliable.

Tanks were first used during the Battle of the Somme (Source **G**) but had little effect on the course of that campaign. The generals had, as yet, no idea how to use them to their best advantage.

**Source F** First World War tank

**Source G** First sight of a tank

September 15th 1916: These astounding machines arrived last night. They are huge armoured forts, weighing over thirty tons. They have no wheels, but move like the caterpillar, on endless chains. They are the most alarming things imaginable and are so heavily armoured that they are impervious to rifle or machine-gun fire. Nothing but a direct hit from a gun can stop them. They are armed with light guns and also machine-guns.

Extract from a memoir by Lt. Col. the Hon. R. G. A. Hamilton printed in *I Was There!*, edited by Sir John Hammerton, The Waverley Book Company, 1938

The short-sighted war minister, Lord Kitchener, had earlier dismissed the tank as 'a pretty mechanical toy' but Sir Douglas Haig, Britain's top general, was sufficiently impressed to encourage further development of the weapon. His faith in the new weapon was fully justified on 8 August 1918 when tanks spearheaded the devastating breakthrough which brought an end to the war (page 35).

1 What were the advantages and disadvantages of using: **a)** poison gas, **b)** heavy artillery and **c)** machine-guns?

2 How did the tank overcome the disadvantages experienced by the foot soldier in the First World War?

3 Which weapons do you think were most feared by the other side?

4 Source **F** on page 17 and Sources **C** and **D** on these pages are from poems written during the war. In what ways can poetry like this be of value to the historian?

*Questions*

# On the Somme and at Passchendaele

**How and why were the battles of the Somme and Passchendaele fought and with what success?**

## First day of the Battle of the Somme

The Battle of the Somme began on 1 July 1916. Germany's highly trained professional and conscript soldiers faced Kitchener's New Army (page 29) of eager volunteers, many of them under fire for the first (and last) time in their lives. By the end of that lovely summer's day, 19,000 British soldiers lay dead. Another 40,000 were missing, wounded, or taken prisoner. Many units were of men from the same town, such as the 1st and 2nd Barnsley Pals, Hull Sportsmen and Grimsby Chums. When a unit, like the Accrington Pals, suffered horrendous casualties, it had a devastating effect on morale at home.

The battle had been well advertised! For weeks, the Allied commanders had made preparations, training soldiers, building railway lines to supply the huge armies involved, and stockpiling ammunition, food and medical supplies. For seven days before the battle began, Allied artillery – some 1500 guns – shelled the German lines continuously (Source **A**). The sound of the barrage was so loud it could be heard in Kent. Even so, there were not enough guns to do the job and the shells they fired were not powerful enough to destroy the deep German dug-outs even if they did wipe out many surface trenches.

When the shelling ended, the Germans, who had been sheltering in deep dugouts, knew what to expect and lay ready in waiting. Some British troops, on the other hand, had been told it would be a walkover (Source **B**) and that Allied troops outnumbered the Germans by seven to one.

▲ **Source A**   Heavy guns firing on the German trenches

British commanders honestly believed their guns had knocked out the German trenches, cut the barbed wire and killed the enemy's front-line soldiers. Even so, they had no excuse for their failure to send reconnaissance parties to check this first (Source **C**).

**Source C**   From *The Official History of the War*
▼

In the early discussions Haig had said that corps were not to attack until their commanders were satisfied that the enemy's defences had been sufficiently destroyed; but this condition seems to have been dropped as time went on.

At 07.30 precisely, the attack by 60,000 men began. You can see what happened next in the sources.

**Source B**   Comforting news for the Newcastle Commercials
▼

You will be able to go over the top with a walking stick. You will not need rifles. When you get to Thiepval, you will find the Germans all dead, not even a rat will have survived.

Quoted in *Wars of the Twentieth Century*, by Susanne Everett, Bison Books, 1985

**Source D**   By a soldier in the Manchester Rifles
▼

At 7.30 we went up the ladders, doubled through the gaps in the wire, and lay down waiting for the line to form up on each side of us. When it was ready, we went forward, not running, but at a walk.

N.C.O. in the Manchester Rifles, *Westminster Gazette*, October 1916

**Source E** 1 July 1916. 07.30. An officer looks at his watch as troops line up to launch the attack

**Source F** By Sergeant Cook of the 1st Somerset Regiment

The 1st Rifle Brigade advanced in perfect order. Everything was working smoothly, not a shot being fired. The first line had nearly reached the German front line, when all at once machine-guns opened up all along our front with a murderous fire, and we were caught in the open, with no shelter. Men were falling like ninepins. I tripped over dead bodies, fell headlong into shell holes. My clothes were torn to ribbons by barbed wire.

Extract from a memoir by Yeoman Warder Cook printed in *I Was There!*, edited by Sir John Hammerton, The Waverley Book Company, 1938

**Source G** By a German officer at the Somme

At 7.30 am the hurricane of shells ceased as suddenly as it had begun. Our men at once clambered up the steep shafts leading from the dugouts and ran singly or in groups to the nearest shell craters. The machine-guns were pulled out of the dugouts and hurriedly placed in position.

Quoted in *The Bloody Game*, edited by Paul Fussell, Scribners, 1991

**Source H** By a German machine-gunner at the Somme

We were very surprised to see them walking. We had never seen that before. When we started firing, we just had to load and reload. They went down in their hundreds. You didn't have to aim, we just fired into them.

**Source I** Stretcher-bearers bring in wounded soldiers from no man's land

**Source J** By Sergeant Cook of the 1st Somerset Regiment

July 2nd 1916: We were roused at 7 am for roll call. No officer who had gone into action (there were 26) was present, 17 were killed, 1 captured and 8 wounded. All Warrant Officers were killed, 7 sergeants survived, 438 other ranks were killed, wounded or missing.

Memoir by Yeoman Warder Cook printed in *I Was There!*, edited by Sir John Hammerton, The Waverley Book Company, 1938

## The Somme campaign

The soldiers were ordered into battle on the following day and every day thereafter for the next 20 weeks. You can see the distance they gained on the map (Source **R**). Haig was later much criticised for this. He and his supporters pointed to the fact that he had pinned down a large part of the German army for nearly six months. He was also under great pressure from the French to continue fighting on the Somme, since the Battle of Verdun, where over a million French and German soldiers were killed or wounded, was still being fought 200 km away (see map – Source **A** – on page 16). A modern historian comments:

'There could be no question of abandoning the offensive, for the first day on the Somme was the 132nd day of the Battle of Verdun.'

1 Write a soldier's letter home describing what happened on the first day of the Battle of the Somme.

2 Make a list of the reasons why so many British soldiers were killed.

3 Why did the British think their advance would be unopposed and why were they mistaken? Who was responsible for the mistakes they made – was it the soldiers themselves, the officers who led them across no man's land, the senior officers who ordered the attack, or Haig, the Commander-in-Chief?

*Questions*

Source K   General Joffre, the French Commander in Chief in 1916

Source L   Field Marshal Haig, the British Commander in Chief in 1916

## Why the Battle of the Somme was fought

## Planning the Somme offensive

### TIMING:

**5 December 1915**: General Joffre (Source **K**) and Field Marshal Haig (Source **L**) plan a joint attack against Germany in 1916 with 40 French and 25 British divisions [each division had about 10,000 men].

**14 February 1916**: Date fixed – end of June 1916.

**21 February 1916**: Savage and unexpected German attack on French fortress town of Verdun. Two main effects:

(1) Joffre wants the Somme offensive to begin as soon as possible to take German troops away from Verdun.

(2) Far fewer French troops take part in the attack on 1 July. From now on the British Army is the senior partner on the Western Front.

**29 June 1916**: Attack scheduled to begin. Cancelled because of weather.

**1 July 1916**: Attack begins.

### TACTICS:

The French and British plan to attack at the point where their two armies meet. Convenient as this is, it is also the strongest sector of the German defences (Source **M**). Haig would have preferred to attack the German right flank in Flanders believing this to be their weakest point.

### STRATEGY:

Joffre's strategy is ATTRITION. He wants to wear the enemy down by causing as many casualties and destroying as many weapons as possible. Haig wants to go for a BREAKTHROUGH, to split the German armies in two and trap them. Fighting a war of attrition and aiming for a breakthrough require different tactics in the field. ATTRITION only works if you have a much bigger army than the enemy and can afford to lose more men and weapons. A BREAKTHROUGH is more likely if you attack the enemy at his weakest, not his strongest, point.

**Source M**   By Field Marshal Haig AFTER the battle

The German defences consisted of several lines of deep trenches, well-provided with bomb-proof shelters and protected by wire entanglements forty yards wide, built of iron stakes interlaced with barbed wire. The woods and villages between the trenches had been turned into veritable fortresses.

Quoted in *World War 1914–18*, by J. A. Hammerton, Amalgamated Press, c. 1934.

**Source N**   By Field Marshal Haig in 1917

By the third week in November the three main objects with which we had commenced our offensive had already been achieved: Verdun had been relieved; the main German forces had been held on the Western Front; and the enemy's strength had been very considerably worn down.

Extract from *Sir Douglas Haig's Great Push*, Hutchinson, c. 1917

**Source O**   Official history of the German 27 Infanterie Division

In the Somme fighting of 1916 there was a spirit of heroism which was never again found in the division. The men in 1918 had not the temper, the hard bitterness and spirit of sacrifice of their predecessors.

Quoted in *The World Crisis*, by Winston Churchill, 1923–27

**Source P**   The British *Official History of the War*

For this disastrous loss of the finest men there was only a small gain of ground to show. Never again was the spirit or the quality of the officers and men so high. The losses sustained were not only heavy but irreplaceable.

**Source Q**   Lloyd George in the 1930s

The Battle of the Somme was not responsible for the failure of the German effort to capture Verdun. The French Commander-in-Chief [Joffre] said in May that the Germans had already been beaten at Verdun. It is claimed that the battle of the Somme destroyed the old German Army by killing off its best officers and men. It killed off far more of our best and of the French best.

Extract from *War Memoirs*, by David Lloyd George, Odhams Press, 1938

**Source R**   Map of the Battle of the Somme

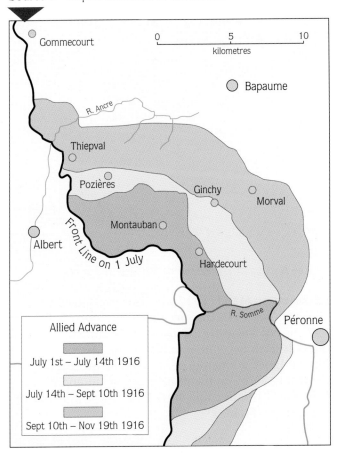

0    5    10
kilometres

Gommecourt

Bapaume

R. Ancre

Thiepval

Pozières

Ginchy

Morval

Montauban

Albert

Front Line on 1 July

Hardecourt

R. Somme

Péronne

**Allied Advance**

July 1st – July 14th 1916

July 14th – Sept 10th 1916

Sept 10th – Nov 19th 1916

## Passchendaele – the Third Battle of Ypres

Despite the huge casualties at Verdun and on the Somme and against the advice of many senior officers, Haig went ahead with the Flanders campaign he had always wanted. The Third Battle of Ypres (Passchendaele) began on 31 July 1917 (see map – Source **A** – on page 16). It ended on 10 November, made little difference to the course of the war, but left another 400,000 British soldiers dead or wounded. Heavy rain as much as German resistance hindered progress and hundreds of men were drowned on the battlefield – in 'shell craters, half-full of yellow, slimy water' (Source **T**). Despite the advice of General Gough, the field commander, Haig pressed on. An army captain said later: 'The generals responsible for prolonging the fight should have been shot.' Lloyd George, the Prime Minister, went to see Haig in September (Source **S**).

**Source S**   By David Lloyd George

Nowhere was there a more ecstatic belief in these imaginary victories than at the chateau and village where the Field Marshal and his staff were quartered. Haig was radiant. He was marching his army step by step surely and irresistibly, overcoming all obstacles. This time it was purely his own. The French could claim no share in this victory.

Extract from *War Memoirs*, by David Lloyd George, Odhams Press, 1938

**Source T**   Haig could see pictures like this in the *Illustrated London News* – on 22 September ('quagmire') – on 13 October ('Mud, shells, chaos, and more mud – and death!')

**1**  What is the difference between fighting to achieve a breakthrough and fighting a battle of attrition?

**2**  Why was the Battle of the Somme fought? How and why did the aims of the generals differ? What effect did this have on the outcome of the battle? How much territory was won (Source **R**)?

**3**  'The English soldiers fight like lions – but they are lions led by donkeys.' Use the sources to say how far this was true of the battles on the Somme and at Passchendaele.

**4**  In what respects do Sources **N** and **Q** disagree? Differences like this are called differences in interpretation. The facts are the same but the importance attached to them can be very different.

**5**  Which of the other sources, if any, support Haig (**N**)? Which support Lloyd George (**Q**)?

Questions

# Ending the stalemate

**What was the nature of the fighting on the other fronts?
How important were they to the course of the war?**

## The Eastern Front

Both sides tried to break the stalemate by attempting a breakthrough on another front. After the Schlieffen Plan failed, the Germans decided to knock Russia out of the war first instead of France. The Tsar's armies had invaded Eastern Prussia in August 1914 but were massively defeated at the Battle of Tannenberg later that month. By the end of 1915, the Russians had suffered appalling casualties and the Germans had occupied most of Russian Poland (Source **B**).

It was a different story to the south where Russian armies captured much of Galicia (Source **A**) until German reinforcements drove them back. Then, in 1916, General Brusilov inflicted an even bigger defeat on the Austrians with a terrible cost in lives. This created such discontent among the soldiers that neither empire – the Russian or Austro-Hungarian –

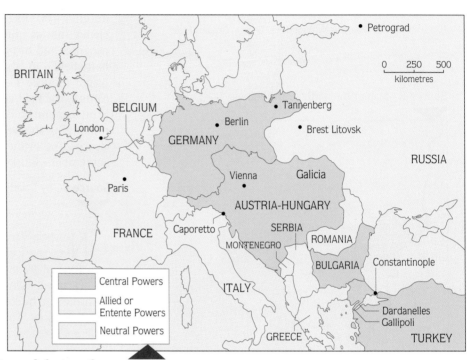

**Source A**  Map of Europe during the First World War

recovered. In March 1917, the Tsar was forced to abdicate (page 54). His successors continued to fight the war but the army fell apart in the summer. After the Bolshevik Revolution in November (page 56), Russia signed a separate peace agreement with the Central Powers – to the dismay of London and Paris. Now the Germans could move their troops to reinforce the Western Front.

## The war against Turkey

In October 1914, Turkey declared war against the Allies, hoping to regain territory in the Balkans. When she stopped Allied war supplies reaching Russia through the Dardanelles (Source **A**), Allied forces launched an attack to capture the straits. The plan was enthusiastically backed by Winston Churchill, who was then in charge of the Royal Navy. After a long but unsuccessful naval bombardment, Allied troops landed at Gallipoli in April 1915. Many came from Australia and New Zealand and were known as the ANZACs (Source **C**).

**Source B**  The war on the Eastern Front was one of movement rather than trench warfare. This picture of German soldiers on the march was published in a German magazine in 1915.

THE NEW STAR
Drawn by TED COLLES, after F. J. Leigh.

**Source C** Cartoon drawn by an Australian in the ANZAC army at Gallipoli

The Gallipoli operation was badly mishandled. Turkish soldiers held most of the higher ground and were difficult to dislodge. The Army High Command had underestimated the strength of Turkish resistance and many of the generals were incompetent and extravagant with the lives of their men (Source **D**).

**Source D** By Digger Craven, a soldier from New Zealand at Gallipoli

We had the trifling task of capturing the Turkish stronghold on Hill 60. After all the lessons and experiences and fiascos and disasters of the Peninsula, the attacking force was called upon to open this crazy offensive by crossing the wide plain of an exposed valley continually swept by the enemy's guns from higher ground, and in broad daylight! It was the last straw! The automatic guns opened up on us before we had gone a few yards.

Extract from a memoir by Digger Craven in *I Was There!*, edited by Sir John Hammerton, The Waverley Book Company, 1938

The Turkish soldiers fought with great bravery and determination under the leadership of German officers. Huge casualties were suffered by both sides. Despite heroic efforts, the Gallipoli campaign was a disaster and the survivors had to be evacuated by sea at the end of 1915. The Allied defeat, meanwhile, had given Bulgaria confidence to declare war on the Allies (September 1915) and Winston Churchill was forced to resign from the government.

## The war in the colonies

The war in Europe spilled over into Africa and Asia when the Allies attacked Germany's overseas empire. The Germans were unable to defend their colonies because the Royal Navy had command of the seas (page 27). Japan seized German-held territory in the Pacific, Australians landed in New Guinea, New Zealand troops occupied Samoa, South Africa (then part of the British Empire) invaded German South-West Africa (Namibia), and British forces seized Togoland and the Cameroons but had to fight a long war in German East Africa (Tanzania) against a very resourceful German commander.

The British also fought in Mesopotamia and the Middle East, long part of the Ottoman (Turkish) Empire. They successfully defended the Suez Canal and used Egypt as a springboard from which to invade Palestine, capturing Jerusalem, Damascus and Beirut. Another British army seized Baghdad, while T. E. Lawrence stirred up an Arab revolt against the Turks.

## The war in the Balkans

In the land where the war first began – Serbia – Austrian forces crossed the frontier in the north while Bulgaria invaded from the south. After occupying much of Serbia, they overran Romania, too, after the latter declared war in 1916.

## The Italian Front

Italy, neutral in 1914, joined the *Entente powers* in 1915, hoping to gain territory after the War. The Allies gave her substantial support since a breakthrough here would have forced the Germans to take troops away from other fronts. But the Italian army had little success and suffered a major defeat at Caporetto in 1917 (Source **A**).

1  What does the cartoon (Source **C**) show? Who is represented **a)** by the moon and **b)** by the new star? Who else is depicted in the picture? Why?

2  What mistakes did the Allies make at Gallipoli?

3  Compare Source **B** with Source **T** on page 23. What differences were there in how the war was fought on the Eastern and Western Fronts? How do you account for this?

4  What effect, if any, did the fighting on the other fronts have on the course of the war? Did they weaken or strengthen the Allied cause?

Questions

# The war at sea and in the air

## ▶ How important was the war at sea and in the air?

### The war in the air

Allied commanders underestimated the part that aircraft could play in the fighting. Britain's air force – the Royal Flying Corps – was part of the army until 1918 when it became the RAF. France's best general, Ferdinand Foch, said aviation was 'good sport but for the Army the aeroplane is worthless.' Yet aircraft soon proved their value. A pilot was the first to detect von Kluck's army switching direction towards the Marne in August 1914 (page 16).

At first, pilots used pistols and rifles to fire on enemy reconnaissance planes. But in 1915 the Germans developed the *Fokker* fighter plane with a synchronised machine-gun mounted in front of the pilot firing between the rotating propeller blades. Fighter planes like this could be used to attack ground targets as well as enemy aircraft (Source **B**).

**Source A** Wartime painting of a British pilot 'looping the loop' to evade German fighter planes

**Source C** A dogfight over Arras

**Source B** By a German soldier at the Battle of the Somme

Already flocks of enemy aeroplanes were humming over us. We were absolutely at their mercy, and with remorseless accuracy they directed the English heavy guns, shell after shell, into our line, and themselves fired with machine-guns at anybody who made the slightest movement below.

Private Karl Gorzel, quoted in *German Students' Letters*, Methuen

Action! The patrol keep close like a pack of hounds on the scent. Six scouts three thousand feet below. Black crosses! The leader sways sideways, as a signal, and suddenly drops. Machines fall scattering, the earth races up, the enemy patrol, startled, wheels and breaks. Each his man! The chocolate thunderbolts take sights, steady their screaming planes, and fire. Two machines approach head-on at breakneck speed, firing at each other, tracers whistling through each other's planes.

Extract from a memoir by Cecil Lewis printed in *I Was There!*, edited by Sir John Hammerton, The Waverley Book Company, 1938

German fighter aces, such as Hermann Göring and Baron von Richthofen (who shot down over eighty Allied planes) did battle with Allied pilots over France (Source **C**).

Aircraft also intercepted the slow-moving German Zeppelins when they bombed London in 1915-18. They did some damage (page 31) but searchlights picked them up as they flew across the city (Source **M** on page 31). Fighter planes firing explosive bullets or

dropping bombs on them from above brought many down in flames. Four-engined bombers replaced Zeppelins in 1918 but by then it was too late to help the Kaiser. The Allies, by contrast, made little use of air raids. In 1918, when the newly-formed RAF had over 20,000 aircraft, fewer than 2% were bombers, even though the munitions factories of the German Ruhr were well within reach.

## The war at sea

The British used the superior strength of the Royal Navy (Source **E** on page 19) to stop the German battle fleet leaving the North Sea. The Royal Navy also stopped merchant ships bringing food and supplies to German ports. This blockade was so successful, it forced the Germans to ration food long before this was necessary in Britain (Source **B** on page 34).

Only one major naval battle was fought – the Battle of Jutland in 1916. Although the short-term effect of this battle (the Royal Navy lost more ships and suffered higher casualties) favoured the Germans, the long-term effect was of far greater consequence. Germany's warships were forced to stay in port for the rest of the war, unable to support their U-boats in the Atlantic, protect their empire, or lift the blockade.

## The U-boat war

Early on in the war, a single German U-boat (submarine) sank three British cruisers off the coast of Holland with the loss of 1600 lives. This grim warning went unheeded by Britain's top naval commanders. They wasted three years before devising an effective method – the convoy system – to deal with the U-boat menace. The Kaiser hoped to starve Britain into surrender. By 1916, U-boats were sinking one ship in every 20, most of them in waters close to the British coast (Source **D**). American sympathy for the German

**Source E**  Sinking of the *Lusitania*, 7 May 1915

cause had earlier fallen sharply when U-boats torpedoed the British liner *Lusitania* off the coast of Ireland, killing 128 US citizens among the 1400 people drowned (Source **E**). The Kaiser promised it wouldn't happen again and the USA continued to remain neutral.

In February 1917, however, Germany began a new campaign of unrestricted warfare on merchant ships trading with Britain and her Allies. The U-boat sinking rate shot up to one ship in four but at a cost. The United States declared war in April (page 34). Later that year, when the convoy system was fully introduced, the sinking rate fell rapidly. Warships protected large numbers of ships sailing together. When a German U-boat fired a torpedo, it gave away its position. The warships immediately concentrated their attack on that part of the ocean, using depth charges to destroy any submarines below. It was very effective. In 1918 only one ship in every 300 was sunk by a U-boat.

**Source D**  German painting of a U-boat off the coast of Ireland.

**1** Which source sums up in a nutshell the main contribution of aircraft to the British war effort? Explain, in your own words, what this contribution was.

**2** Which source is more useful as a record of an aerial dogfight – the painting (Source **A**) or the written account (Source **C**)? Explain your reasons.

**3** Which of the two sources **D** or **E** would you select to illustrate the war at sea? Why?

**4** How effective was Britain's command of the sea in helping to win the war?

*Questions*

# The Home Front

 **What was the impact of the war on government, everyday life and the position of women? How did attitudes to the war change?**

## Wartime government

After the war began, the government had to organise the many activities needed at home to fight the war. These included: recruiting men into the army; organising supplies of food, uniforms and other necessary resources for the armed forces overseas (Source **A**); increasing output of munitions (weapons and ammunition); bringing in censorship to prevent useful information reaching the enemy; publishing propaganda to make everyone do their utmost to help the war effort; raising money to pay the huge cost of running the war. Later on, conscription had to be introduced in 1916 and food rationed in 1917-18.

## Restricting freedom

A more sinister development was DORA – the Defence of the Realm Act. This could be used to take action against anyone accused of helping the enemy. But it was also used, unfairly, to curb criticism. A Londoner was fined £100 for saying: 'We shall see the Germans in the Mile End Road yet'. People were taken to court for giving out leaflets urging soldiers not to fight. Critics were worried at the way in which traditional freedoms were being taken away from the people, such as free speech and freedom of movement.

Strikes were banned in munitions factories and a policy of directed labour was introduced. Workers could be ordered to move from one factory to another if this was thought to be in the national interest. Trade union workers bitterly complained when strikers in some industries (exempt from military service because of their work) were threatened with conscription if they didn't return. They got very little sympathy. 'It makes me feel sick,' wrote an officer in the trenches, 'to hear of people clamouring for more while the country is engaged upon this murderous struggle.'

## Political changes

The war also affected the political parties. In December 1916, Herbert Asquith, the Liberal Prime Minister since 1908, was forced out of office and replaced by Lloyd George (Source **B**). Asquith was thought to be

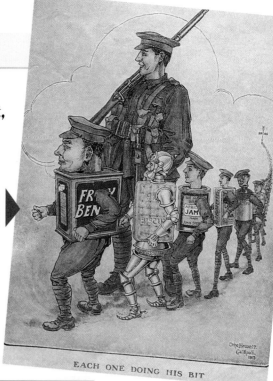

**Source A**
Cartoon drawn by an ANZAC soldier serving in Gallipoli in 1915.

EACH ONE DOING HIS BIT

**Source B**
David Lloyd George

### DAVID LLOYD GEORGE (1863–1945)

David Lloyd George, one of the most outstanding leaders of the century, was Welsh, a lawyer and a Liberal MP from 1890 to 1945. He soon gained a reputation as a persuasive speaker and became a cabinet minister in 1905. He excelled in conducting difficult negotiations and in getting things done. His forceful manner and policy helped to focus the British war effort. Hitler later said he was 'the man who won the war.' In 1919 he played the leading role in negotiating the Treaty of Versailles (page 36).

weak and to lack the drive and personality needed to lead the country to victory. Lloyd George's new coalition government included many Conservatives as well as Liberals and members of the Labour Party. But some Liberals continued to support Asquith. The feud between the two leaders split the Liberal Party in two. It never recovered. From 1922 onwards, Labour became the main opposition party to the Conservatives.

**Source C** Lord Kitchener

**Source D** Picture postcard in 1914

"THIS LITTLE PIG STAYED AT HOME."

**Source E** From the Reverend Andrew Clark's diary

Tuesday, 15 September 1914. There is a great village feeling against lads who are of age and physique to enlist and who have not done so.

**Source F**

Sunday, 9 May 1915. The resentment of farm labourers at being badgered to enlist is shown by the fact that every recruiting poster from the Rectory to Lyons Hall has been torn down.

Extract from *Echoes of the Great War*, edited by James Munson, Oxford, 1985

## Your country needs you!

Although many people thought the war would be over by Christmas 1914, Lord Kitchener, the War Minister (Source **C**), thought otherwise. He launched a massive recruiting campaign for volunteers and within four weeks raised an army of over half a million – Kitchener's New Army. Posters played on the emotions of potential young recruits with slogans such as 'Women of Britain say – GO!' and 'Daddy, what did YOU do in the Great War?' The first men to join up were *The First Hundred Thousand*. After nearly eight times that number died in the war, they were called *The Lost Generation* instead.

Music hall stars joined the recruitment drive, singing the hit numbers of the day, such as 'Oh, we don't want to lose you, but we think you ought to go,' and 'I'll make a man of you'. Some employers tried to coerce their employees by telling them to join up or face the sack. Some tried bribery. A West End store said it would pay half the salary of any employee who joined and promised to keep his job open. Patriotic women blackmailed 'slackers' by sending them four white feathers – the traditional sign of cowardice (Source **D**). Entries in an Essex clergyman's diary give some indication of the pressure put on young men at this time (Sources **E** and **F**).

When the number of new recruits began to fall, conscription was introduced at last in January 1916. Under the new regulations, all men in the 18-41 age group had to serve in the forces. Those who refused to do so because their consciences would not let them kill were called *conscientious objectors*.

1  Explain the cartoon (Source **A**).

2  Why was the postcard (Source **D**) published?

3  Does Source **F** add anything to Source **E**?

4  How did the war greatly increase the control the government had over people's lives? In what new ways were people no longer free to do as they wished?

Questions

## Propaganda and censorship

Newspapers and soldiers' letters were censored if they contained anything that could help the enemy or lower morale (Source **G**). It was only in the late 1920s that people fully realised how much the soldiers had suffered during the war.

**Source G**   By a war correspondent

At first the censorship office let us mention the fact that following a battle the dead of both sides were noticeable. A time came when it allowed only German dead on the battleground. Later still, no dead were permitted.

Extract from a memoir by H. M. Tomlinson printed in *I Was There!*, edited by Sir John Hammerton, The Waverley Book Company, 1938

The popular newspapers spread abuse, rumours, lies and half-truths about the *Huns, Boche* and *Germ-huns*. The invading German soldiers were accused of atrocities, such as beheading Belgian children or raping French nuns. Even after the war, the image persisted of German brutality (Source **H**) although most of it was greatly exaggerated and greatly resented by the ordinary German soldier.

**Source H**   German 'war crimes' in 1920

Without doubt the World War was the greatest crime in history. Germany's inhuman brutality, her innumerable and in many cases indescribable cruelties to old men, women and children, prisoners and wounded, her diabolical inventions of air-warfare, and of the still more infamous submarine warfare, and the wholesale use of poison gases, made up together an immense villainy too bad for description.

Extract from *Croydon and the Great War*, 1920

## Changing attitudes to the war

Attitudes to the war changed as the casualty lists mounted. At the start of the war, people on both sides had seemed to welcome a fight (Source **I**).

By 1917, sentiments like these were being mocked. Arthur Graeme West wrote: 'God how I hate you, you young cheerful men.' Soldiers, in particular, resented the bias of the press (Source **J**).

By 1917, a minority of politicians wanted to end the war. 'Peace has got to come some time or other,' said an MP. 'We ought to take every chance to try to bring this horrible war to a close.'

**Source I**   By Francis Grenfell

August 15th 1914: We go by train today at 1 pm and hope to reach France tonight. Everyone is so full of enthusiasm. I have had the happiest possible life, and have always been working for war, and I have just got into the biggest in the prime of life as a soldier.

Extract from 'Francis and Riversdale Grenfell', by John Buchan. Quoted in *Vain Glory*, edited by Guy Chapman, Cassell, 1937

**Source J**   Letter from Arthur Conway Young (killed 16 August 1917)

September 9th 1916
You read no end of twaddle in the papers at home about the spirit in which men go into action. You might almost think they revelled in the horror and the agony of it all. One correspondent spoke of men in a reserve regiment almost crying with rage because they couldn't take part in the show. It is rubbish like this which makes people in England think that war is great sport.

Extract from a letter by 2nd-Lieut. Arthur Conway Young printed in *I Was There!*, edited by Sir John Hammerton, The Waverley Book Company, 1938

**Source K**   Women in essential industries got help so they could do their work. This day nursery was used by the children of munitions workers.

## Full employment

Many people were better off financially than before the war. Families of men in the services were paid allowances while the wages of the poorest workers, such as farm workers and labourers, increased because employers were short of staff. There was little unemployment and the widespread use of women (Source **K**) and older children often meant that two or more wages were going into homes where only one or none had gone before the war.

## Rationing

People's health improved as living standards rose but the success of the U-Boat campaign caused serious food shortages in 1917-18. Working people resented the fact that some shopkeepers kept back scarce items for their wealthier customers. This led to demands for rationing to ensure everyone got an equal share. Sugar was the first commodity to be rationed in 1917. It was followed early in 1918 by meat, butter, margarine, coal, electricity and gas.

**Source L**  Victoria Station in wartime with soldiers returning to the trenches after a spot of leave

## Increasing output

The wholesale slaughter of young men affected everyone deeply. Many tried to escape from grief by living for the moment. Dance halls, cinemas, music halls and theatres were full. Soldiers on leave (Source **L**) made the most of their time. Alcohol was blamed for absenteeism at work. This was particularly worrying when, it was claimed, it affected output from the munitions factories. Lloyd George called it 'our greatest enemy'. The Bishop of London even claimed 'the men who drink at home are murdering the men in the trenches'. This is why the Government decided to control the times when pubs could open. British Summertime was also introduced, in May 1916, to help increase output from the wartime industries.

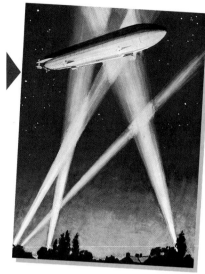

**Source M**  Zeppelin raider caught by searchlights

## Air raids

The first air raid took place in January 1915 when a German Zeppelin dropped bombs on Great Yarmouth and King's Lynn in Norfolk. These airships, filled with inflammable gas and driven by propellers, were over 200 metres long but very slow and vulnerable to attack (Source **M**). All told, there were just over a hundred air raids on Britain. They did some damage, disrupted production in factories and in total killed about 1500 people. This was far fewer than died in a single hour on the Somme but the horrific effect of each raid gave further substance to the propaganda campaign against the evil 'Hun'.

## Money

The war affected everyday life in many other ways. Inflation more than doubled in only four years. Goods costing £3 in 1914, cost £7 on Armistice Day. The war also had a disastrous effect on Britain's trade, since many of the factories which had exported goods now made shells, guns, vehicles and uniforms for the army. To pay for imports and the colossal cost of running the war, the Government had to borrow large sums from America. Income tax was drastically increased and people were encouraged to put money into a special savings scheme called War Loan.

1  Write a sentence beginning: 'Without doubt the Battle of the Somme was …' as it might have been written by **a)** a British soldier and **b)** a newspaper correspondent. Why was censorship thought necessary during the war?

2  How far do you think the writer of Source **H** was justified in his view of German war crimes?

3  What was the impact of the war on government and everyday life? Make use of these words in your answer: DORA, strikes, recruitment, conscription, propaganda, censorship, employment, rationing, inflation, air raids.

4  What are the main differences between Sources **I** and **J**? How and why did attitudes to the war change?

Questions

## Suffragettes at war

The outbreak of war in August 1914 brought a truce between the suffragettes (page 8) and the Government. Emmeline Pankhurst rallied the women behind the war effort. On 10 August 1914, she told them,

'What is the use of fighting for a vote if we have not got a country to vote in?'

In return, all existing suffragette prison sentences were pardoned. It was the end of the suffragette campaign of violence. Henceforth, Mrs Pankhurst used her formidable energy to organise meetings and processions to publicise the part women could play in the war effort.

Some employers were reluctant to see women working in their factories or on the land. Trade unions fighting for the rights of the skilled male worker were reluctant to let unskilled female workers do the same jobs. They called this dilution of labour. Emmeline and Christabel Pankhurst and other leading suffragettes led a huge procession of 40,000 women through London under the slogan 'WE DEMAND THE RIGHT TO SERVE' to demonstrate the strength and determination of women to aid the war effort. You can see some of the jobs women did in these sources.

**Source N** Wartime painting depicting a nurse as an angel of mercy in a hospital for wounded soldiers.

**Source O** Numbers of women employed in making munitions

| 1914 | 200,000 |
|------|---------|
| 1915 | 250,000 |
| 1916 | 500,000 |
| 1917 | 800,000 |
| 1918 | 950,000 |

**Source P** Women factory workers proved beyond all doubt that women could do the same jobs as men. The downside came after the war when munitions were no longer needed and the returning soldiers wanted their jobs back.

**Source Q** The New Woman – from the *Sphere*, 4 May 1918

She has entered practically all the professions. She has a vote. You meet her at every turn. A postwoman brings your morning letters and a girl brings the milk for your morning tea. There are girls, uniformed or not, at the wheels of half the cars that pass. If you go by train, women will handle your luggage. If you choose bus or tram, the conductress in her smart uniform has long been a familiar figure in our streets. Familiar, too, are the blue-overalled window-cleaner with her ladder, the myriad messenger girls, the khaki-clad members of the WAAC, besides the legion of Government clerical workers. You can even be shaved by a woman.

From *The Sphere*, 4 May 1918

**Source R** Land Army girls picking fruit. Farm work was very important since it was vital to grow as much food as possible.

**Source S** Women's Army Auxiliary Corps (WAAC) driver on the Western Front in 1917. Other women joined the Women's Royal Naval Service (WRNS) or the Women's Royal Air Force (WRAF).

## Votes for women – at last!

In 1917, the prime minister, David Lloyd George said women's war work had changed people's opinion on the subject of women's suffrage. When the War was over he said, Parliament would decide the matter.

'I have not the faintest doubt what the vote of the House of Commons will be.'

He was right. In 1918, the Representation of the People Act gave the vote to all women over 30 (Source **T**) and all men over 21. It was no longer necessary to own property or be a householder. Parliament had recognised, at long last, that all people had an equal right to say how their country should be governed. Nonetheless, it still wasn't fair. Women had to wait until they were 30 to vote simply because Parliament wanted to make sure the majority of electors were male. When the Bill was debated in the House of Lords, Lord Finlay asked why, if the vote was a reward for war work, was it not given to the younger women who did most of the work in the munitions factories?

As a consequence, the electorate trebled in size from 7.7 million before the war to 21.8 million in 1918. It greatly boosted the chances of the Labour Party (page 47), because it gave the vote to working men too poor to qualify under existing rules. Women were also given the right to stand for Parliament. The first woman MP was Lady Astor.

(page 47)

**Source T** Women voting for the first time in 1918.

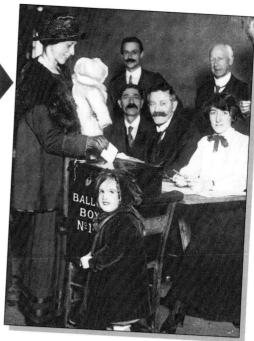

**Source U** Charles Graves in 1922

The Vote was won, not by burning churches, mutilating pictures, or damaging pillarboxes, but by women's work in the War. It was not a concession to violence, but an acknowledgement of patriotic service.

**Source V** Roger Fulford in 1957

The idea that women won the vote by their work in the war was one of those easy sayings which bore no approximation to the truth. Changes had been happening in the years before the war began. Women had become independent in circumstances and outlook to an extent which would have startled a pioneer of the 1860s.

Extract from *Votes for Women*, by Roger Fulford, 1957

### Questions

1 Use the sources on these pages to make a list of the new job opportunities for women during the First World War.

2 Which of the arguments of the opponents of women's suffrage (pages 8–9) were answered by women's work in the War?

3 How far does the judgement in Source **V** differ from the one in Source **U**?

4 Write a paragraph summing up the different ways in which the First World War changed the position of women in Britain. Was this progress or just women doing something different?

## *The defeat of Germany*

 **How was the stalemate broken?**
**What were the reasons for Germany's defeat?**

**Source C**
Cartoon – The
Hydraulic Press

### Close to defeat

By November 1917, the Germans had every reason to think the tide was turning in their favour. The Battle of Passchendaele had greatly increased British casualties for very little gain, the French army had mutinied, the Russian army was in tatters, the Italians had been well-beaten at Caporetto, and the German U-boat campaign was sinking more Allied ships than ever before.

Only the distant prospect of fresh American troops reinforcing the Western Front brought any real hope to the Allies. British leaders tried to get the USA to enter the war earlier but the Americans stayed neutral for three years, even after the *Lusitania* sank (page 27). This attitude changed in 1917 when Germany waged unrestricted war on all shipping in the Atlantic. News that Germany supported Mexican claims to American territory further incensed Americans. They entered the war on 6 April 1917 (Source **A**).

**Source A**   David Lloyd George in his *War Memoirs*

The inexplicable stupidity of the Germans in provoking a quarrel with America and bringing that mighty people into the War against them just as they had succeeded in eliminating another powerful foe – Russia.

### Life in Germany

Despite their apparent success, all was not well in Germany, either (Source **B**).

**Source B**   A 10-year old girl in Berlin in the last year of the war

In the end we could hardly buy a pea without a ration card. No fat, no milk, no eggs. Fritz and I needed them so urgently. Our growing bones were bare of flesh and only covered with a greyish skin. Day after day we had to queue up for the barest necessities of life. Shivering with cold and weariness, I looked more like a scarecrow than a little girl.

Extract from a memoir by Lilo Linke printed in *I Was There!*, edited by Sir John Hammerton, The Waverley Book Company, 1938

The Allied blockade caused massive food shortages in Germany and Austria (Source **C**). Soup kitchens distributed free soup to children and artificial substitutes replaced everyday items of food, such as Ersatz-Kaffee tasting of 'dish-water' and Ersatz-Sauce.

### The German Spring Offensive in 1918

In the spring of 1918, the German High Command decided to launch a major effort to win the war before American troops could reinforce the Allied armies. It began on 21 March 1918 and was so successful it pushed the Allies back to the Marne once more (Source **D**).

**Source D**   By Rudolf Binding, a senior German officer

March 23, 1918. We are going like hell, on and on, day and night. One or two hours' halt, then on again.
March 27, 1918. We are through the awful crater-field of the Somme.
March 28, 1918. The difficulties of reinforcement are beginning. Our former camp is fifty to sixty miles behind us and the new camp has not yet been chosen.

Extract from a memoir by Rudolf Binding printed in *I Was There!*, edited by Sir John Hammerton, The Waverley Book Company, 1938

Eventually the Allied armies held firm. By now Germany's armies and her people were far too exhausted to withstand any further onslaught. The Allies began a counter-offensive in July and August. Over 400 tanks and 800 aeroplanes spearheaded the Allied attack which broke through the German lines at the Battle of Amiens on 8 August 1918 (Sources **E**, **F** and **G**). In September, the Germans recognised the inevitability of defeat. They began talks to try to negotiate an armistice.

**Source E** Tanks leading the Allied breakthrough in August 1918

**Source F** Tank Driver Bacon at the start of the Battle of Amiens, 8 August 1918

4.20 am. Gosh it was quiet. There was a fine mist which cloaked all movement. The silence was painful. Crash! Hell was let loose. Thousands of screaming shells raced overhead and swamped the German trenches. I drove immediately towards the sound of the nearest German machine-gun. The tank crushed the German wire defences and left a clear pathway through which the infantry followed. When the mist lifted, what a sight met our eyes! The enemy had retreated all along the line.

Extract from a memoir by A. Bacon printed in *I Was There!*, edited by Sir John Hammerton, The Waverley Book Company, 1938

**Source G** The Battle of Amiens by General von Ludendorff, the German commander

August 8th was the black day of the German Army, the worst experience I had to go through. The report of the battle shocked me deeply. I was told of deeds of great bravery, but also of behaviour which I should not have thought possible in the German Army. Whole groups of our men had surrendered. I thought the war must be ended.

Extract from a memoir by General von Ludendorff printed in *I Was There!*, edited by Sir John Hammerton, The Waverley Book Company, 1938

One by one Germany's allies deserted her. Bulgaria surrendered in September and Turkey in October. The Italians defeated the Austrians at Vittorio Veneto, a victory which helped to hasten the end of the Austro-Hungarian Empire. Czechoslovakia, the future Yugoslavia and Hungary all declared their independence towards the end of October. By now Socialists were marching through the streets of Berlin. Revolution was in the air (Source **H**).

**Source H** By Paul Schubert

Mutinous sailors left Kiel to spread the revolution. On Monday [*4 November 1918*] they were in mighty Hamburg. They scattered through the city, gathering crowds, making speeches, rallying the workers to their cause. The police made no attempt to stop them. By Tuesday night Hamburg was afire with revolution.

Extract from a memoir by Paul Schubert printed in *I Was There!*, edited by Sir John Hammerton, The Waverley Book Company, 1938

The Kaiser abdicated on 9 November and two days later, at the eleventh hour, on the eleventh day, of the eleventh month, 1918, the armistice came into being. The war was over.

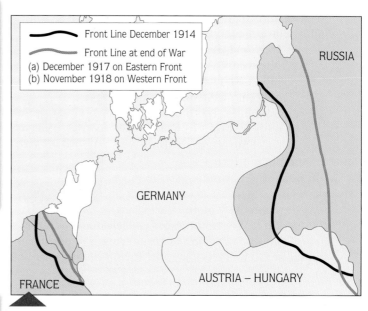

**Source I** Map showing how the front line changed 1914-18

**Q**uestions

1 Look at the map (Source **I**) and at the map on page 16 (Source **A**). What territorial gains had been made by the German and Allied armies by the time of the Armistice?

2 What was the point of the cartoon (Source **C**)?

3 What part did each of the following play in Germany's defeat: **a)** the entry of the United States, **b)** the Bolshevik Revolution (page 56), **c)** the Allied Naval Blockade, **d)** the failure of the German Spring Offensive, **e)** the Allied use of tanks and **f)** the collapse of Germany's allies?

4 Use Sources **E** and **F** and the information on pages 18–23 to explain why the Battle of Amiens was a success and the Battle of the Somme a failure.

# 4 Hopes for a lasting peace: 1918-31

## The Peace Treaties 1919-23

▶ *What were the motives, aims and attitudes of the Allies towards the defeated countries?*
*What were the main terms of the Paris Peace Treaties 1919–20 and the Treaty of Lausanne 1923. Were they fair?*

### A Dictated Peace

A separate peace treaty was drawn up and signed by each of the five Central Powers in and around Paris in 1919-20. The Allied powers, mainly Britain, France, Italy and the United States, dictated the terms. Germany was not consulted. She was told to accept the treaty as it stood or face the consequences. The other treaties with Austria, Hungary, Bulgaria and Turkey were also imposed under threat of force. This infuriated the Germans, especially since they were also made to admit that they, and they alone, started the war. In addition, the Allies cancelled all Germany's gains from Russia at Brest-Litovsk (page 58) but did not bother to invite Communist Russia to take part in the peace talks in Paris.

**Source A** The Palace outside Paris where the Treaty of Versailles was signed on 28 June 1919 - exactly five years to the day since the assassination of the Archduke Franz Ferdinand in Sarajevo in 1914.

### A Just and Lasting Peace

For much of the time, the conference delegates argued among themselves (Sources **B** and **C**).

**Source C** By Frances Stevenson, secretary and close companion of David Lloyd George

▼

March 14th 1919. President Wilson arrived. He has started to annoy David already by talking of matters that have already been settled. Clemenceau cannot tolerate him at any price.
March 28th 1919. A most unpleasant scene between Wilson and Clemenceau.
April 19th 1919. The Italian claims are giving a certain amount of trouble, the Italians being very obstinate. They say that Germany promised them more than this if they remained neutral and Orlando naturally feels he cannot go back to Italy empty-handed.

Extract from *Lloyd George: A Diary*, by Frances Stevenson, edited by A. J. P. Taylor, Hutchinson, 1971

**Source B** The Big Three Allied leaders at Versailles. British and French prime ministers, David Lloyd George (left) and Georges Clemenceau (centre) with US President Woodrow Wilson (right). All are wearing top hats.

The fighting in northern France had destroyed towns and villages and left fields and woods littered with corpses, craters and live ammunition. Hundreds of thousands of French people were homeless. Nearly 1.5 million French soldiers had been killed and 2.5 million wounded. Clemenceau spoke for the French people as a whole when he demanded peace terms which would use German money to help restore and rebuild France. The French wanted revenge. They wanted to punish the Germans and weaken Germany so much that it would never again be strong enough to wage war.

Britain itself had suffered little damage but the loss of the 750,000 men killed had caused immense suffering. Most people had little sympathy for the defeated 'Hun' or 'Boche'. Some wanted to hang the Kaiser. Lloyd George was also restricted by his election promise in December 1918 when he said he would 'squeeze the German lemon until the pips squeak.' Yet at Versailles (Source **A**) he tried to soften French demands for revenge (Source **D**).

**Source E**  Lloyd George signs the Treaty at Versailles

**Source D**  By Frances Stevenson, secretary and close companion of David Lloyd George

March 25th 1919. The great topic is Poland. David is dead against the 'corridor' system, under which a large slice of Germany containing 3 million Germans is lopped off and put under the Poles. David says it will simply mean another war. The French are furious with him for opposing the idea. David says the peace must be a just peace and we must prepare such terms for the Germans to sign that we shall feel justified in insisting upon them. To add this corridor to Poland is simply to create another Alsace Lorraine.

Extract from *Lloyd George: A Diary*, by Frances Stevenson, edited by A. J. P. Taylor, Hutchinson, 1971

Lloyd George wanted a peace settlement which would exact fair compensation from the Central Powers without reducing them to poverty and causing anarchy, such as the ill-fated Spartacist uprising in Berlin in January 1919 (page 72).

By contrast, the United States, entering the war late, had lost just over 100,000 men - far too many, but insignificant compared with the other participants in the war. Moreover, many Americans had made immense profits (page 92). It was easy for Wilson to be moderate and seek 'a just and lasting peace.' Many people in the USA had little interest in the affairs of Europe (page 90).

The final peace settlement which the delegates signed on 28 June 1919 (Source **E**) pleased no one. It was not a recipe for peace, neither was it tough enough to satisfy the French (Sources **F** and **G**, see page 38). Some of the other victorious allies were very disappointed. China refused to sign. Orlando of Italy walked out in disgust. Italy claimed Fiume and had wanted colonies overseas in addition to the gains she made at Austria's expense. The final straw came when the US Senate (page 41) refused to accept the Treaty because signing it would mean agreeing to join the League of Nations as well (page 40).

Questions

1  Why was it easier for Lloyd George and Woodrow Wilson to talk about a 'just and lasting peace' than it was for the French delegates?

2  What evidence is there that some of the victors did not get everything they wanted?

3  Explain what Lloyd George meant when he said a Polish Corridor would 'create another Alsace Lorraine'.

4  Which do you think was Lloyd George's true position - his election promise to squeeze the German lemon dry or the desire to see a 'just peace' recorded by Frances Stevenson in her diary (Source **D**)? Explain the reasons for your choice.

**Military Provisions:**
**Army** – reduced to 100,000 men. No conscription. Guns strictly limited. No armed forces in the Rhineland – to act as a buffer separating Germany from her neighbours, France, Belgium and the Netherlands.
**Navy** – reduced to 15,000 sailors, 6 battleships, 6 light cruisers, 12 destroyers and 12 torpedo boats. No submarines.
**Air Force** – not allowed after October 1920. Many planes destroyed.
**Reparations:**
Germany to pay over 30,000 million US dollars in compensation by 1951 – a sum far beyond her capacity to pay since the Germans, too, had been drastically affected by the war. The demand for reparations caused rampant inflation (page 73). Germany also had to replace Allied merchant ships sunk in the war, pay for the upkeep of the Allied armies of occupation and restore the areas of France and Belgium destroyed by her invading armies.
**Loss of territory** (see map – Source **G**)
**Fate of the German Empire** (see map – Source **G**):
German overseas possessions to be governed by the great powers as mandates of the new League of Nations. All German interests in Morocco, Egypt and China to be renounced.
**Guarantees of independence:**
Germany to guarantee the independence of Czechoslovakia, Poland and Austria. *Anschluss* (union with German-speaking Austria) forbidden.

**Source G** Maps showing the frontier changes imposed by the Paris Peace Treaties

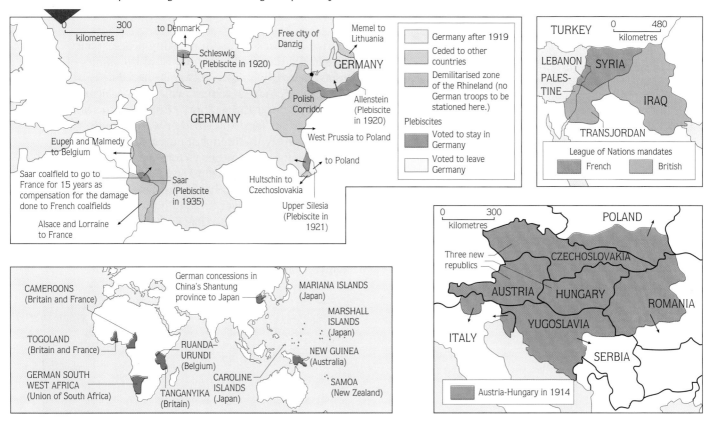

## Verdicts on the Treaty of Versailles

**Source H** British Socialist writer, Beatrice Webb

May 10th 1919. A hard and brutal peace. What disgusts me most is the fact that Great Britain adds most to her territory, prestige and power.

**Source I** South African statesman Jan Smuts

I view it as a thoroughly bad peace – impracticable in the case of Germany, absolutely ludicrous in the case of German Austria [*because it prevented union with Germany*]

**Source J**  Friedrich Ebert, Socialist President of Germany

We shall never forget those who are to be severed from us. They will be torn from the Reich, but they will not be torn from our hearts.

**Source K**  British statesman, David Lloyd George

In many respects terrible terms to impose upon a country .... We shall have to fight another war all over again in twenty-five years at three times the cost.

**Source L**  Marshal Foch of France

This is not a peace. It is an armistice for twenty-one years.

**Source M**  Colonel House (President Wilson's adviser, Versailles)

While I should have preferred a different peace, I doubt whether it could have been made. No one can say with certainty that anything better could have been done at this time.

**Source N**  The Editor of *The Graphic*, 5 July 1919

Nobody involved is competely satisfied – not those who wish to punish the evil-doers and least of all, of course, the evil-doers. The Germans may even yet treat the Peace Treaty as another Scrap of Paper.

**Source O**  King George V

The Treaty of Peace will be received with deep thankfulness throughout the British Empire.

**Source P**  Perceval Landon in *The Daily Telegraph*, 30 June 1919

The Treaty is signed. Militarism, with all its disciplined brutality and unbridled lust of conquest, is at an end. At an end, too, is the German Empire. The world looks forward from today to a full generation of peace.

## The other Paris peace treaties

Peace treaties with the other Central Powers were also signed in Paris in 1919-20. Like Germany, each country had to pay war reparations and limit its armed forces. Frontier changes were also made, moving large numbers of German-speaking peoples to other countries and breaking up the Austro-Hungarian and Turkish empires (Source **G**):

**St Germain – AUSTRIA – September 1919:** South Tyrol to Italy, Sudetenland, Bohemia and Moravia to Czechoslovakia.

**Neuilly – BULGARIA– November 1919:** Western Thrace to Greece – depriving her of a southern coastline. Western Borderlands to Yugoslavia.

**Trianon – HUNGARY – June 1920:** Large areas of the old Hungarian kingdom given to Czechoslovakia, Romania and Yugoslavia.

**Sèvres – TURKEY – August 1920:** Control of Dardanelles taken away. Parts of Thrace, Smyrna and the Aegean Islands to Greece. Palestine and Mesopotamia to Britain and Syria and Lebanon to France – as mandates of the League of Nations.

## Treaty of Lausanne: July 1923

The severity of the Treaty of Sèvres caused a revolution in Turkey led by Kemal Atatürk. When the Greeks claimed their gains in Western Turkey, they were defeated. The Allies had to call a new conference at Lausanne. Smyrna and Eastern Thrace were given back, reparations were cancelled but Britain and France held on to the Middle East.

1 List the terms imposed by the Paris Peace Treaties aimed at: **a)** preventing Germany going to war again, **b)** punishing Germany for starting the war, **c)** returning territories taken by Germany in the past and **d)** rewarding the Allies for fighting against the Central Powers.

2 Why were the defeated Germans so incensed by the Treaty of Versailles?

3 What effect did the long-term causes of the war (page 10) have on the Treaty of Versailles?

4 How and why were the verdicts of Marshal Foch and Lloyd George similar but for different reasons?

5 Draw up a table with three columns labelled FOR/AGAINST/UNDECIDED. Enter the name of the author of each source (**H** to **P**) in one of the three columns. Write a paragraph saying how and why their verdicts on the Paris Peace Treaties differed.

*Questions*

## The League of Nations

 **What were the key features of the League of Nations and to what extent was it a success before 1931?**
**What were the other main triumphs and failures of diplomacy in the 1920s?**

### Setting up the League of Nations

Before 1920 there was no international organisation which could be used to help resolve disputes between nations. The appalling loss of life in the war convinced many people that something had to be done to bring nations together, not set them apart from one another. The leading statesman pressing for such an organisation – a League of Nations – was US President Woodrow Wilson (Source **A**). The attitude of the other statesmen in Paris, however, was less encouraging (Sources **B** and **C**).

**Source B** By Frances Stevenson, secretary and close companion of David Lloyd George

March 14th 1919. President Wilson arrived, and David says he can think and talk of nothing else but his League of Nations.

Extract from *Lloyd George: A Diary*, by Frances Stevenson, edited by A. J. P. Taylor, Hutchinson, 1971

**Source C** By South African statesman Jan Smuts at Versailles

The League of Nations is our best hope, but the diplomats are all against it, regarding it as a toy to amuse and mislead the public, but intending all the time to carry on their old game just as before.

Quoted in *The Political Diaries of C. P. Scott*, edited by Trevor Wilson, Collins, 1970

Despite the apparent lack of enthusiasm, the Allies needed some way of ensuring that Germany and the other defeated powers kept strictly to the terms of their respective treaties. This is why the League of Nations was created and given the job. A Covenant agreeing to join and to abide by the League's decisions was made part of the Treaty (Source **D**). As a consequence, every country signing the treaty joined the League at the same time.

**Source A** Picture on the front page of *The Sphere* magazine, 22 February 1919, after President Wilson made a major speech at the Paris Peace Conference. The main caption read: 'THE REIGN OF FORCE IS OVER' – PRESIDENT WILSON ANNOUNCES THE BIRTH OF THE LEAGUE OF NATIONS – 'Wrong has been defeated. Men are looking eye to eye and saying, "We are brothers, and have a common purpose."'

**Source D** Covenant setting up the League of Nations

OBLIGATIONS OF MEMBERSHIP:
reduce armaments; respect and preserve international frontiers and the independence of all Members of the League;
in cases of aggression accept the Council's ruling on how to deal with the aggressor, including the joint use of force, if necessary;
accept that any war or threat of war is a matter of concern for the League, who will take appropriate action to safeguard the peace;
agree to submit any dispute with another Member to arbitration or inquiry by the Council;
accept that if another Member goes to war, this is an act of war against the League as a whole, the Members of which will immediately sever all trade links and dealings with the covenant-breaking State;
agree to contribute troops to any joint armed force formed to protect the covenants of the League;
agree to support measures directed against slavery; the persecution of indigenous peoples; traffic in women, children and drugs; and disease.

## Ratification

In November 1919, when President Wilson tried to get the Treaty of Versailles ratified (agreed) by the US Congress, he was defeated in the Senate. Senators were worried that under the terms of the Covenant (Source **D**), US troops could be sent automatically into battle without the prior approval of Congress. When Warren Harding became President in 1921, he confirmed to Congress that the USA would not be joining. As a result, the richest and most powerful nation in the world never became a member of the League of Nations. Since neither Germany nor Russia was invited to join in 1920, either, the League began life as a tiger without teeth.

THE GAP IN THE BRIDGE.

**Source E** *Punch* cartoon 'The Gap in the Bridge'

**Source F**

### HOW THE LEAGUE OF NATIONS WAS ORGANISED

The ASSEMBLY met once a year. Each country had one vote, whatever its size. It decided policy and controlled the League's finances.

The COUNCIL met regularly and made most of the important day-to-day decisions. At first, it had four permanent representatives (Britain, Japan, Italy, France) and four representatives elected by the Assembly. Each member had one vote. When Germany joined the League in 1926 she became the fifth permanent member. When she left in 1933, her place on the Council was taken by the Soviet Union.

The SECRETARIAT ran the day to day business from the League's headquarters in Geneva in Switzerland.

The COURT OF INTERNATIONAL JUSTICE with fifteen judges from fifteen different countries met in The Hague in the Netherlands and tried cases brought before it by countries complaining about infringements of international law.

### Questions

1 Describe the main features of the League of Nations.

2 Look at Source **D**. What actions did Members of the League promise to take: **a)** to reduce the likelihood of war, **b)** if they had a quarrel with another member state and **c)** if a Member of the League went to war and ignored the League's solution to the problem?

3 What was the point of the *Punch* cartoon (Source **E**)?

4 Adopt the point of view of any one of the following in 1919: **a)** an American, **b)** a Serb or a Belgian, **c)** a German or **d)** a French or British citizen. *Either* form a discussion group, *or* write down the arguments you would use, to argue FOR or AGAINST the Covenant setting up the League of Nations.

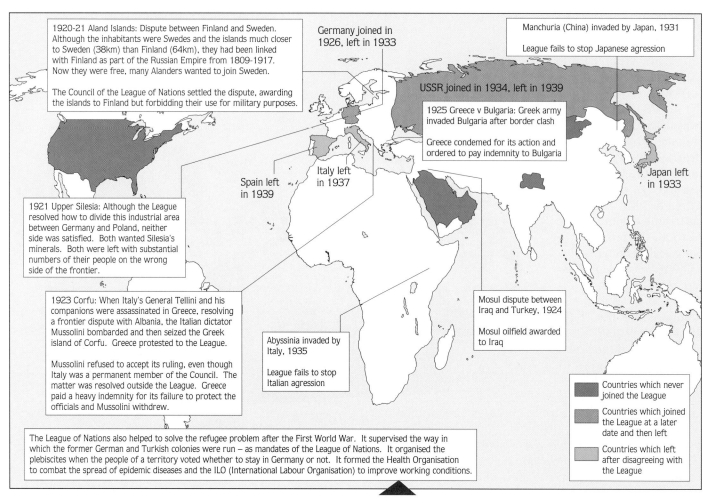

1920-21 Aland Islands: Dispute between Finland and Sweden. Although the inhabitants were Swedes and the islands much closer to Sweden (38km) than Finland (64km), they had been linked with Finland as part of the Russian Empire from 1809-1917. Now they were free, many Alanders wanted to join Sweden.

The Council of the League of Nations settled the dispute, awarding the islands to Finland but forbidding their use for military purposes.

Germany joined in 1926, left in 1933

Manchuria (China) invaded by Japan, 1931

League fails to stop Japanese agression

USSR joined in 1934, left in 1939

1925 Greece v Bulgaria: Greek army invaded Bulgaria after border clash

Greece condemned for its action and ordered to pay indemnity to Bulgaria

Spain left in 1939

Italy left in 1937

Japan left in 1933

1921 Upper Silesia: Although the League resolved how to divide this industrial area between Germany and Poland, neither side was satisfied. Both wanted Silesia's minerals. Both were left with substantial numbers of their people on the wrong side of the frontier.

1923 Corfu: When Italy's General Tellini and his companions were assassinated in Greece, resolving a frontier dispute with Albania, the Italian dictator Mussolini bombarded and then seized the Greek island of Corfu. Greece protested to the League.

Mussolini refused to accept its ruling, even though Italy was a permanent member of the Council. The matter was resolved outside the League. Greece paid a heavy indemnity for its failure to protect the officials and Mussolini withdrew.

Mosul dispute between Iraq and Turkey, 1924

Mosul oilfield awarded to Iraq

Abyssinia invaded by Italy, 1935

League fails to stop Italian agression

Countries which never joined the League

Countries which joined the League at a later date and then left

Countries which left after disagreeing with the League

The League of Nations also helped to solve the refugee problem after the First World War. It supervised the way in which the former German and Turkish colonies were run – as mandates of the League of Nations. It organised the plebiscites when the people of a territory voted whether to stay in Germany or not. It formed the Health Organisation to combat the spread of epidemic diseases and the ILO (International Labour Organisation) to improve working conditions.

**Source G** Map of some of the disputes which came before the League of Nations

## The work of the League

In the 1920s, the League's decisions were often criticised but usually accepted (Source **G**). It eventually failed because its lack of authority as a peace-maker was exposed by the actions of some of the permanent members of the Council in the 1930s (pages 105-6). One by one, the major powers left the League (Source **G**). Member states were afraid intervention might lead to a wider war. After its most spectacular failure – the Second World War – the League was wound up but its organisations bore a strong resemblance to the UN General Assembly and UN Security Council.

## Treaty of Locarno

Because the Americans, Germans and Russians were not members of the League in the early 1920s, diplomats had to look elsewhere in order to reach agreement on matters of common concern. The Treaty of Locarno, signed by Germany, France and Belgium in Switzerland in December 1925, was a notable diplomatic breakthrough at a time of international tension. French and Belgian troops had earlier occupied the Ruhr coalfield in Germany, accusing the Germans of delaying payment of reparations (page 38). Two statesmen – Gustav Stresemann of Germany (page 76) and Aristide Briand of France (Source **H**) – won the Nobel Peace Prize in 1926 for their work in seeking reconciliation.

**Source H** Aristide Briand

All three countries agreed to confirm existing frontiers and to abide by arbitration, not war, if any dispute arose between them. The main difference with the Treaty of Versailles was Germany's willingness to negotiate and sign the treaty of her own accord. Other agreements were also signed at Locarno between Germany, Poland and Czechoslovakia.

## The Kellogg-Briand Pact

In 1927, Briand went further. He wanted to involve isolationist America (page 90) in the peace process as well. He suggested to the US Secretary of State, Frank Kellogg (Source **I**), that France and the United States should jointly renounce war as a means of settling international disputes. Kellogg, fearing this would be seen as an alliance with France, proposed, instead, that other nations should be invited to sign the declaration as well.

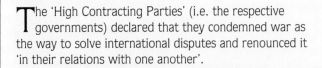

**Source I**  Frank Kellogg, US Secretary of State (foreign minister)

On 27 August 1928, the Kellogg-Briand Pact was signed in Paris. Nine nations (Germany, the United States, Belgium, France, Britain, Italy, Japan, Poland and Czechoslovakia) took part. Over 60 nations eventually signed the Pact, including the Soviet Union. Its provisions were very simple (Source **J**).

**Source J**  The Kellogg-Briand Pact

> The 'High Contracting Parties' (i.e. the respective governments) declared that they condemned war as the way to solve international disputes and renounced it 'in their relations with one another'.

They agreed to settle all disputes between them by peaceful means.

The Kellogg-Briand Pact had two fatal flaws. (1) There was no way of enforcing the Pact. (2) The great powers signed the Pact on the understanding that it did not stop them using force in self defence. Kellogg himself said:

> 'any nation has the right to defend its interests anywhere in the world'.

Since most wars begin with some incident which a warmonger can interpret as an excuse to declare war, the Pact was meaningless. But many people at the time thought differently (Source **K**).

**Source K**  Newspaper account of the signing the Kellogg-Briand Pact

> Short and simple as were the proceedings, the ceremony was most impressive, and those who were present will not easily forget the occasion when the plenipotentiaries of the greatest Powers of the modern world 'solemnly declared', in the names of their respective peoples, that they condemned recourse to war for the solution of international controversies, and renounced it as an instrument of national policy in their relations with one another.
>
> *The Times*, 28 August 1928

## Disarmament

One of the fundamental causes of the First World War had been rearmament, the heavy build-up of weapons, warships and conscripted armies in the years up to 1914. After the War the great powers made a number of efforts to reduce and limit stocks of weapons and the recruitment of armed forces. Germany and the other Central Powers had been forced to do so under the terms of the Paris Peace agreements (page 38) but no such restriction had been placed on the Allies although President Wilson had urged that this be done. In 1921, the Washington Conference agreed to limit the size of the British, US and Japanese navies. But the members of the League of Nations, charged with the duty of securing general disarmament, dragged their feet. It was not until 1932 that a Disarmament Conference eventually met in Geneva (page 108). By then, it was too late.

Questions

1  Why was *The Times* impressed by the signing of the Kellogg Pact (Source **K**)?

2  Look at Source **G**. Were the diplomatic efforts and the work of the League of Nations a success or a failure in the first ten years or so after the war?

3  Explain why the Locarno and Kellogg-Briand Pacts were thought necessary when their terms appeared to be much the same as those agreed to at Versailles.

4  Would the Kellogg-Briand pact have prevented the start of the First World War? Which of the following could have justified using force 'to defend its interests' in 1914: **a)** Austria-Hungary, **b)** Serbia, **c)** Russia, **d)** Belgium, **e)** France, **f)** Britain, **g)** Germany?

# 5 Britain between the wars

## Effects of the First World War

▶ **What were Britain's main economic and industrial problems after the First World War?**
**What were the special problems faced by the mining industry?**

### Effects of the First World War

The First World War had a disastrous effect on the British economy. Prices doubled (page 31), while large sums were borrowed from the USA and income tax was increased to pay the huge cost of the war. When it ended, manufacturers found that other countries, such as Japan and the USA, had taken some of their customers. British goods were expensive to produce compared with those from abroad. There were too many small mills and factories, too many old and antiquated machines, too few modern industries and too great a dependence on imported raw materials, such as wool, cotton, timber and iron ore. Since fewer goods were exported, factories cut back on production and unemployment rose rapidly to about one in every ten members of the workforce.

### Problems of the coal-mining industry

Coal-mining, too, lost markets to the United States, Germany and Poland (Source **C**). The fact that Britain had been a pioneer in the coal-mining industry worked against her. British coal was more difficult to mine since the easily-won coal had been taken hundreds of years earlier. Magazine articles explained why (Sources **B**, **C** and **D**).

**Source A** Colliery and miners in the 1920s

**Source B** *The Graphic*, April 1921

American coal is easy to obtain and can be mined cheaply because it is near the surface and in thick, easily worked seams in inexhaustible quantities. British coal is hard to obtain because it is very deep, often in thin seams, at a great distance from the pit-shaft and therefore expensive to mine.

**Source D** Working conditions in a colliery – from *The Sphere*, March 1919

**Source C** Coal production in tonnes – from *The Graphic*, May 1921

|      | US coal output | US coal exports | UK coal output | UK coal exports |
|------|----------------|-----------------|----------------|-----------------|
| 1913 | 517 million    | 12 million      | 287 million    | 77 million      |
| 1920 | 556 million    | 34 million      | 205 million    | 39 million      |

Coal-cutting machinery was standard in the United States but not in British pits (Source **D**). Britain's 2500 mines were run by 1400 small and inefficient companies. They did not have the cash to make the big improvements which were needed. Since profits in the mining industry depended on exports, the employers had to make the coal cheaper to produce. The miners wanted the Government to nationalise the pits and install up-to-date machinery. The owners had a simpler solution – cut wages and lengthen the working day. There were a number of damaging strikes and lock-outs (when the pit-owners closed down production to force the miners to give in). The miners tried to get their colleagues in the Triple Alliance (page 7) to help (Source **E**).

**Source F**  Sheffield in the 1920s. So long as works and factories used coal as their main fuel, miners were sure of a job. But, as you can see, this was only achieved at a terrible cost to the health of the community.

**Source E**  Miners' plea to their fellow workers

> Make no mistake. It will be your turn next. The miners are locked out in the great war on wages. Are you going to refuse them support? Your place is in the firing-line. Your safety, your standards, your wages, depend upon action now.

A National Strike by railwaymen and transport workers in support of the miners was called off at the last moment – on Black Friday, 15 April 1921 – by timid union leaders. The Cripple Alliance, as it was now called, collapsed. Future negotiations were handled by the General Council of the TUC (the Trades Union Congress).

## The Samuel Commission

Falling demand in 1925, partly due to the fact that German coal competed with British coal after the Dawes Plan was signed (page 73), brought renewed demands from the pit-owners. They got a short, sharp reply from the miners' leader, A. J. Cook. '*Not a penny off the pay! Not a minute on the day!*' Other workers were afraid their employers would demand pay cuts or longer working hours as well, so the TUC backed the miners. All movement of coal by land or water would be stopped. Stanley Baldwin's Conservative government had no alternative. On Red Friday – 31 July 1925 – they agreed to pay a subsidy to maintain the miners' wages until an Official Commission, led by Sir Herbert Samuel, had studied the problem.

Meanwhile, the Government built up stocks of coal and petrol and formed the OMS (Organization for the Maintenance of Supplies) to distribute essential supplies if a general strike was called.

When the Samuel Commission reported back, it recommended modernisation of the pits but backed cuts in wages and longer hours. The miners refused to accept this, so the mine-owners closed the pits. TUC delegates voted overwhelmingly in favour of a General Strike. Union leaders were sure agreement could be reached in last-minute talks with the Government. They were wrong. Baldwin ruled out a compromise. The Labour Party, although sympathetic to the workers' cause, stood on the sidelines. Its leader, Ramsay MacDonald, said he would 'have nothing to do at all' with general strikes, since they called into question the right of the electorate to determine who ran the country.

**Questions**

1  How can you guess from Source **E** that it was written shortly after the end of the First World War? In your own words, explain **a)** what the miners wanted, and **b)** what arguments they used.

2  Explain why **a)** 'Black Friday' and **b)** 'Red Friday' were so named.

3  Use Sources **B** and **C** to explain why Britain's coal mines were no longer able to compete successfully with those in the USA.

4  What were the long-term causes of the General Strike?

## The General Strike

▶ **What was the General Strike, what were its consequences and how close did Britain come to revolution at this time?**

### The Strike begins

The General Strike began on Monday, 3 May 1926, but, at first, only printing, power and transport workers were called out in support of the miners. The Government immediately put its own plans into operation. Soldiers were sent to likely troublespots. Armoured cars and troops with machine-guns protected food convoys. The OMS distributed essential supplies from a depot in London's Hyde Park (Source **B**) using thousands of motor vehicles and even trains driven by volunteers (Source **C**).

Only one person was killed in the first week but there were many scenes of violence – police baton charges, stone-throwing, attempted derailment of trains, overturned lorries and buses. At other times it was more like a holiday. Strikers beat police 2-1 at football in Plymouth. Although people in general had been sympathetic to the miners, they tended to support the Government in the general strike (Source **D**).

### Government versus TUC

Newspapers published during the Strike were often no more than a single sheet of paper. Winston Churchill edited *The British Gazette* to give the Government point of view while the TUC published *The British Worker* (Source **E**) in reply.

**Source A**  Picture of the General Strike painted in 1953

**Source D**  Left-wing writer, Beatrice Webb, in 1926

▼

*M*ay 4th. Such methods cannot be tolerated by any government. If it succeeded it would mean that a militant minority were starving the majority into submission to their will and would be the end of democracy.

Extract from *The Diary of Beatrice Webb*, edited by Norman and Jeanne MacKenzie, The Belknap Press of Harvard University Press, 1984

**Source E**  Rival newspaper headlines

▼

*T*he *British Worker*. Thursday 6 May 1926: WORKERS CALM AND STEADY – Firmer and Firmer Every Day of Strike – BLACKLEGS FAIL.
*The British Gazette*. Friday 7 May 1926: VITAL SERVICES IMPROVING – All Obstacles Being Progressively Surmounted – RESULT OF THE STRIKE NOW BEYOND DOUBT.

*The British Worker*. Monday 10 May 1926: Nothing could be more wonderful than the magnificent response of millions of workers to the call of their leaders.
*The British Gazette*. Wednesday 12 May: ORDER AND QUIET THROUGH THE LAND. Growing Dissatisfaction Among Strikers. INCREASING NUMBERS OF MEN RETURNING TO WORK.

**Source B** Milk churns at the Hyde Park food depot

**Source C** Volunteer driving a bus with a police escort

## Ending the Strike

Talks to end the Strike went on behind the scenes. When Sir Herbert Samuel slightly modified his proposals, they were accepted. When the miners refused to climb down, the TUC called off the Strike. A senior TUC official, asked why, replied: 'There were some people on the General Council who thought it was going too far' (Sources **F**, **G** and **H**). The miners carried on until November, when distress in the mining communities forced them back to work.

**Source F** By the TUC General Secretary

It became apparent that Arthur Cook, the miners' leader, had made up his mind to fight to the finish, and wouldn't settle for any terms within reasonable sight. When I saw the miners' attitude I felt it best to avoid useless sacrifice. The strike had to end, even though we could have gone on for at least another week.

Lord Citrine, quoted in *The General Strike 50th Anniversary Souvenir*, edited by Rick Hosburn, New English Library, 1976

**Source G** Speech in Parliament by railway union leader J. H. Thomas

May 13th 1926: What I dreaded about this strike more than anything else was if by any chance it should have got out of the hands of those who would be able to exercise some control.

Quoted in *The General Strike* by Julian Symons, The Cresset Press, 1957

**Source H** By the historian Margaret Morris in 1973

The General Strike was, in fact, becoming increasingly effective in halting industrial production. Even factories not directly involved were closing down for lack of raw materials or transport. Nor does it seem to have been true that the strike was falling into the hands of revolutionaries.

Extract from *The British General Strike*, by Margaret Morris, Historical Association, 1973

## Reasons for failure

The General Strike failed partly because the Government had public opinion on its side. Most newspapers supported the Government, and BBC radio broadcasts, impartial as they tried to be, left out the news the Government didn't want people to hear. OMS ensured adequate supplies of food and fuel, while the non-violent methods of most strikers minimised clashes with the police. Who knows what might have happened had soldiers opened fire with their machine-guns?

## Effects of the Strike

Calling off the General Strike lowered confidence in the TUC. Many workers were penalised when they returned to work. Ringleaders were sacked. Others had to accept inferior terms of employment. The miners were especially bitter and felt betrayed. Fears of revenge were soon realised when Baldwin's government passed a new law (Source I).

**Source I** The Trade Disputes and Trade Unions Act, 1927

Any strike is illegal if it has any object other than or in addition to the furtherance of a trade dispute within the trade or industry in which the strikers are engaged; and is a strike designed or calculated to coerce the Government either directly or indirectly or by inflicting hardship upon the community.

Trade unions could no longer use members' union dues to support Labour. Workers had to 'contract in' instead of 'contracting out' (page 7). TUC membership fell from 5.5 million in 1925 to 3.75 million in 1930. If anyone gained from the Strike, it was probably the Labour Party, since the lack of common purpose among the unions strengthened those who sought change through the ballot box.

**Questions**

1  How did the two newspapers contradict each other (Source **E**)?

2  Why was Beatrice Webb (Source **D**) against the General Strike?

3  Use Sources **D**, **F**, **G**, **H** and **I** to explain the consequences of the General Strike. In your own words, explain **a)** why it was called off, and **b)** whether or not it was a failure.

4  To what extent is the painting in Source **A** biased in favour of the trade unions rather than the Government?

5  Imagine you are *either* a trade unionist, *or* a right-wing MP. Use these sources to write a short speech supporting or opposing the idea that Britain was close to revolution in 1926.

## The years of depression

► **What effect did the Depression have on Britain?**
**How effective was the Government in dealing with the country's problems?**

### Effects of the Depression

For most of the years between the two world wars, the unemployment rate in Britain (Source **A**) was never less than one in ten of the workforce. It reached its peak in 1932 when nearly one worker in four was out of a job. The years after 1929 were known as the Depression years – a period when large-scale unemployment was common all over the world (page 78).

Many of the reasons for the slump in trade were the same as in Germany (page 78) and the USA (page 96). But there were differences. The value of the pound was too high. This made British exports expensive abroad. The Wall Street Crash (page 96) only made it worse. It was even harder now to sell British goods abroad, such as coal, cloth, steel and pottery. Most of these goods were made in the North. The industries of the Midlands and South-East England were far less affected by the slump, so unemployment rates in these areas were low (page 50). In 1934 only 6% of Birmingham's workforce was out of work and even fewer (4%) in St Albans, on the fringe of London.

Shipbuilding towns were especially hard hit, since the worldwide decline in trade meant that fewer cargo ships were needed. Jarrow on Tyneside had 68% of its

**Source B**  A writer visits Jarrow in 1933

> Wherever we went there were men hanging about, not scores of them but hundreds and thousands of them. The whole town looked as if it had entered a perpetual penniless bleak Sabbath. The men wore the drawn masks of prisoners of war.
>
> Extract from *English Journey*, by J. B. Priestley, Heinemann, 1934

workforce unemployed in 1934 (Source **B**). In 1936, the unemployed shipyard workers of Jarrow went on a much publicised protest march to London – the Jarrow Crusade – to bring their plight to the attention of the Government.

Coal-mining communities were also deeply affected by the Depression since most industries used coke or coal-fired steam-power as their main sources of energy. Merthyr Tydfil on the South Wales coalfield was nearly as badly hit as Jarrow in 1934, with 62% out of work. Many other hunger marches were organised to try to force the Government into doing something to help the depressed areas (Source **D**).

**Source A**  Unemployment in Britain 1919-39

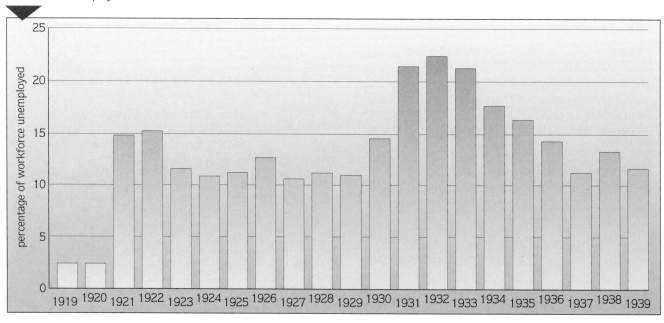

**Source D** Report in the *Manchester Guardian*, Friday 28 October 1932

It is difficult to recall any demonstration in Hyde Park during recent years that has touched the imagination of the onlookers more than did the march of the unemployed today. The crowd showed most interest in the men who walked with haversacks on their shoulders and boots or other oddments hanging from the haversacks, but its sympathy increased as the local men came by, men in a great many cases of poor physique, with pale, pinched faces and a look of worry in their eyes – young men with the stamp of despair on them and elderly men beside whom the hunger-marchers, chosen for their powers of endurance, looked fresh and vigorous.

Extract from *The Guardian Omnibus 1821-1971*, chosen and edited by David Ayerst, Collins, 1973

**Source E** Sandwich board carried by an unemployed worker

I know 3 trades
I speak 3 languages
Fought for 3 years
Have 3 children
And no work for
3 months
But I only want
ONE JOB

## Reactions to the Depression

Government spending increased in 1931 with the rapid rise in the numbers of unemployed claiming benefit. As a result, the value of the pound began to fall. Instead of letting this happen, Ramsay MacDonald's Labour government borrowed money from foreign banks to keep up its value – but at a drastic price. They had to agree to reduce government expenditure. They did this by making savage cuts in state benefits and in the wages of public employees. Most of MacDonald's colleagues refused to support him, so he formed a National Government instead, backed by the Conservatives and Liberals. It took the Labour Party many years to recover from this split and the pound was devalued a month later anyway.

Unlike Roosevelt in the USA (page 100) or Hitler in Germany (page 87), the National Government did not spend public money on large-scale building works to create new jobs to boost the economy. If anything, it did the opposite, cancelling the construction of new roads and new schools. You can see what it did do on page 50.

Sir Oswald Mosley, a former Labour minister, was convinced that the Depression could lead to a Communist revolution. He wanted the Government to create new jobs. This is why he formed the New Party in 1931. The moderates in his party soon left when Mosley veered to the extreme Right, stirring up anti-Semitism and recruiting a black-shirted youth movement like Hitler's Stormtroopers (page 74). He renamed the party the National Front and there were frequent street clashes with Britain's Communists who wanted the Government to adopt Stalin's methods (page 66), for example by taking factories and railways into state ownership. Neither Mosley's Fascists, nor the Communists, ever commanded enough support from the British public to threaten the Government.

### Questions

1 Use the graph (Source **A**) to write a brief account of the rise and fall in unemployment between the two wars.

2 Use sources **B**, **C**, **D** and **E** to help explain the effects of the Depression on Britain in the early 1930s.

3 What does Source **C** tell you about, **a)** the Depression, **b)** the photographer who took the picture?

4 Design a 1935 election poster on unemployment to be used in support of a parliamentary candidate, *either* **a)** standing on behalf of the National Government (such as a Conservative, Liberal or Labour supporter of Ramsey MacDonald) *or* **b)** representing the Labour Party.

# GOVERNMENT ACTION TO HELP BRITAIN OUT OF THE DEPRESSION

ON THE DOLE: Unemployment benefit was cut by 10%. It was now more difficult to get state help. After six months, you had to apply for Public Assistance – the dole. How much you got depended on a Means Test. You lost benefit if you had other income, any savings, or if members of your family had a job.

INTEREST RATES: In June 1932 the Government lowered the bank interest rate to only 2%. This is called cheap money because it makes it cheap to take out a loan. It helped industry to borrow money to buy new machinery and encouraged people to borrow money from their banks to buy homes, cars and domestic appliances. The increased demand for goods created more jobs.

REARMAMENT: The rearmament programme, started in 1935 as a response to the growing threat to peace from Hitler, helped further to reduce unemployment. Making tanks, armoured cars and aeroplanes increased the demand for metals, such as steel and aluminium – and therefore for fuel to heat the furnaces – and electricity to power the machinery.

PUBLIC SPENDING CUTS: Public spending was reduced in 1931, mainly by cutting the wages of public employees, such as postal workers, soldiers, teachers and civil servants. Teachers could still talk resentfully about these pay cuts over twenty years later.

HELP FOR FARMING: Farming suffered when world wheat prices halved between 1929 and 1931. This is why the Government tried to fix wheat prices and founded marketing boards in 1931-3 to control the supply and sale of milk, meat, eggs, potatoes and bacon. By 1939, farming was recovering. Farm values increased and wages rose.

DEVALUATION: The pound was devalued less than a month after the National Government was formed. It was now worth about 70% of its previous value. This helped to make British exports cheaper abroad, making them more competitive. But it pushed up the cost of foreign imports, such as food.

IMPORT DUTIES ACT: In 1932, the Government put a tariff (tax) of 10% on all foreign imports other than foods and raw materials. They also made special trade agreements with countries of the Empire (Imperial Preference). On balance, however, historians cannot agree whether these tariffs did Britain's trade any good.

SPECIAL AREAS ACT: In 1934, the Government encouraged firms to build new factories in the areas worst affected by the slump, such as parts of Wales, Cumbria and Tyneside. In 1934, these regions were called Special Areas and were given money and later the power to build industrial estates, such as in Gateshead. They were not a success. Fewer than 15,000 new jobs were created.

## Recovery

In the end, recovery came when people began to spend more money on products made in Britain, such as electrical goods. Twelve times as many people were using electricity in 1938 compared with 1920. Buying a car boosted the coal and steel industries as well as the growing motor industry.

Three million new houses were built in the 1930s, most of them in the Midlands and South-East where light industry was booming, rather than in the heavy industrial districts of the North. The housing boom reduced unemployment in the brick, glass and timber industries as well as in the building trade. It also gave a fillip to the light industries themselves, since new house-owners were more likely to buy carpets, paint, light fittings, furniture, domestic appliances and electrical goods.

At the same time, people in employment were having much smaller families while their wages were increasing. This meant their living standards were rising. Successive governments also improved the country's social services, improving Old Age Pensions in 1925, abolishing the old workhouse and the Poor Law system in 1929, building council houses, encouraging private housing, providing free school milk (1934), extending the provisions of the existing insurance scheme (1936) and building ante-natal clinics and welfare centres.

## North versus south

As you have seen, the decline in world trade affected the older traditional export industries (coal, steel, textiles and ships) much more than it did the newer industries which made products (such as vacuum cleaners, radios and cars) primarily for the home market. Demand for household goods rose sharply in the 1930s as factories became more efficient and prices fell. Many of the new industries were attracted to the Midlands, London and the South East rather than to the coalfields of the North (Sources **G** and **H**).

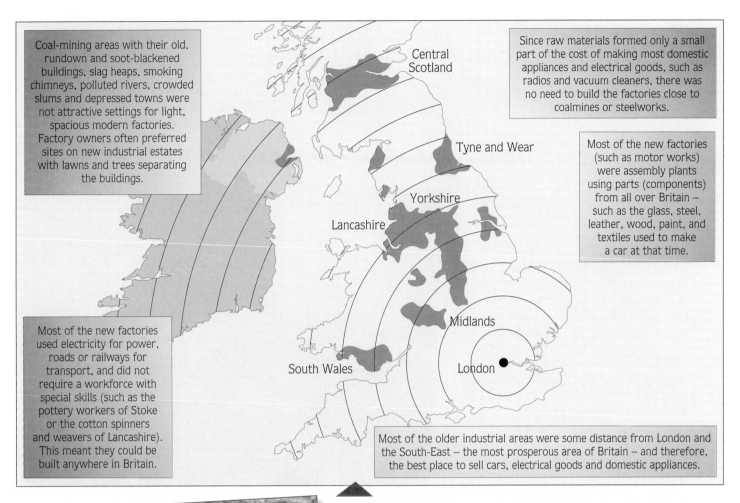

Coal-mining areas with their old, rundown and soot-blackened buildings, slag heaps, smoking chimneys, polluted rivers, crowded slums and depressed towns were not attractive settings for light, spacious modern factories. Factory owners often preferred sites on new industrial estates with lawns and trees separating the buildings.

Since raw materials formed only a small part of the cost of making most domestic appliances and electrical goods, such as radios and vacuum cleaners, there was no need to build the factories close to coalmines or steelworks.

Most of the new factories (such as motor works) were assembly plants using parts (components) from all over Britain – such as the glass, steel, leather, wood, paint, and textiles used to make a car at that time.

Most of the new factories used electricity for power, roads or railways for transport, and did not require a workforce with special skills (such as the pottery workers of Stoke or the cotton spinners and weavers of Lancashire). This meant they could be built anywhere in Britain.

Most of the older industrial areas were some distance from London and the South-East – the most prosperous area of Britain – and therefore, the best place to sell cars, electrical goods and domestic appliances.

Central Scotland

Tyne and Wear

Yorkshire

Lancashire

Midlands

South Wales

London

**Source G**   Why industries were attracted to the Midlands and South-East

**Source H**   The writer J. B. Priestley visits Coventry in 1933

Coventry seems to have acquired the trick of keeping up with the times, a trick that many of our industrial cities find hard to learn. It made bicycles when everybody was cycling, cars when everybody wanted a motor, and now it is also busy with aeroplanes, wireless sets, and various electrical contrivances, including the apparatus used by the Talkies.

Extract from *English Journey*, by J. B. Priestley, Heinemann, 1934

**Source F**   The Prince of Wales visited the home of a Durham miner in 1929 to see for himself what life was like for the unemployed

Questions

1   Make a list of the reasons why the Depression hit the North and West much harder than it hit the South-East and the Midlands.

2   What was the trick (Source **H**) that the other industrial cities found 'hard to learn'? Was this a fair criticism of the northern towns?

3   What measures did the Government take to deal with the Depression and with what success?

# 6 The rise of communism in Russia

## Tsarist Russia

▶ *What were the causes, significance and effects of the 1905 revolution?*

### Russia in 1905

Although Russia in 1905 was modernising fast with a growing middle class, expanding railway system, new factories and rising industrial towns, it was still a vast, backward nation of poor peasants ruled by an autocratic Tsar and controlled by an upper class of nobles and rich landowners. Tsar Nicholas II ruled by decree and appointed his own ministers without the advice or help of a parliament. This meant that everyone had to obey the regime. A growing number of Russians wanted a say in how they were governed. Some wanted a revolution to overthrow the Tsar. They had to be careful what they said. Suspected opponents of the Tsar were hunted down by the *Okhrana* (secret police) and exiled to Siberia. This is why opposition groups usually met in secret or abroad – like Lenin's Bolsheviks.

**Source A**   Bloody Sunday, 22 January 1905

**Source B**   Report in *The Sphere*, 28 January 1905

> It was in the great square in front of the royal palace that Father Gapon and his followers desired to present their petition to the Tsar personally. When the procession of strikers reached the entrance to the square they pleaded with the Cossacks to allow them to proceed, but were eventually fired upon, and many fell at these points, staining the snow of the square with their blood.

### Bloody Sunday

In January 1905 there was widespread unrest in Russia. Fighting a disastrous war against Japan (1904-5) had led to rising prices and higher taxes – and demands for higher wages. Food shortages and a series of humiliating defeats added to the people's grievances. Matters came to a head on 22 January 1905 – Bloody Sunday. Workers on strike in St. Petersburg decided to take their grievances to the Tsar himself rather than to his corrupt and reactionary ministers (Source **B**). They were led by Father Gapon, an Orthodox Priest and trade union official. Some took their families with them, carrying pictures of the Tsar and singing the national anthem 'God Save the Tsar'.

The Tsar had stayed away and his ministers knew only one answer – brutal suppression. Weeks later, workmen with shovels cleared away traces of bloodstained ice uncovered during a thaw. Over 1000 people died (Sources **A** and **B**).

People were appalled. The unrest spread rapidly. Within weeks, there were strikes in many other Russian cities. The Grand Duke Sergius (the Tsar's uncle), 'the best-hated man in Russia', was assassinated. The crew of a battleship – the *Potemkin* – mutinied in June. But although there were many protesters, there was no one leader or political party to co-ordinate the opposition. Only hatred of the Tsarist system held together the mixed bag of discontented peasants, strikers, soldiers, liberals, intellectuals, terrorists and revolutionaries.

## The Tsar's reforms

In October a general strike by 3 million workers paralysed the country. The railway system, factories and even shops, shut down. Massive crowds rampaged through the streets of the big cities carrying red flags. Leon Trotsky, a Marxist, became President of the first Soviet (an elected council or committee of workers) in St Petersburg. Trotsky told them to prepare for armed revolution. But on 30 October 1905, the Tsar gave in and issued the October Manifesto (Source **C**).

**Source C**   The October Manifesto 1905

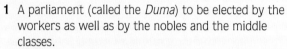

> **1** A parliament (called the *Duma*) to be elected by the workers as well as by the nobles and the middle classes.
> **2** No law to be passed without first being approved by the Duma.
> **3** Freedom of speech and worship, and freedom to hold meetings.

The moderates called off the general strike but some of the extremists continued their protests, doubting whether the Tsar would keep his word. Serious fighting broke out in Moscow in December when local soviets put up street barricades, set buildings on fire and fought pitched battles with soldiers and the police. Hundreds were killed and many more arrested, executed or exiled.

In 1906, the Tsar kept his promise up to a point. But the voting system for the Duma favoured the rich landlords and middle classes in the towns while the peasants – the vast majority of the people – got less than half the votes. The extremists who had distrusted the Tsar were proved right when he later limited the powers of the Duma. Government ministers were responsible to the Tsar, not the Duma. He alone had the right to dissolve the Duma and declare war. When the Duma met, it demanded greater power and sweeping reforms, such as the break-up of large estates. The Tsar rejected these proposals and dissolved the Duma – safe in the knowledge that the police and army were back in control (Source **D**).

## Stolypin

Peter Stolypin, the Russian prime minister from 1906 to 1911, had a simple solution. He changed the electoral laws to give the landlords a greater share of the votes and to ban extremists. The new Duma was much easier to control and stayed in office until 1912. Stolypin ruthlessly suppressed any further opposition to the Tsar. But at the same time, he introduced a

**Source D**   Soldiers patrolling the streets of St Petersburg in 1905

number of important reforms to get liberal support. Land reform made it easier for peasants to put their scattered holdings together and use more efficient farming methods. Other reforms included free primary schools, better secondary schools, and accident and health insurance for workers.

**Questions**

1 Use Sources **A** and **B** to explain what happened on Bloody Sunday.

2 What were the causes of the 1905 revolution and what were its effects?

3 Use Source **C** to explain how the Tsar survived the 1905 revolution.

4 In your own words, describe the ways in which Russia could be seen to be moving towards democracy by 1914.

# The March revolution of 1917

▶ **Why was the revolution of March 1917 successful?**
**What were the weaknesses and strengths of the Provisional Government?**

## Revolution!

Despite bitter memories of the 1905 revolution, patriotism inspired Russians when war was declared in August 1914 (page 13). But by March 1917, they had many new grievances to add to their earlier problems (Source **B**). Millions of Russians despaired of a solution to their misery or an end to the war.

The Tsar ignored the signs of unrest. On 7 March 1917 he left St Petersburg (renamed *Petrograd* in 1914) for the Front. The following day, Thursday, 8 March 1917, bread shortages brought many people on to the streets. Workers downed tools in factories. The police did little to stop the demonstrations. Even bigger crowds demonstrated on the Friday. Many soldiers joined the protests. By Saturday, there were over 250,000 demonstrators in the streets. The situation was rapidly getting out of control (Sources **A** and **C**).

**Source A** Banners carried by the workers

> 'DOWN WITH THE TSAR!'
> 'DOWN WITH THE WAR!'
> 'WE WANT BREAD!'

**Source B** Causes of the March 1917 revolution

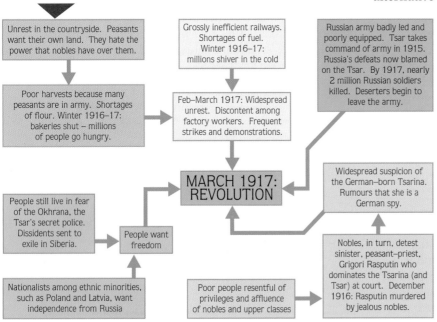

**Source C** By an eyewitness during the March Revolution

> **M**arch 10th 1917 The entire civil population was united against the enemy – the police and the military. Proclamations were quite openly torn down from the walls. Factories were at a standstill. No trams were running. Near the gates of a factory, I met a small group of workers. 'What do they want?' said one grim-looking fellow. 'They want bread, peace with the Germans, and equality,' another replied. 'Right in the bull's eye,' I thought.
>
> Extract from *The Russian Revolution 1917, A Personal Record*, by N. N. Sukhanov, June-August 1921; edited, abridged and translated by Joel Carmichael, Oxford, 1955

Two days later, on Monday, 12 March, protesters set fire to public buildings and attacked police stations and army barracks (Source **D**). By now police and soldiers were openly siding with demonstrators. The Tsar dissolved the Duma but it was too late. The Duma formed its own Provisional Government instead. At the same time, the Petrograd Soviet of Workers' and Soldiers' Deputies was also being formed as an alternative government, elected by army units and factory workers. The Tsar had little choice and abdicated on 15 March 1917.

## The Provisional Government

Next day the Provisional Government, led initially by Prince Lvov and later by Alexander Kerensky, announced measures agreed with the Petrograd Soviet of Workers' and Soldiers' Deputies (Source **E**).

These were tremendous gains when compared with the rights enjoyed by Russians under the Tsar. But a serious problem arose in April when a number of exiled Bolsheviks returned home to Russia. They were led by a dynamic Marxist, baptised Vladimir Ilyich Ulyanova, but far better known as Lenin.

**Source D** Street fighting in Petrograd in 1917

**Source E** The first reforms

1 Amnesty for all political prisoners.
2 Free speech and freedom to strike and join a trade union.
3 Equality for all, irrespective of class, religion or nationality.
4 A Constituent Assembly, elected by secret ballot, to determine the new constitution.

He was greeted in Petrograd, on 3 April 1917, by cheering crowds. Next day he announced his programme (Source **F**). There would be no government of national unity. The Bolsheviks were committed to overthrowing the regime, however liberal. Lenin said the Russian soldiers wanted PEACE. The Russian peasants wanted LAND. The industrial workers wanted a decent wage and enough BREAD.

**Source F** Lenin's April Theses

The real revolution was yet to come. The second stage would come next – the seizure of power by the peasants and workers. The Provisional Government should not be supported. The Soviet of Workers' and Peasants' Deputies was 'the only possible form of revolutionary government' in Russia. All land and all the banks should be owned by the State. Railways, factories and mines should be controlled by the Soviet.

## Continuing the war

The Provisional Government pressed on with the war, even though it was now very unpopular. When Kerensky became war minister in the summer, his aims clashed with those of Lenin (Sources **G** and **H**). He began a new offensive in June, but thousands of Russian soldiers took Lenin's advice and fled or deserted the army. 'They brought back guns and Bolshevik leaflets,' recalled one villager.

**Source G** Lenin's appeal to the army

We summon you to a social revolution. We appeal to you not to die for others, but to destroy others – to destroy your class enemies on the home front!

**Source H** Kerensky's appeal to the army

It's easy to appeal to exhausted men to throw down their arms and go home, where a new life had begun. But I summon you to battle, to feats of heroism – I summon you not to festivity, but to death; to sacrifice yourself; to sacrifice yourselves to save your country!

Extract from *The Kerensky Memoirs*, Alexander Kerensky, Cassell, 1965

## The July Uprising

In July 1917, a half-baked Bolshevik uprising against the Government failed. Trotsky went to prison but Lenin escaped to Finland. Others, who were not so fortunate, were shot. The Provisional Government closed down *Pravda*, the Bolshevik newspaper. For a moment the Bolshevik threat had been crushed. The Socialist, Alexander Kerensky, became Prime Minister. But when the right-wing General Kornilov led a revolt against the Government in September, Kerensky had to call on the Petrograd Soviet and the Bolsheviks to help suppress it.

1 Use Sources **A**, **B** and **C** to explain the causes of the March 1917 revolution. Which of these sources provides evidence of what the demonstrators wanted?

2 How did the Russian Army respond to **a)** Lenin, and **b)** Kerensky in the Summer of 1917? Use Sources **G** and **H** to explain their responses.

3 In your own words, summarise the differences between the 1905 revolution and the March 1917 revolution. Draw a cartoon, poster or chart to explain why the latter succeeded where the former failed.

4 What fundamental differences were there between the reforms of the Provisional Government (Source **E**) and Lenin's April Theses (Source **F**)?

## The Bolshevik revolution

▶ **How were the Bolsheviks able to seize power in November 1917?**

### Growing Unrest

Food and fuel shortages in the autumn of 1917 led to further strikes and protests. Russia was fed up with the war. In many rural areas there was anarchy when peasants began to seize land from the estates of the nobles. The Bolsheviks decided to strike at once and take over the Government. Incredibly, it took them less than two days, between 7 and 8 November. It was called the October Revolution because the Russian calendar was thirteen days behind the rest of Europe. Trotsky did much of the planning. For weeks the Bolsheviks built up their support among the industrial workers and soldiers of Petrograd. They set three main targets (Source **B**).

**Source B**  Bolshevik targets in Petrograd: 7-8 November 1917

▼

The main bridges across the river Neva and the telegraph station were seized early on Wednesday 7 November 1917.
The four main railway stations to the south of the Winter Palace (the centre of the Government), the electricity power station and two bridges close to the Winter Palace were taken later on Wednesday.
The Winter Palace, the main prison and railway stations north of the Neva were captured on Wednesday night/Thursday morning, 8 November 1917.

**Source C**  Armoured car manned by Bolsheviks blocking off a street during the October Revolution

**Source A**  Lenin

**Source D**  By N. N. Sukhanov, an eyewitness during the October Revolution 1917

▼

No resistance was shown. Beginning at 2 in the morning the stations, bridges, lighting installations, telegraphs, and telegraphic agency were gradually occupied. From evening on there were fanciful rumours of shootings and of armed cars racing round the city attacking Government pickets. The decisive operations were quite bloodless; not one casualty was recorded. The city was absolutely calm.

Extract from *The Russian Revolution 1917, A Personal Record*, by N. N. Sukhanov, June-August 1921; edited, abridged and translated by Joel Carmichael, Oxford, 1955

**Source E**  Proclamation by the Military Revolutionary Committee at 10.00 am, 7 November 1917

▼

To the citizens of Russia: The Provisional Government is overthrown. The State power has passed into the hands of the Military Revolutionary Committee on behalf of the Petrograd Soviet of Workers' and Soldiers' Deputies. The cause the people have been fighting for – a democratic peace, the elimination of private property in land, workers' control of production, and the formation of a Soviet Government – is assured.

Extract from *The Russian Revolution 1917, A Personal Record*, by N. N. Sukhanov, June-August 1921; edited, abridged and translated by Joel Carmichael, Oxford, 1955

**Source F** By a British eyewitness, Dr David Soskice

When I arrived at the Winter Palace on the morning of November 7, I found that the guards had left, being unable to get food. Kerensky had set out on a dangerous mission to bring loyal troops from outside the city. The Ministers gathered from time to time to watch the crowds on the bridges. The situation grew more and more critical. Five thousand sailors arrived from Kronstadt, and the cruiser Aurora entered the Neva and lay with guns directed upon the Winter Palace. The Fortress of St. Peter and St. Paul was now in the hands of the Bolsheviks, and its guns were also turned upon the Palace. The Government offices on the other side of the square were gradually surrendering to the Bolsheviks, whose troops were little by little surrounding the Palace itself.

**Source H** Soviet painting of the assault on the Winter Palace, 7-8 November 1917

**Source I** Reasons for the failure of the Provisional Government

KERENSKY failed to:
end the war;
solve the food and fuel shortages;
call the promised Constituent Assembly;
appreciate the threat posed by the Petrograd Soviet;
crush the Bolsheviks in the summer when he had the chance;
recognise the threat posed by Lenin and Trotsky;
solve the problem of the peasants and the great landed estates.

**Source G** By Dr Soskice after leaving the Winter Palace

During the night [*7-8 November*] the booming of guns began. I knew they were the guns of the Aurora bombarding the Palace. An ultimatum was sent to the Ministers to surrender. They refused. Bolsheviks began to penetrate into the Palace. A battle ensued, during which there were some hundred casualties on either side. The Palace was pillaged and devastated from top to bottom by the Bolshevik armed mob, as though by a horde of barbarians.

*Manchester Guardian*, Thursday, 27 December 1917

In another part of Petrograd, the Second All-Russia Soviet Congress was told by Lenin that a Council of People's Commissars had been set up and that decrees would soon be issued, firstly to claim the land for the peasants, secondly to give workers control of the factories, and, thirdly, to start negotiations with the Germans to end the war. Remarkably, this epoch-making revolution, which had incalculable consequences for the history of the modern world, was achieved with very little bloodshed and little reaction or opposition from the Russian people. The newspapers even appeared as usual the next day. Workers, peasants, students, soldiers, clerks and teachers alike had little criticism to make of Lenin's Bolsheviks. They were prepared to see them try (where Kerensky and the Tsar before him had failed) to bring the war to an end and give them the food they desperately needed.

Questions

1 Why did the Bolsheviks choose the targets listed in Source **B**? Was the announcement in Source **E** strictly accurate? How did the Bolsheviks achieve victory so quickly and shedding so little blood?

2 Imagine you are an eyewitness of the Bolshevik Revolution. Write a message to fit on the back of a picture postcard (no more than 50 words) describing what you have seen. (Sources **C**, **D**, **E**, **F**, **G** and **H**)

3 In what ways do Sources **G** and **H** agree or disagree in their portrayal of the storming of the Winter Palace?

4 What problems might arise in using Source **H** as historical evidence?

# Lenin's Russia

## How did Lenin impose Communist control on Russia?

### Keeping Lenin's promises

**1 LAND** One of Lenin's first acts was to sign a Land Decree. This abolished ownership in land without compensation, giving the peasants the right to use the land, but placing its ownership in the hands of the State. A second decree (27 November 1917) gave workers control over the running of their factories.

**2 FREEDOM** Minority national groups, until then part of the Russian Empire, were given the right to break away from Russia. But the promised constituent assembly never met again after the Bolsheviks were defeated when the election was held.

**3 BREAD** Food shortages soon caused a terrible famine, partly as a result of a new policy called War Communism which discouraged peasants from growing surplus corn.

**4 PEACE** An armistice was agreed in December and the Treaty of Brest-Litovsk was signed in March 1918. The treaty was cancelled at Versailles in 1919, but if Germany had defeated the Allies, the humiliating terms agreed by the Bolsheviks would have meant Russia losing a third of her population, a third of her farmland and two-thirds of her heavy industry.

### State security

The Bolsheviks had many opponents, such as Kerensky's Socialists, former landowners, Russians still loyal to the Tsar and army officers who resented the humiliation of Brest-Litovsk. To deal with this, Lenin formed a secret police organisation – the *Cheka* – to

### Lenin (1870-1924)

Lenin was the dynamic and charismatic leader who made the Bolshevik Revolution possible. He spent his life working to 'liberate the working class'. After his release from exile in Siberia in 1900, he lived abroad, planning the revolution to come. Cold, calculating and ruthless in person yet adored by peasants and workers alike, he died of overwork in 1924, worn out after six years of struggling against anarchy, foreign intervention, civil war and famine.

THE LIBERATORS.

FIRST BOLSHEVIK. "LET ME SEE; WE'VE MADE AN END OF LAW, CREDIT, TREATIES, THE ARMY AND THE NAVY. IS THERE ANYTHING ELSE TO ABOLISH?"
SECOND BOLSHEVIK. "WHAT ABOUT WAR?"
FIRST BOLSHEVIK. "GOOD! AND PEACE, TOO. AWAY WITH BOTH OF 'EM!"

**Source A** 'The Liberators'. Cartoon published in *Punch*, 20 February 1918

deal ruthlessly with 'enemies of the State'. Like the Tsar's *Okhrana*, it had the power to exile dissidents to Siberia, suppress free speech and prevent demonstrations.

### The Civil War

The opposition to the Bolsheviks turned into full-scale civil war. Opponents of the regime joined the White Armies gathering on the frontiers of the country (Source **B**). General Kornilov and General Denikin led armies in the Ukraine. In the east an army commanded by Admiral Kolchak took control of a large part of Siberia. Another army, led by General Yudenich, advanced to within striking distance of Petrograd. It looked as if they would crush the Bolsheviks with ease, especially since they received aid at different times from the French, British, American, Japanese, Polish and Finnish armies. Russia's separate peace with Germany had infuriated the Western Allies (page 24) and Trotsky made no secret of the fact that he wanted to export Soviet Communism across the world. The Comintern was founded in Moscow in 1919 to do just that – make Russia the centre of world revolution.

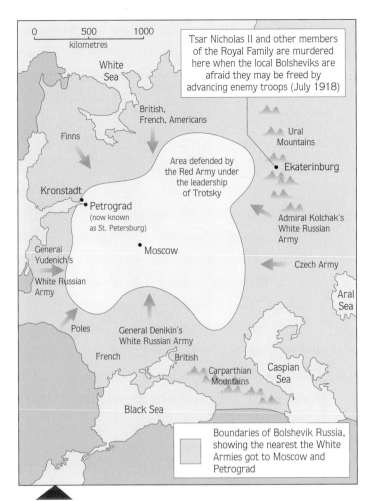

Tsar Nicholas II and other members of the Royal Family are murdered here when the local Bolsheviks are afraid they may be freed by advancing enemy troops (July 1918)

**Source B** Map of the Russian Civil War

## The Red Army

Trotsky became Commissar for War with the job of raising and training a Red Army to defend Bolshevik Russia. A new policy – War Communism (page 60) – was brought in to support the forces defending the homeland.

Trotsky built the Red Army into a formidable fighting force. He toured the country in a special train and used propaganda to get the recruits needed. His efficient organisation of the Red Army played a major part in the eventual victory. Each army unit had a party member as Commissar to keep an eye on the officers and men and ensure they did not desert to the other side (Source **D**). In the end, the Red Army defeated the White Armies one by one. Vast distances separated the enemy armies opposing them (Source **B**), so it was difficult for one White Army to reinforce another. Nor were Lenin's opponents agreed on what they would do if they won. All they had in common was hatred of Communism. The real losers were the million Russians who died, many of them brutally and in cold blood – executed as Bolsheviks by the White Armies or as enemies of the State by the Red Army or *Cheka*. Afterwards, Communist historians gave their reasons for the collapse of the Civil War (Source **E**).

**Source C** Lenin with a broom

**Source D**
Trotsky's orders to the Red Army – 14 August 1918

I give this warning: if a unit retreats, the first to be shot will be the commissar, the second will be the commanding officer. Cowards, profiteers and traitors will not escape bullets. I answer for this pledge before the whole Red Army.

Quoted in Victor Serge, *Year One of the Russian Revolution*, Allan Lane, 1972

**Source E** Reasons why the Red Army won – by a Communist Party committee in Moscow in 1939

1 Lenin had the support of the whole country.
2 The Red Army was loyal and faithful to the people of Russia.
3 The Bolshevik Party formed the core of the armed forces.
4 The Red Army was able to produce talented commanders like Voroshilov.
5 The political education of the Red Army was in the hands of men like Lenin, Stalin, Molotov, Kaganovich, Kirov, Mikoyan, and Khruschev.
6 Each army unit had a military commissar from the Communist Party.

Adapted from *History of the Communist Party of the Soviet Union*, edited by a Commission of the Central Committee, Moscow, 1939

1 Explain the reasoning behind the two cartoons (Sources **A** and **C**). In what ways are they biased for or against the Bolsheviks?

2 Did Lenin fulfil his promise of PEACE, LAND and BREAD for the people?

3 Why did the Red Army triumph over the White Armies? Which of the reasons given in Source **E** seem to you to be acceptable explanations of the Bolshevik victory?

Questions

## War Communism

War Communism put the whole of the country on a war footing to repel the invaders. Small industries were taken over by the State and peasants were forced to sell their surplus grain at fixed prices well below the market value. Many peasants tried to conceal their grain, but soldiers scoured the country seizing supplies from resisting peasants. Some did not even bother to harvest the corn or plant new seed. The end result proved disastrous for Russia. Grain production fell instead of rising. The problem was aggravated by prolonged drought in the main grain-growing areas. Output in 1920 was half that of Russia under the Tsar. There was widespread famine, and many Russians died of starvation (Sources **F** and **G**).

**Source F** Woman dying of starvation in Petrograd. Artist's impression for *The Sphere* – based on 'personal notes and sketches' made by a writer who had escaped 'the grip of the Red Terror.'

**Source G** British eyewitness in Russia in October 1921

There was no grain because it had been burned in its seed time by a terrible drought, leaving the peasants without food because their reserves had been taken up to feed the Red Army. The villages were as quiet as death. No one stirred from the little wooden houses, though now and again we saw faces at the windows – pallid faces with dark eyes staring at us.

Philip Gibbs, *The Pageant of the Years*, Heinemann, 1946

**Source H** From *The Graphic*, 29 May 1920

The people live under a perpetual Reign of Terror without parallel in Russian history. Murder stalks abroad in the land. Outrages are committed everywhere. The industrial life of the great nation has been paralysed. Famine has been added to the horrors of the people.

Although compassion was shown by people in the West to Russia's plight, there was also much gloating. Hatred of Bolshevism coloured news reports (Source **H**).

**Source I** Strip cartoon in *The Graphic*, 29 May 1920. Part of a sequence of pictures claiming to be 'an accurate description of what has been happening all over Russia' under the Soviet Government. The pictures told the story of how Vassily became a Bolshevik official and confiscated 'all poor Peter's belongings' in the name of the State.

A RUSSIAN BURLESQUE OF BOLSHEVISM
THE HUMOURS OF THE VILLAGE UNDER THE SOVIET GOVERNMENT

PETER WORKED HARD ON HIS CORNFIELD

WHILE VASSILY WAS DRUNK BOTH NIGHT AND DAY

## The Mutiny at Kronstadt

Even when the Civil War came to an end the policy of 'War Communism' continued, leaving Russia desperately short of food, raw materials and manufactured goods. The Mutiny at Kronstadt in March 1921 alerted Lenin to the problem: 'It was the flash which lit up reality better than anything else,' he said. Kronstadt was a large naval base protecting Petrograd. The men who served there, many of them peasants, wanted to get back to their farms. Discontent turned into mutiny. The mutineers demanded 'Soviets without Communists', an end to strict government control of agriculture and industry and freedom for political prisoners.

Trotsky's reaction was little different from that of the Tsars. He sent troops across the frozen ice to Kronstadt, saying:

'I am issuing orders for the suppression of the mutiny and the subjection of the mutineers by armed force.'

An American noted the effect of this order in his diary (Source **J**).

**Source J** The Kronstadt Mutiny is crushed

March 17th 1921: Kronstadt has fallen today. Thousands of sailors and workers lie dead in its streets. Summary execution of prisoners and hostages continues.

## The New Economic Policy

Lenin took the events at Kronstadt to heart, recognising there was substance in these grievances and that the appalling shortages in Russia desperately needed new and effective solutions. He introduced the New Economic Policy (Source **K**) less than a week after the start of the mutiny.

**Source K** The New Economic Policy (NEP)

Forcible seizure of surplus grain to be abolished. Instead a fixed percentage of the output from the land to be taken each year as tax. Peasants free to sell any surplus grain on the open market. Small private businesses to be permitted in future. But the 'commanding heights of the economy' – heavy industry, power and transport – to be run by the State.

Later Communists, brought up to believe that Lenin could do no wrong, had to justify the fact that he had abandoned War Communism in favour of free enterprise (Sources **L** and **M**).

**Source L** The NEP by the revisionist Russian Communist leader Nikita Khruschev in 1971

This was a bold, decisive, and dangerous – but absolutely necessary – step to take. It meant the restoration of private property and the revival of the middle class, including the kulaks [*successful peasant farmers*]. Naturally this was, to some extent, a retreat on the ideological front, but it helped us to recover from the effects of the Civil War. As soon as the NEP was brought in, the famine began to subside. The cities came back to life. Produce started to reappear in the market stalls, and prices fell.

Extract from *Khruschev Remembers*, translated by Strobe Talbot, Andre Deutsch, 1971

**Source M** The NEP by a hardline Communist Party committee in Moscow in 1939

The correctness of the New Economic Policy was proved in its very first year. Kulak robbery was almost completely wiped out. Agriculture soon began to forge ahead. Industry and the railways could record their first successes. An economic revival began, still very slow but sure. The workers and the peasants felt the Party was on the right track.

Extract from *History of the Communist Party of the Soviet Union*, edited by a Commission of the Central Committee, Moscow, 1939

Questions

1 In your own words, explain the differences between the New Economic Policy and War Communism.

2 How and why do the two verdicts on the NEP (Sources **L** and **M**) differ? On what points, if any, do they agree?

3 Examine Sources **F**, **H** and **I**. To what extent is each biased against the Bolshevik regime? How far are they reliable sources of information about:
a) Bolshevik Russia, b) British attitudes to Lenin's Russia at that time?

4 What was the effect of War Communism on Russia?

## Stalin's dictatorship

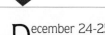 **How did Stalin gain and hold on to power in Communist Russia?**

### Death of Lenin

The New Economic Policy helped Russia regain her strength. But there was tension among the leaders. Lenin and Trotsky often took opposing views. When Lenin died in 1924, he left no obvious successor. No one man or woman commanded the full support of all the other Communist leaders. The brilliant, efficient and dynamic Trotsky was the most effective of the men at the top but was difficult to like with his arrogance and ice-cold contempt for those who tried to thwart him. None of the others – Kamenev, Zinoviev, Bukharin or Stalin – had the same brilliance. It looked as if control of the Soviet Union would be left in the hands of the collective leadership at the top – the *Politburo* – rather than under the control of a dictator like Lenin.

### Man of Steel

Josef Vissarionovitch Dzhugashvili, who later took the name of Stalin ('man of steel'), had other plans. He had earlier built up support among the non-Russian peoples of the USSR. He himself came from Georgia in the south and not from Russia itself. In 1922 he became General Secretary of the Central Committee of the Communist Party. This gave him control of the Party organisation and meant that he could plan the work of committees so they reached decisions he had

**Source A**  Lenin's view of Stalin

December 24-25th 1922:  Comrade Stalin, having become Secretary General, has concentrated unlimited authority in his hands and I am not certain whether he will always be capable of using that authority with sufficient caution.

January 4th 1923:  Stalin is too rude and this defect, although quite tolerable in our midst and in relations among us Communists, becomes intolerable in the post of Secretary General. That is why I suggest that comrades think of a way of removing Stalin from that post and appointing another man to replace him.

V. I. Lenin, quoted in *The Russian Revolution and the Soviet State 1917-1921 Documents*, edited by Martin McCauley, Macmillan, 1975

already made. He skilfully out-manoeuvred his rivals, playing one off against the other. Kamenev, Zinoviev, Bukharin and Trotsky were slow to see Stalin as a rival until it was too late. Lenin (Source **A**) had – but he was dead.

Stalin survived. He first allied himself with Kamenev and Zinoviev against Trotsky, the extremist who wanted to abandon the New Economic Policy. Having discredited Trotsky, he allied himself with Bukharin, a right winger, against Kamenev and Zinoviev. Lastly, he allied himself with Voroshilov and Molotov against Bukharin. By 1929, he was the unchallenged dictator of the Soviet Union and acclaimed on his 50th birthday as 'True Successor of Lenin'. Three cities had already been named after him – Stalino, Stalingrad and Stalinabad.

### Socialism in One Country

In his dispute with Trotsky, Stalin had stressed the need to strengthen the Communist Party at home. 'Socialism in one country' was his motto. By this he meant that the first essential for Russia was to complete the Socialist transformation of the Soviet Union. A successful Soviet Union would be the perfect model of a Communist society and encourage other countries to do the same. A strong Soviet Union could better defend Communism against its enemies. Trotsky thought differently. He wanted to encourage Communists in other countries at once and to give them all the support necessary to help them overthrow their leaders. Stalin feared this would give their many enemies the excuse they needed to invade the Soviet Union. In any case, Russia needed all the outside assistance it could get (Source **B**).

**Source B**  Stalin's comments on Trotsky's idea of world revolution

We have had enough of this idiotic slogan. Without the assistance of the outer world, Russia cannot exist.

Extract from 'These Tremendous Years', *Daily Express*, 1938

Source C Lenin and Trotsky (in uniform, on the right) at a meeting in 1920

Source D A photograph taken at the same time, in the version authorised by Stalin when leader

## Retribution

Stalin's rivals paid dearly in the end. Trotsky was sacked as Commissar for War in 1925. Henceforth, it was Stalin who controlled the army and the secret police. Trotsky had lost his all-important power base. Those who opposed Stalin were spied on by his agents. When Zinoviev spoke of 'the crimes of Stalin' at the funeral of a party member in 1927, Stalin was sent a report of the speech. Trotsky, Kamenev and Zinoviev were expelled from the Party they had helped to found. Trotsky was later exiled from Russia in 1929 and murdered in Mexico in 1940 by Soviet agents. Kamenev, Zinoviev and Bukharin were executed as enemies of the State in the 1930s. Stalin's hatred of Trotsky even extended to trying to erase the role he had played in Soviet history – as you can see by comparing the photographs (Sources **C** and **D**).

1 Write a long caption explaining the difference between the two photographs (Sources **C** and **D**), adding sufficient background information to make your explanation clear to someone with little knowledge of Russian history.

2 How and why did Stalin become supreme leader of the Soviet Union, despite Lenin's warnings to the Russian Communist Party (Source **A**)?

3 Was 'socialism in one country' a sensible policy for Russia to adopt in the 1920s?

Questions

**Source E** Soviet poster of Stalin at a parade

**Source F** News item in *The Times*, 17 January 1935

## The Purges

On 1 December 1934, Sergei Kirov, a friend of Stalin and Communist Party Boss in Leningrad, was assassinated. Stalin ordered the trial of all those held responsible for the crime and their prompt execution if found guilty. This was the beginning of the *Purges*, the name given to the time between 1936 and 1938 when hundreds of thousands of Russians were executed. Show trials were staged in Moscow so that the accused could confess their crimes in public. Former heroes of the Revolution made little attempt to defend themselves (Source **F**). After sentence was passed, they were shot in the neck in a Moscow prison. Many of the families of the victims never discovered the truth, having been told the accused had been exiled 'without the right to receive or send letters'. Top party officials (70 of the 133 members of the Central Committee in 1937), leading civil servants and scientists, senior police and army officers, all Lenin's closest colleagues (apart from the exiled Trotsky) and military commanders of the highest rank (such as Marshal Tukhachevsky and Admiral Orlov) were executed.

Zinoviev, Kamenev, Yevdokimov, and 16 others are charged with complicity in an anti-Stalinist and terrorist plot, including the murder of Kirov on 1 December 1934. A large part of the indictment consists of extracts from the prisoners' alleged confessions of repentance. Under the decree of December the participation of defending counsel at these trials is prohibited, and no appeal against sentence is allowed. If a tribunal passes sentence of death the victims must be shot immediately.

Estimates of how many died vary from one million to fifteen million. The Purges seriously reduced the effectiveness of the Soviet armed forces, as Stalin found to his cost in 1941 when Hitler invaded the USSR. Soviet propaganda effectively concealed the truth (Sources **G** and **H**) – until in 1956 the newly-appointed First Secretary of the Communist Party, Nikita Khruschev, set up a Commission to investigate the Purges. He shocked the Twentieth Party Congress when he revealed the Commission's findings at a secret session in 1956 (Source **I**).

## Josef Stalin (1879-1953)

Stalin trained to become a priest, was exiled to Siberia as a revolutionary, helped plan the Bolshevik Revolution and had succeeded Lenin by 1928. He achieved a great deal during his twenty-five years as Soviet Dictator but at a terrible cost in terms of lives and human suffering. Millions died or were killed as a result of collectivisation and during the Purges. Yet, Stalin founded modern Russia and created the industrial and technological base which enabled the Soviet Union to become a superpower after 1945. Russian propaganda at the time presented him as a father-figure leading his country to greatness. In reality, those close to him loathed and certainly feared him. He was reviled after his death in 1953. His statues were pulled down and the five cities named after him all changed their names.

**Source G** From a Communist history published in Moscow in 1939

The chief instigator and ringleader of this gang of assassins and spies was Judas Trotsky. The 1937 trials brought to light the fact that the Trotsky-Bukharin fiends, in obedience to the wishes of their masters – the espionage services of foreign states – had set out to destroy the Party and the Soviet state. These Whiteguard pigmies, whose strength was no more than that of a gnat, apparently flattered themselves that they were the masters of the country. These Whiteguard insects forgot that the real masters of the Soviet country were the Soviet people. These contemptible lackeys of the fascists forgot that the Soviet people had only to move a finger, and not a trace of them would be left.

Extract from *History of the Communist Party of the Soviet Union*, edited by a Commission of the Central Committee, Moscow, 1939

**Source H** From a history of the USSR published in London in 1950

In the late spring of 1936, a series of arrests of Nazi agents and Trotskyist conspirators revealed the existence of a much wider organization – a central terrorist committee which included, not only Zinoviev and Kamenev, but several leading Trotskyists. Preliminary investigations and evidence given at their trial (in August 1936) revealed that the organisation was in close contact with the German Gestapo.

Extract from *A History of the USSR*, by Andrew Rothstein, Penguin, 1950

**Source I** From the speech by First Secretary Nikita Khruschev in 1956

The Commission has become acquainted with a large quantity of materials in the NKVD [*Secret Police*] archives and with other documents and has established many facts relating to false accusations and glaring abuses of Soviet law which resulted in the death of innocent people. Many Party, Soviet and economic activists who were branded in 1937-38 as 'enemies' were actually never enemies, spies, wreckers, etc., but were always honest Communists. Often, no longer able to bear barbaric tortures, they charged themselves with all kinds of grave and unlikely crimes.

Extract from *Khruschev Remembers, Memoirs of the Soviet Leader*, translated by Strobe Talbott, Andre Deutsch, 1971

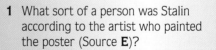

**Questions**

1  What sort of a person was Stalin according to the artist who painted the poster (Source **E**)?

2  What did the writer of Source **G** mean by the phrases, **a)** 'Whiteguard insects', **b)** 'Judas Trotsky', **c)** 'lackeys of the fascists'?

3  How and why do Sources **G**, **H** and **I** differ in their verdicts on the Purges? Which of the three sources are biased? Which are misinformed? What do you consider to be their value as historical evidence?

4  How did Stalin hold on to power in Communist Russia? Were the Purges necessary? What damage did they do?

## Stalin's economic policies

▶ **Why did Stalin introduce the Five Year Plans and what effect did they have on making Russia a great power?**

### Modernising Soviet industry

Stalin wanted to make the Soviet Union strong to deter others from armed invasion. To do this he had to expand production of the raw materials and energy sources used by the factories making the warships, aeroplanes and vehicles needed by the Red Army. He couldn't afford to wait. Russia lagged behind the rest of Europe. The New Economic Policy had been a half-hearted attempt at Communism. Now was the time for change. In 1930 he was able to claim:

> 'We are on the eve of the transformation of our country from an agricultural to an industrial country'.

The existing industrial heartland of the Soviet Union was in the Ukraine and, therefore, vulnerable to attack from Eastern Europe. Stalin decided to build new iron and steelworks at Magnitogorsk in the Ural Mountains some 1000 miles to the east of Moscow. His foresight was vindicated when the Germans occupied the Ukraine in 1941-2. Such a disaster would have crippled the Soviet war effort if this had been the only Russian source of steel and coal. Many other industrial projects were undertaken. Tractor factories were built at Kharkov and Chelyabinsk to mechanise Soviet agriculture. Vast hydro-electricity schemes were constructed on the river Dnieper. Foreign experts were recruited to provide advice and technical skills. The Russians also developed their own system of technical and university education to train experts and technicians. Scientific and engineering research was encouraged. New canals, roads and railways were built to speed up delivery of goods and aid communications across the Soviet Union. Electricity pylons criss-crossed the country.

### The Five Year plans

In order to ensure swift progress, Stalin drew up a Five Year Plan in 1928 setting production targets for each industry. Coal and steel production would be doubled; production of chemicals trebled. These targets were used by planners in each industry to set goals for individual mines and factories to meet. Some of the

**Source A**
Soviet poster praising the industrialisation of the Soviet Union

production targets were impossibly high and factory managers failing to meet them were punished. Each manager, in turn, used the production target to define the norms which had to be achieved by individual workers in the factory.

### The Stakhanov Movement

Workers, too, were punished if they failed to meet their norms but rewarded if they greatly exceeded them. One worker – Alexei Stakhanov – surpassed all existing norms and became a role model for Soviet industry as a whole (Sources **B**, **C**, **D** and **E**).

**Source B** From a Soviet history published in 1939

> On August 31, 1935, Alexei Stakhanov, a coal-hewer in the Central Irmino Colliery (Donetz Basin) hewed 102 tons of coal in one shift and thus fulfilled the standard output fourteen times over. This started a mass movement of workers and collective farmers to raise the standards of output, for a new advance in the productivity of labour.
>
> Extract from *History of the Communist Party of the Soviet Union*, edited by a Commission of the Central Committee, Moscow, 1939

**Source C** Josef Stalin in a speech at the First All-Union Conference of Stakhanovites held in the Kremlin in Moscow, November 1935

> The significance of the Stakhanov movement lies in the fact that it is a movement which is smashing the old technical standards, because they are inadequate and is thus creating the practical possibility of converting our country into the most prosperous of all countries.

**Source D** Propaganda poster for the Stakhanovite movement

**Source E** Rupert Cornwell in *The Independent*, 17 October 1988

**Source F** Industrial output in the Soviet Union 1928–39

Soviet propaganda made much of the achievements of Stakhanov. All workers were encouraged to do likewise. There were subsidised holidays on the Black Sea, free tickets and special privileges for those who succeeded. The majority of the Soviet people, however, were deprived of consumer goods during this time since the emphasis was on heavy industry. Food was short, discipline strict. Many were worse off than they had been under the Tsars. But there was little unemployment and, taken as a whole, Soviet industry showed a remarkable rate of growth (Source **F**) at a time when other countries were suffering the effects of the Depression (page 48).

The First Five Year Plan (1928-32) was succeeded by the Second Five Year Plan (1933–7). This allowed Russian factories to make more consumer goods than had been permitted under the First Five Year Plan. But war loomed ahead. When the Third Five Year Plan (1938-42) was announced, it placed far greater emphasis on the manufacture of guns, planes, tanks and munitions. When Hitler invaded the USSR in 1941, the Soviets had the industrial might to recover from heavy initial losses. Whatever the human cost of the Five Year Plans, there can be little doubt they saved the USSR from defeat.

Fedorov, an engineer, drawing on unpublished archives from the mine, has revealed that two assistants shored up the tunnel and removed the coal while Stakhanov worked at the face with hammer and pick. The event was deliberately organised by the local party to meet Stalin's requests for 'heroes'.

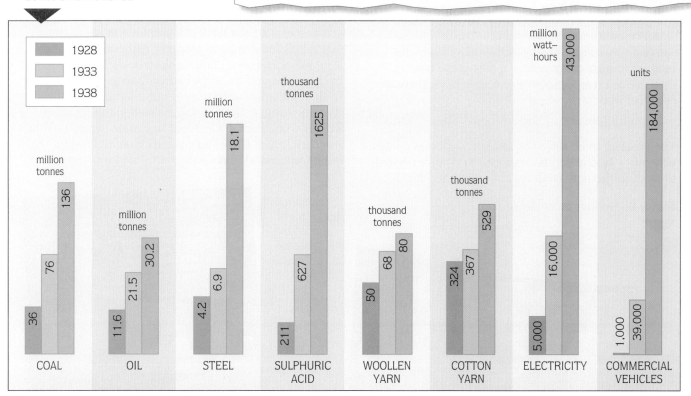

**1** What message did the poster in Source **A** convey to the Soviet people?

**2** Why did Stalin concentrate on expanding heavy industry? Use Source **F** to measure the extent of his success. Which industries expanded most? Which expanded least?

**3** Use Sources **B**, **C**, **D** and **E** to write an October 1988 TV news item saying who Stakhanov was and why he was important to the Soviet Union. Explain why his achievement is now known to be not fully justified by the facts.

*Questions*

# The Collectivisation of Soviet Agriculture

▶ *Why did Stalin introduce collectivisation of agriculture and what effect did this have on the Soviet economy and on the Soviet people?*

## Increasing productivity from the land

In 1928 Soviet agriculture had changed little since the days of the Tsars. Farming methods were primitive, yields low and overall output inadequate to meet the growing needs of the Soviet people. Lenin had earlier suggested 'the advantages of common, collective, co-operative, cultivation of the soil'. This solution – collectivisation – was taken up again by Stalin in 1927 (Source **A**).

**Source A**  Stalin at the Fifteenth Party Congress in December 1927

▼

The way out is to unite the small and scattered peasant farms slowly but surely, not by pressure, but by example and persuasion, into large farms based on common, co-operative, collective cultivation of the soil with the use of agricultural machines and tractors and scientific methods of intensive agriculture. There is no other way out.

The problem to be solved by collectivisation – 'no other way out' – had arisen because peasants were needed to work in the new factories and industries. But if peasants were taken from the land, less food would be grown on their farms to feed the growing numbers of factory workers, not more. Without a radical shake-up of Soviet agriculture, the Five Year Plans would fail.

## Collective Farming

In the end, Stalin abandoned the idea of gradual progress and friendly persuasion. The land was seized – by force where necessary – and merged to form huge farms, often thousands of hectares in extent. The biggest losers were the richer peasants, the kulaks, many of them thrifty and hard-working with extensive holdings, who saw their life's work disappear with scant compensation.

In most districts, collectivisation took several years. Many kulaks were not prepared to see their farms become common property without an armed struggle. Some even chose to destroy their homes, barns, crops and livestock rather than hand them over to the State. But Stalin would not tolerate opposition. 'We must smash the kulaks!' he said – and meant it. Kulaks who resisted were sent to labour camps or shot. In February 1930, Stalin's agents were reported to be killing up to 40 kulaks a day.

**Source B**  Workers on a collective farm

▼

**Source C**
Soviet poster praising the mechanisation of agriculture

In 1928, Russia had had 25,000,000 individual farm holdings. Four years later these had been merged to form 250,000 huge, government-owned farms. There were two types. State farms were run by the Government, paying farm workers a fixed wage. Collective farms, on the other hand, were run by committees of farm workers. Each worker had a small plot of land on which to keep a cow, grow a few vegetables and keep hens and a pig or two. In addition he, or she, took a share of the profits from the collective farm in direct proportion to the amount of work put in. The State took its share of the profits, too. In return it provided the machinery which the peasants had been unable to afford in the past. Fedor Belov, a leading official on a collective farm in the Ukraine, saw these changes for himself (Source **D**).

**Source D**  Setting up a commune in 1928

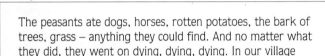

A commune was set up, using two former kulak farms as a base. The commune consisted of thirteen families, with a total of seventy persons, the majority of whom were poor peasants, hired farmhands and orphans. The farm tools taken from the 'dekulakised' farms were turned over to the commune, since its members had almost none of their own. Income was divided in accordance with the principles of 'Co-operative Communism.'

Extract from Fedor Belov, *The History of a Soviet Collective Farm*, Praeger, 1955

## Gains and Losses

In theory, collectivisation meant that farming could be more efficient, since tractors, combine harvesters, heavy ploughs and other implements were shared and could be used more efficiently on the huge fields of the collectives. What is more, they were easier to control. The Government could plan farm production in advance. It could direct the collectives to produce more meat, milk or grain as and when the situation warranted it. But there were also drawbacks. The workers on the collectives no longer had a motive to work long hours. Many devoted more time and energy to their private plots of land than to their official duties on the collective.

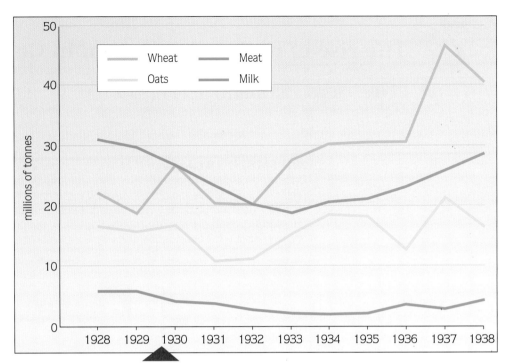

**Source E**  Soviet agricultural production. Collectivisation caused a sharp fall in agricultural production between 1928 and 1932. But by 1934, output was rising again.

The disturbances in the countryside caused a drastic initial fall in farm output (Source **E**). This rebounded on the peasants when Stalin's agents scoured the countryside for grain to feed the industrial workers in the towns, leaving the peasants to starve (Source **F**).

**Source F**  The famine of 1932–3 by Fedor Belov

The peasants ate dogs, horses, rotten potatoes, the bark of trees, grass – anything they could find. And no matter what they did, they went on dying, dying, dying. In our village alone the famine claimed 479 lives.

Extract from Fedor Belov, *The History of a Soviet Collective Farm*, Praeger, 1955

1   In your own words, explain the ways in which agriculture was always a problem for Russia's leaders – from the Tsar and Kerensky to Lenin and Stalin. Use Source **A** to describe how the Communist solution was different.

2   Using Sources **B**, **C** and **D**, write an account explaining how the first collective farms were set up, who benefited and who lost out.

3   Look at the graph (Source **E**). To what extent does it justify Stalin's policy of collectivisation?

4   What were the advantages and disadvantages of Stalin's policy on agriculture?

*Questions*

# 7 The rise of national socialism in Germany

## Overview: Germany 1918–39

**NOVEMBER 1918 (page 72)**
Germany in despair; widespread discontent; a defeated and demoralised army; people starving; strikes and protests; mutiny in the Navy. Kaiser Wilhelm II abdicates. Germany becomes a republic with a President instead of an Emperor. A provisional government is formed by the Socialist Friedrich Ebert and a new system of government – the Constitution of the Weimar Republic – is drawn up.

**JANUARY 1919 (page 72)**
Communists take advantage of the chaos, hoping to repeat the success of the Bolsheviks in Russia. The Spartacists erect barricades and fight in the streets;

ex-officers and soldiers join a makeshift army – the *Freikorps* – which helps the Government to suppress the rebellion. The Spartacus leaders, Rosa Luxembourg and Karl Liebknecht are murdered in cold blood.

**JUNE 1919 (page 73)**
Germans are furious after the Allies impose harsh terms at Versailles.

**1919–20 (pages 73–4)**
Adolf Hitler joins the German Workers' Party and turns it into the Nazi Party; recruits ex-soldiers into his private army of Stormtroopers, the SA. In March 1920, the *Freikorps* try in vain to overthrow the Socialist government.

**APRIL 1922 (page 73)**
Germany, excluded from the League of Nations, seeks friends. Left-wing Jewish Foreign Minister, Walter Rathenau, signs treaty with Bolshevik Russia.

**JUNE 1922 (page 73)**
Anti-Semitic, anti-Communist German Nationalists are furious. Rathenau is assassinated by two right-wing extremists.

**JANUARY 1923 (page 73)**
Germany falls behind with reparation payments. French and Belgian soldiers occupy Ruhr seeking payment in kind (e.g. coal and steel). Instead of fighting back, workers offer passive resistance. Factories shut down as Germans sabotage works, strike and refuse to co-operate.

**OCTOBER 1923 (pages 73–4)**
Inflation, rising steeply since the end of the war, gets out of hand; German mark is worthless; workers and people with savings or small businesses despair. There is widespread discontent throughout Germany. People turn to the extremist parties.

In the Rhineland, a left-wing coalition of Communists and Socialists is in control;

Bavaria, at the other extreme, has turned to a right-wing dictator, Gustav von Kahr, who defies Berlin.

**NOVEMBER 1923 (pages 74–5)**
Hitler and the Nazis try to get von Kahr to join the Munich *Putsch* (an attempt to overthrow the Berlin Government) but it is crushed and Hitler is sent to jail.

**NOVEMBER 1923 (page 73)**
Chancellor Gustav Stresemann replaces the worthless mark with a new German Rentenmark to end inflation; it gives German people confidence once more.

**APRIL 1924 (page 76)**
A committee chaired by American banker Charles Dawes puts forward a plan to loan money to Germany to help industry recover so reparations can be paid. Prosperity as rich investors put money into German businesses.

**1925 (page 76)**
Hitler, released from prison, revives Nazi Party. The SA parade through towns. Hitler decides to contest elections. At first, only a handful of Nazis are elected to the Reichstag (German Parliament).

**1926 (page 77)**
Germany takes its place in the League of Nations after signing the Treaty of Locarno cementing friendship with France and Belgium.

**1929 (page 78)**
Wall Street Crash in New York sparks off worldwide Depression; American bankers want their money back; rapid rise in unemployment. Widespread despair once more. Nazis, Social Democrats (Socialists) and Communists use the Depression to urge Germans to vote for them at elections to the Reichstag. Frequent street fights, many started by the Nazis, the party of law and order!

**JULY 1932 (page 79)**
Almost as many Germans vote for the Social Democrats and Communists as vote for the Nazis.

**JULY 1932 (page 79)**
Many moderates vote for Hitler since the Nazis promise action to restore law and order and positive steps to end unemployment.

**JANUARY 1933 (page 80)**
After the Nazis become by far the biggest single party in the Reichstag, President Hindenburg reluctantly askes Hitler to become Chancellor. He immediately calls a new election using his control of radio and press to convince Germans that the Nazis will make Germany great once more.

**1933 (pages 80–2)** Hitler uses his power as Chancellor to crush the Communists after a Dutch Communist is accused of setting fire to the Reichstag building in Berlin. Communists, Socialists and trade union leaders are rounded up and sent to concentration camps. The Nazis have effectively closed down all left-wing activity in Germany.

**MARCH 1933 (page 81)**
Moderates in the Reichstag pass the Enabling Bill after Stormtroopers and the SS intimidate members into voting with the Nazis. It enables Hitler to become a dictator. Political parties are banned. Persecution of Jews begins; Gestapo is formed; concentration camps are opened. Trade unions are banned.

**JUNE 1934 (page 83)**
Hitler deals with his enemies in the Blood Purge or 'Night of the Long Knives' when over 1000 Nazis are murdered, many of them leaders of the SA.

**SEPTEMBER 1935 (page 85)**
The Nazis bring in the Nuremberg Race Laws, making it a criminal offence for Jews to marry non-Jews.

1 Russia experienced three revolutions in twelve years (in 1905 and in March and November 1917). Which, if any, of the changes in Germany in 1918–39 do you think could also be called revolutions and in which years? Give your reasons.

2 What were the problems of the Weimar Republic, 1918-33, and why did it collapse?

*Questions*

**1935 (pages 86–7)**
Unemployment falls rapidly as Nazi Germany rearms and prepares for war. Industrial output rapidly increases. Most Germans are happy; they have jobs and workers get free or subsidised holidays with the *Strength Through Joy* movement. There is order and discipline in the streets.

**NOVEMBER 1938 (page 85)**
Kristallnacht. The SA smash the windows of Jewish shops after a Nazi diplomat is killed by a young Jew in Paris. Many Jews are beaten up and synagogues are set on fire. Many more Jews flee from Germany.

# The Weimar Republic

▶ **How did defeat by the Allies affect Germany in 1918-23? What was the Weimar Republic and what were its main problems?**

## Spartacists and *Freikorps*

After the Kaiser abdicated in November 1918, Friedrich Ebert, a Socialist, headed a new government. This was a time of chaos and confusion in Germany (Source **A**). Rosa Luxembourg and Karl Liebknecht led a workers' rebellion in Berlin – the Spartacist revolt – in January 1919 (Source **B**). Armed Communists occupied most of the key buildings in Berlin. The rebellion was suppressed by the Socialist government (Source **C**) assisted by the *Freikorps* – a freelance army of extremist ex-soldiers led by discontented former officers.

▼ **Source B** Eyewitness account of the Spartacus revolt

January 15th 1919: Lieutenant M – – – told me there were machine-guns at every corner, and more than once the people in the street threatened to shoot him, and one day smashed the window of the taxi he was in with a hand-grenade. The lack of food, the high prices, the universal demoralization amongst the German people is the best soil possible for the spread of Bolshevism.

Evelyn, Princess Blücher, *An English Wife in Berlin*, Constable, 1921

▲ **Source A** The Kaiser's ruined palace in Berlin

Meanwhile, at Weimar, well away from Berlin and its troubles, Germany's politicians devised a new constitution or system of government (Source **D**). It gave small parties the chance to sit in the Reichstag but hindered future governments, since they had to get the support of different parties with different points of view. In an emergency, however, they could rule without the Reichstag if the President agreed.

**Source C** Communist notice in Berlin in January 1919

Workers! Comrades! The Ebert Government is seeking to uphold its power with the bayonet. Your freedom, your future, the fate of the Revolution are at stake. Down with the tyranny of Ebert. Long live international Socialism!

Quoted in *Germany from defeat to conquest*, W. M. Knight-Patterson, Allen and Unwin, 1945

**Source D** Elections under the Weimar Constitution

▼

At an election all the

GERMAN PEOPLE
(including women)

vote by proportional representation
(where seats are allotted to the men and women on each party list in direct proportion to the number of votes cast)

for parties to represent their interests and make laws in the

REICHSTAG
(the German parliament)

where the leader of the largest party is usually chosen by the

GERMAN PRESIDENT
(elected separately for 7 years)

to head the government as

GERMAN CHANCELLOR

## Rumblings of Discontent

The humiliation of defeat hit Germany hard. Socialists and aristocrats alike resented the attitude of the Allies. How could Germany afford to pay reparations? It was intolerable that a tenth of the German people would no longer live in Germany. After President Ebert infuriated many Germans by accepting the harsh peace terms at Versailles (page 38), the *Freikorps*, tried to overthrow the Government and named Wolfgang Kapp as Chancellor. When workers called a general strike, the Kapp *Putsch* (attempted takeover) collapsed.

Excluded from the League of Nations (page 40), Germany needed friends. A start was made when the Jewish Foreign Minister, Walther Rathenau, negotiated the Treaty of Rapallo in April 1922. This was a treaty of friendship with Russia, re-establishing diplomatic links between the two countries, abandoning claims for war damage and promising economic co-operation. The Allies were furious since the Russians were refusing to pay back money borrowed under the Tsar. Ten weeks after Rapallo, Rathenau was assassinated by two anti-Semitic, anti-Communist, German Nationalists working for the *Freikorps*. It was an ominous portent for the future.

In 1923, Germany's delay in paying reparations to France and Belgium sparked off a new crisis. French and Belgian soldiers crossed the frontier and occupied the Ruhr coalfield, demanding payment in coal and steel. Workers were told to resist peacefully and to show the French and Belgian troops they were unwelcome. German heavy industry almost came to a standstill. The raw materials needed by other industries dried up.

## Inflation

Rising wages and rising prices had been a growing problem since the war. In January 1922, the annual inflation rate was 200%. A year later it was 2000%. Passive resistance undermined the currency even further and by October 1923, the mark was worthless. Factory workers were paid twice a day. Prices changed daily (Source **E**). Shopkeepers stuffed the day's takings

**Source F** 'The Pillars of Society'. Although Nationalists like Hitler were on the extreme RIGHT, many other Germans were moderate Socialists like President Ebert or Communists on the extreme LEFT, like the painter George Grosz who painted this picture of the people he despised most in German society in the early 1920s.

in tea chests. Small businesses, farmers and thrifty citizens suffered most. Their savings were worthless.

On 26 September 1923, Gustav Stresemann, the new Chancellor, ended the policy of passive resistance and resumed payment of reparations since it was hurting Germany more than it was France and Belgium. This further infuriated Hitler and other Nationalists (page 74). In November, Stresemann replaced the old worthless mark with a new unit of currency, the *Rentenmark*. Later the same month, Stresemann had to resign and Charles Dawes, a leading American politician and banker, began an investigation which was soon to put Germany back on her feet (page 76).

**Source E**  By a student

You could go to the baker in the morning and buy two rolls for twenty marks, but go there in the afternoon, and the same two rolls were twenty-five marks. The baker didn't know why rolls were more expensive in the afternoon. It had something to do with the Jews.

Karl-Heinz Abshegen, *Schuld und Verhängniss*, quoted in *Nazism1919–45*, edited by J. Noakes and G. Pridham, University of Exeter, 1983

1 Find the following 'pillars of society' in the painting by George Grosz (Source **F**): **a)** German Nationalist; **b)** journalist; **c)** President Ebert (with a chamberpot for a head); **d)** priest; **e)** soldiers. Why do you think Grosz portrayed Ebert in this way? What did he think of the other people in the picture?

2 Use Sources **A**, **B**, **C**, **D** and **E** to describe the problems faced by the Weimar Republic in the period up to 1923.

*Questions*

# The Munich Putsch

▶ **How, why and with what consequences did Hitler and the Nazi Party attempt to seize power in Munich in 1923?**

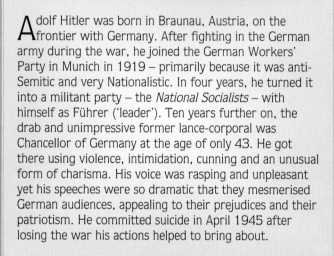

## The NSDAP

Soon after joining the German Workers' Party, Hitler suggested a change of name to *National Sozialistischen Deutschen Arbeiter Partei* ('National Socialist German Workers' Party') – NSDAP for short. In 1920 he played a leading part in drawing up the party's policy – the Twenty-Five Points (Source **B**).

**Source B** The Twenty-Five Points (some have been omitted)

- union between Germany and Austria;

- cancellation of the Treaty of Versailles;

- colonies to grow food and provide living space for Germans;

- only Germans as citizens NOT Jews;

- interests of State to come before the individual;

- nationalisation of all large companies;

- generous improvements in old age pensions;

- a new curriculum in schools to teach nationalistic ideas;

- improvement in people's fitness;

- a people's army of conscripts instead of a professional army;

- control and censorship of the press;

- freedom of religion for all but Jews;

- strong central government.

### Adolf Hitler (1889-1945)

Adolf Hitler was born in Braunau, Austria, on the frontier with Germany. After fighting in the German army during the war, he joined the German Workers' Party in Munich in 1919 – primarily because it was anti-Semitic and very Nationalistic. In four years, he turned it into a militant party – the *National Socialists* – with himself as Führer ('leader'). Ten years further on, the drab and unimpressive former lance-corporal was Chancellor of Germany at the age of only 43. He got there using violence, intimidation, cunning and an unusual form of charisma. His voice was rasping and unpleasant yet his speeches were so dramatic that they mesmerised German audiences, appealing to their prejudices and their patriotism. He committed suicide in April 1945 after losing the war his actions helped to bring about.

When the inflation crisis in September 1923 (page 73) led to widespread despair and a nationwide state of emergency, Hitler got the opportunity he was seeking. He intended to 'persuade' the Bavarian dictator, Gustav von Kahr, to join the Nazis in overthrowing the Berlin government. On Thursday evening, 8 November 1923, as von Kahr addressed a meeting in Munich's Burgerbräu Keller, Hitler surrounded the building with 600 armed men. 'The national revolution has broken out,' he told them. He and war hero General Ludendorff (a recent Nazi convert), forced von Kahr and other Bavarian leaders – at pistol point – to join them. Next day, the SA seized key positions, such as Ernst Röhm's group of Brownshirts at the War Ministry, while Hitler issued a Proclamation (Source **C**).

**Source C** Hitler's Proclamation

Proclamation to the German People! The Government of the November Criminals in Berlin has today been deposed. A provisional German National Government has been formed.

In November 1921, Hitler became Führer of the NSDAP. By now it had 3000 members. Ex-soldiers and volunteers were recruited to form a private army, the *Sturmabteilung* ('Stormtroopers') or SA for short. They bought their own jackboots, brown uniforms and swastika armbands. Ostensibly, the Brownshirts brought order to the streets. In reality, they were thugs who broke up rival meetings.

But the Proclamation was premature. After being freed, von Kahr alerted the army and the police. Hitler wanted to abandon the *putsch* but was too late. Stormtroopers were already pouring into Munich (Source **D**). So Hitler and Ludendorff marched into the city centre (Source **E**) and tried to reach the Residenz where armed police and soldiers were waiting (Source **F**).

**Source D**  By a British eyewitness in Munich

The streets were filled with Hitler's men posting up proclamations. The bridges were all heavily guarded. At the Burgerbräu Keller uniforms, rations and equipment were being issued. Outside rows of lorries were drawn up, which moved off at intervals with troops, munitions or supplies.

Quoted in *Prologue*, edited by M. Christine Walsh, Cassell Australia, 1968

**Source E**  Nazi re-enactment of the Munich *Putsch*. Hitler, Göring and Julius Streicher (leading the procession) march again through Munich.

**Source F**  Official Bavarian Police account of the *Putsch*

The column of National Socialists about 2000 strong, nearly all armed, moved across the Marienplatz, the majority going down the Perustrasse to the Residenz. Suddenly, a National Socialist fired a pistol at a police officer from close quarters. The shot went past his head and killed Sergeant Hollweg standing behind him. Even before it was possible to give an order, the comrades of the sergeant who had been shot opened fire as the Hitler lot did, and a short gun battle ensued. After no more than thirty seconds the Hitler lot fled.

From the Official Bavarian Police account, quoted in *Nazism 1919-45*, edited by J. Noakes and G. Pridham, University of Exeter, 1983

**Source G**  Outside the Residenz in Munich where the Stormtroopers were killed. Hitler erected a monument to the 16 Nazi martyrs who died here. Today, only an official plaque set in the paving (right), records the death of the three policemen.

Three policemen and sixteen Nazis were killed and several others were seriously wounded, including Göring. Hitler, Ludendorff and other Nazi leaders were arrested and charged with treason. The Munich *Putsch* was over.

## Mein Kampf

On 26 February 1924, Hitler was tried for High Treason before sympathetic judges and sentenced to five years imprisonment while Ludendorff was acquitted. Hitler only served nine months in Landsberg Prison before being released. He spent his time there writing *Mein Kampf* ('My Struggle') – the bible of the Nazi movement.

1  Which, if any, of the Twenty-Five Points listed in Source **B** were forbidden by the Treaty of Versailles (page 38)?

2  What did the Nazi Party stand for in the 1920s?

3  Use Sources **C**, **D**, **E**, **F** and **G** to draw a strip of small pictures telling the story of the Munich *Putsch*. Use captions and comments (like those in a comic) to show what is happening in each picture.

4  Why did Hitler try to seize power? How and why did the *Putsch* fail?

## Germany recovers

▶ **How and why did Germany recover after 1923 and what effect did this have on the Nazis? What were the achievements of the Weimar period?**

### The Dawes Plan

Germany's problem in finding the money to revive industry and pay war reparations was solved when the introduction of the Rentenmark by Stresemann (Source **A**) helped to bring inflation under control and the proposals of the Dawes committee (page 73) were accepted in April 1924. Under this plan, American banks made a huge loan to Germany to put the economy back on a sound footing. Only by earning a surplus from exports could Germany hope to pay the massive cost of war reparations. Very soon American money was helping German industry recover. As poverty retreated, the attractions of the Communists and Nazis diminished. In 1929, the Young Plan made further reductions in the amount of reparations to be made by Germany to the Allies. The future for Germany looked rosy. The country had a fine new democratic system of government and a flourishing cultural life which was becoming the envy of Europe.

**Source A** Gustav Stresemann

### Hitler bides his time

Hitler, meanwhile, found Germany had changed on his release from prison in December 1924. There was none of the despair of 1923. He decided to rebuild the Nazi Party (Source **B**). Goebbels and Himmler helped him strengthen the NSDAP. Men like the Berliner, Horst Wessel, became Stormtroopers – attracted by the uniform and violent lifestyle. When Wessel was killed in a street brawl in 1930, he became yet another Nazi martyr. A song he had written became a Nazi anthem and marching song (Source **C**).

**Source B**
Nazi poster announcing the rebirth of the National Socialist Party in 1925. The poster warns: 'Jews (Juden) will not be admitted.'

**Source C** The Horst Wessel song

> Hold high the flag! Close up the ranks!
> The SA marches at a steady pace.
> Comrades, shot by the Red Front and the Reactionaries,
> March on in spirit within our ranks.
> Make way! Clear the streets for the Brownshirt Battalions!
> Make way! Clear the streets for the SA!
> Millions look to the Swastika full of hope,
> The day of Freedom and Bread is dawning.
>
> Translated from the German by Rachel Sauvain.

Hitler, however, had doubts about the loyalty of the SA, fearing their power could be used against him one day. He formed the Blackshirts – the black-uniformed, *Schutzstaffel* (SS) – as an elite corps of guards owing allegiance to him personally as Führer. But none of this worried the complacent German Government (Source **D**).

**Source D** Secret German Government report on the Nazi Party in 1927

In spite of their very well prepared and thoroughly organised propaganda, this is a party that isn't going anywhere. It is a numerically insignificant, radical, revolutionary splinter group incapable of exerting any noticeable influence on the great mass of the population or on the course of political developments.

Quoted in Thomas Childers, *The Formation of the Nazi Constituency*, Croom Helm, 1986

So long as people continued to buy everything that German industry and agriculture produced, there was, indeed, little to worry about. The international situation had also changed for the better. Gustav Stresemann, as Foreign Minister, had re-established Germany as a major power in Europe. His greatest triumph came with the signing of the Treaty of Locarno on 1 December 1925 (page 42) and the admission of Germany to the League of Nations in 1926. Harmony reigned at last in Europe.

## Culture in the Weimar Republic

The period of the Weimar Republic gave the German people their first real taste of democracy. It was a time for other freedoms as well. The senseless slaughter of the trenches, anarchy in the postwar years and the fanatical extremism of the Freikorps and Nazis, deeply affected artists and writers. Some German painters, such as Otto Dix and George Grosz (Source **E** and Source **F** on page 73), painted violent and distorted images of everyday scenes to startle people and make them think. Writers did so, too, with plays and novels. The novelist, Thomas Mann, attacked the Nazis. The Communist playwright, Bertolt Brecht, and his collaborator, the composer Kurt Weill (a Jew), shocked audiences who flocked to see their jazz-inspired *The Threepenny Opera* in 1928. German film directors did the same with horror films, such as *The Cabinet of Dr Caligari*, and with films which offended people's sense of morality like *The Blue Angel*, starring Marlene Dietrich. The outstanding American anti-war film *All Quiet on the Western Front* was based on a novel by the German writer Erich Maria Remarque who had served in the trenches.

Ultra-modern architecture also flourished in the Weimar Republic. Walter Gropius founded the Bauhaus ('building house') school of architecture and modern design in Weimar in 1919. It taught architects and designers to think of technology and design as one, whether designing furniture or even

**Source E** *The Agitator* (1928). In this painting by George Grosz, Hitler promises higher living standards (food and wine) to gullible voters, while violent images, such as the jackboot and truncheon, indicate the reality behind his words.

factory buildings. All these movements in art and culture were denounced by the Nazis when they came to power. Many of the artists, composers and writers concerned fled from Germany, many of them to America.

### Questions

1  Why did Germany recover after 1923? Use Sources **B**, **C** and **D** to explain how this affected Hitler and the Nazi Party.

2  What were the cultural achievements of the Weimar period? Why do you think they were of great importance to Germany at that time?

3  What do the paintings of George Grosz (Source **E** and Source **F** on page 73) tell you: **a)** about the painter, and **b)** about the Weimar Republic? How can paintings like these be used as historical evidence?

## The Nazis at the polls

▶ **How did Hitler increase support for the Nazi Party by 1932?**

### The Great Depression

In October 1929 the Wall Street Crash in New York (page 96) changed everything. The value of American stocks and shares plunged sharply and many businesses were ruined. This, in turn, affected Germany, because the American banks called in the money they had loaned Germany under the Dawes Plan (page 73). German manufacturers could no longer sell their goods so easily abroad. Mines, factories and works closed, or severely cut back on employees. Unemployment figures rose steeply from under 2 million in 1929 to nearly 6 million in 1932. Poor people sifted through slag heaps in search of coal. Queues of people lined up for charity. Banks failed.

### Nazi election promises and methods

What was to be done? The extremist parties of the Left and Right had simple answers. The Communists pointed to Russia. The Five Year Plan (page 66) was putting people to work, not throwing them on the scrapheap. Hitler promised strong authoritarian government and a cure for unemployment. You can see how he persuaded Germans to vote for the Nazi party in the sources which follow.

**Source A** German Socialist poster in 1932

**Source B** Nazi Election Promises (by a Communist writer in 1941)

The Nazis promised higher wages to the workers, higher profits to industry, and well-paid jobs to the unemployed. They promised land to the farmhands, tax exemption and higher income to the farmers and government subsidies and cheap labour to the landowners. They promised to outlaw strikes and at the same time supported every strike to curry favour with the workers. They ranted against capitalism and bargained with captains of industry behind the scenes.

Jan Valtin, *Out of the Night*, Alliance Books, 1941

**Source C** The Nazi Election Campaign in July 1932 (by a former Nazi)

The Party flag was everywhere in evidence. Huge posters and Nazi slogans screamed from windows and kiosks, blazoning forth messages about honour and duty, national solidarity and social justice, bread, liberty, and the beauty of sacrifice.

Extract from *I Knew Hitler*, by Kurt Ludecke, Hutchinson, 1938

**Source D** Nazi election poster. 'Women! Millions of men without work. Millions of children without food. Vote Adolf Hitler!'

**Source E** Zdenek Zofka in 1986

Basically we know that it was not the workers or unemployed who gave Hitler their votes but the middle classes, white-collar employees, artisans, shopkeepers and peasants whose economic and social existence seemed threatened.

Translated by Thomas Childers in *The Formation of the Nazi Constituency*, Croom Helm, 1986

**Source F** Nazi painting of a martyred Stormtrooper

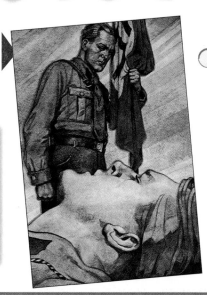

**Source G**  How the SA broke up rival meetings – from the *Manchester Guardian*, 30 March 1932

> If there is any trouble, the lorry dashes to the spot, the storm troops leap down, blows from cudgels, knives, preservers, knuckle dusters are dealt out right and left, heads are cut open, arms raised in self defence are broken or bruised and crouching backs or shoulders are beaten black and blue.
>
> Quoted in *The Guardian Omnibus 1821-1971*, edited by David Ayerst, Collins, 1973

**Source H**  An SA Parade (by Albert Speer, one of Hitler's leading Ministers)

> It must have been during these months [1930–1] that my mother saw an SA parade in the streets of Heidelberg. The sight of discipline in a time of chaos, the impression of energy in an atmosphere of universal hopelessness, seem to have won her over. At any rate, without ever having heard a speech or read a pamphlet, she joined the party.
>
> Albert Speer, *Inside the Third Reich*, translated by Richard and Clara Winston, Weidenfeld and Nicolson, 1970

**Source I**  By a German woman aged 9 in 1932 – in an interview in about 1990

> No money, no work, no bread. As for us, we begged, very horribly, begged. We had nothing. Then came 1932. My mother and father heard Adolf Hitler in a great speech. The next morning they told us how he wanted to be on the side of the unemployed. My mother wept for joy.
>
> Quoted in *Frauen*, by Alison Owings, Rutgers University Press, 1993; Penguin Books, 1995

**Source J**  Elections to the German Reichstag 1928–32 – Percentage Share of the Vote

The number of seats in the Reichstag was in direct proportion to each party's share of the vote

| | 20 MAY 1928 | 14 SEPT 1930 | 31 JULY 1932 | 6 NOV 1932 |
|---|---|---|---|---|
| Nazi Party | 2.6% | 18.3% | 37.3% | 33.1% |
| Social Democratic Party | 29.8% | 24.5% | 21.6% | 20.4% |
| German Communist Party | 10.6% | 13.1% | 14.5% | 16.9% |
| Centre Party | 12.1% | 11.8% | 12.4% | 11.9% |
| German Nationalist Party | 14.2% | 7.0% | 5.9% | 8.3% |
| Other Parties | 30.7% | 25.3% | 8.3% | 9.4% |

**Source K**  Nazi election poster – Building for the future. The three Nazi foundation stones are shown here: ARBEIT (work), FREIHEIT (freedom) and BROT (bread). The alternative is on the right – Jews, Socialists and Communists with their 'empty promises, breakdown of law and order, unemployment, emergency decrees, social decay, corruption, terror, propaganda, lies'.

## Electoral success

First results were disappointing. Only 12 Nazis were elected to the Reichstag in 1928 – when Germany was prosperous. Two years later, the National Socialists had 107 seats (Source **J**). The struggle between Left and Right in the Reichstag made it impossible for Chancellor Heinrich Brüning (a moderate), to get his legislation approved. He had to govern by decree with President Hindenburg's approval. On 31 July 1932, at the height of the Depression, the electoral strength of the National Socialists increased dramatically. This time they took 230 out of the 608 seats in the Reichstag and had the support of far more Germans than any other party. Hitler was now close to government.

### Questions

1  Draw graphs to show the election results in Source **J**. What was the percentage share of the vote of each of the following at the four elections listed: **a)** the RIGHT WING parties (Nazis, German Nationalists), and **b)** the LEFT WING parties (Social Democrats, Communists)?

2  What was the Socialist message for the German people in Source **A**?

3  Use Sources **B**, **C**, **D**, **F**, **G**, **H**, **I** and **K** to explain the methods used by the Nazis to persuade people to vote for them.

4  Which sources tell you, **a)** who voted for Hitler, **b)** from whom the Nazi Party themselves expected to get their support? How do you explain their success?

# The Nazi dictatorship

▶ **How did Hitler change Germany from a democracy to a dictatorship and what were the main features of totalitarian government under the Nazis?**

## Hitler becomes Chancellor

After the July 1932 election, Hitler had good reason to expect the President to invite him to form a government. The Nazis had more votes in the Reichstag than the next two biggest parties combined. But Hindenburg was not yet ready for such a major change in German politics, even after a second election in November 1932 confirmed support for Hitler. Since neither Franz von Papen (the President's first choice as Chancellor), nor his successor, General Kurt von Schleicher, could get the support of the Reichstag, Hindenburg had little choice in the end. Hitler became Chancellor on 30 January 1933.

He immediately used his power as Chancellor to control the media, armed forces and police, and to set in motion plans to turn Germany into a one-party state. To do this, he had to get a two-thirds majority in the Reichstag to pass an Enabling Bill giving him authority to rule as a dictator. In January 1933, however, the combined vote of the Nazi (33%) and German Nationalist parties (8%) was nowhere near enough to overcome the opposition of the Socialists (20%) and Communists (17%).

**Source B** Nazi Party policies

▼

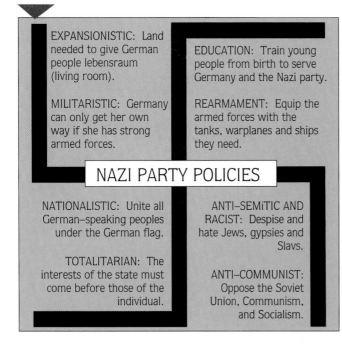

EXPANSIONISTIC: Land needed to give German people lebensraum (living room).

MILITARISTIC: Germany can only get her own way if she has strong armed forces.

EDUCATION: Train young people from birth to serve Germany and the Nazi party.

REARMAMENT: Equip the armed forces with the tanks, warplanes and ships they need.

### NAZI PARTY POLICIES

NATIONALISTIC: Unite all German–speaking peoples under the German flag.

TOTALITARIAN: The interests of the state must come before those of the individual.

ANTI–SEMITIC AND RACIST: Despise and hate Jews, gypsies and Slavs.

ANTI–COMMUNIST: Oppose the Soviet Union, Communism, and Socialism.

**Source A** Chancellor Adolf Hitler with President Hindenburg

## Hitler's policies

Nazi policies were well known (Source **B**). In public, Hitler reassured the German people. He intended to 'revive in the nation the spirit of unity and cooperation', eradicate unemployment, secure world peace and overcome 'the destroying menace of communism in Germany.' But he revealed his real intentions at a secret meeting with top military commanders on 3 February 1933 (Source **C**).

**Source C** Notes made by a general at the secret meeting with Hitler, 3 February 1933

▼

*AT HOME*: Elimination of Marxism lock, stock and barrel. Training of the youth and strengthening military preparedness by all possible means. Strongest authoritarian leadership. Abolition of the cancerous democracy!

*ABROAD*: Fight against Versailles. Equality of rights in the League of Nations. Useless if the nation is not prepared to accept military action. Rebuilding of German Armed Forces a top priority. General conscription must be reintroduced.

Notes made by Lieutenant-General Liebmann at a meeting on 3 February 1933. Translated in *Fragen an die deutsche Geschichte*, the German Bundestag, 1984

## The Reichstag Burns

Hitler called a general election for 5 March 1933. Goebbels was optimistic: 'Radio and Press are at our disposal. We shall achieve a masterpiece of propaganda,' he wrote. During the run-up to the election, Nazi political meetings went unmolested

**Source D** February 1933 – the German Reichstag on fire

**Source F** Election, 8 March 1933

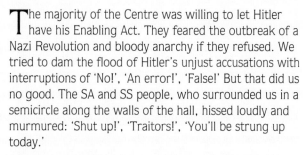

|  | Total votes (millions) | % share of poll | seats in Reichstag |
|---|---|---|---|
| Nazi Party | 17.3 | 43.9% | 288 |
| Social Democrat Party (Socialists) | 7.2 | 18.3% | 120 |
| German Communist Party | 4.8 | 12.3% | 81 |
| Centre Party | 4.4 | 11.2% | 74 |
| German Nationalist Party (Right Wing) | 3.1 | 8.0% | 52 |
| Other parties | 2.7 | 6.3% | 32 |

**Source E** By Josef Goebbels in his diary

*February 27th 1933*: The whole building is aflame. There is no doubt that Communism has made a last attempt to cause disorder by means of fire and terror, in order to grasp power during the general panic. Now we have to act. Göring at once suppresses the entire Communist and Social Democrat Press. Officials of the Communist Party are arrested during the night.

Josef Goebbels, *My Part in Germany's Fight*, Hutchinson, 1935

**Source G** From Josef Goebbels's diary

The Führer delivers an address to the Reichstag. He is in good form. The leader of the Socialists, Wels, complains of terrorism and injustice. The Führer mounts the platform and demolishes him. An incredible success! Only the Socialists vote against.

**Source H** By a Social Democrat

The majority of the Centre was willing to let Hitler have his Enabling Act. They feared the outbreak of a Nazi Revolution and bloody anarchy if they refused. We tried to dam the flood of Hitler's unjust accusations with interruptions of 'No!', 'An error!', 'False!' But that did us no good. The SA and SS people, who surrounded us in a semicircle along the walls of the hall, hissed loudly and murmured: 'Shut up!', 'Traitors!', 'You'll be strung up today.'

Quoted in *Nazism 1919–45*, edited by J. Noakes and G. Pridham, University of Exeter, 1983

while those of Communists and Socialists were broken up. By a stroke of luck, the Reichstag caught fire ten days before the election (Sources **D** and **E**).

At the time, most people thought the Nazis set fire to the Reichstag themselves. It now seems clear that a Dutch Communist called van der Lubbe was probably guilty. Whatever the cause, it gave the Nazis the chance to eliminate the Communist opposition. Hindenburg signed a Presidential Decree giving the police the power to arrest thousands of Communists and take them into 'protective custody' (concentration camps).

## Hitler Seizes Power

Despite a campaign of intense propaganda, intimidation and bias in the State-controlled media, the Nazis still had only 44% of the vote – a long way yet from the 67% needed to pass the Enabling Bill (Source **F**). But Hitler was nothing if not cunning. He used Hindenburg's Presidential Decree to ban the 81 Communists elected to the Reichstag. Had he done so BEFORE the election, the left-wing vote would have gone to the Social Democrats! All that remained was to ensure the parties of the Centre voted with the Nazis when the Reichstag met on 24 March 1933 (Sources **G** and **H**).

So, in March 1933, the centre parties voted with the Nazis giving Hitler unlimited power. Germany ceased to be a democracy. The Enabling Law turned Germany into a one-party state. When Hindenburg died in 1934, Hitler became Head of State as well – as Führer.

1 What was National and what was Socialist about the policies of the National Socialists (Source **B**)?

2 Use Sources **C**, **D**, **E**, **F**, **G** and **H** to explain how and why Hitler obtained the Enabling Law. Did he gain power legally or illegally, honestly or dishonestly?

3 How do Sources **G** and **H** differ in describing the same event? For each source say, **a)** which statements are facts and which are opinions, **b)** whether you regard it as being reliable historical evidence.

*Questions*

## One Party State

Hitler moved swiftly to deal with his opponents. On 14 July 1933, he banned all opposition to the regime with the decree: 'The National Socialist German Workers' Party constitutes the only political party in Germany.' Goebbels censored the press, closed down leftwing newspapers and burned books by Socialists, Communists and Jews (Source **J**).

**Source I**  Nazi poster. 'One people, one country, one leader'. After July 1933, it was also 'one party'.

**Ein Volk, ein Reich, ein Führer!**

## Nazi justice

People's Courts were set up to try cases of High Treason. The Nazis treated anything as lawful if it served the State. Anything which harmed the State was unlawful. In April 1933, Hermann Göring ordered the formation of a secret police force to deal with political crimes. This later became the GESTAPO – GEheime STAats POlizei ('Secret State Police'). Heinrich Himmler, commander of the SS and Munich police chief, later took charge of the Gestapo and established an unenviable reputation for ruthless efficiency. Himmler opened the first concentration camp at Dachau near Munich in March 1933 (Sources **K**, **L** and **N**). It was run by SS guards and held the people the Nazis had taught the Germans to hate.

**Source J**  Berlin, 10 May 1933, by Louis P. Lochner

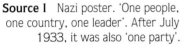

I was a witness. All that afternoon Nazi raiding parties had been going into public and private libraries, throwing on to the streets such books as Dr Goebbels in his supreme wisdom had decided were unfit for Nazi Germany. Columns of Nazi beer-hall fighters took them to the Franz Joseph Platz. Here the heap grew higher and higher, and every few minutes another howling mob arrived, adding more books to the impressive pyre.

Louis P. Lochner, in his introduction to *The Goebbels Diaries*, Hamish Hamilton, 1948

**Source K**  German newspaper report, Tuesday, 21 March 1933

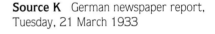

On Wednesday the first concentration camp is to be opened near Dachau with room for 5000 people. All Communists and Socialists who threaten state security are to be concentrated here, since in the long term it is not possible to keep them in the state prisons without overcrowding them. On the other hand these people cannot be released because they persist in their efforts to agitate and organize as soon as they are released.

*Münchner Neueste Nachrichten*, adapted from a translation in the *Official Handbook to Dachau Concentration Camp*, International Dachau Committee, 1978

**Source L**  Dachau concentration camp, near Munich

**Source M**
Nazi Stormtrooper breaking up a meeting

**Source N** Dachau by a former inmate

Physical punishment consisted of whipping, frequent kicking (abdomen or groin), slaps in the face, shooting, or wounding with the bayonet. These alternated with attempts to produce extreme exhaustion, staring for hours into glaring lights and kneeling for hours on end.

Extract from Bruno Bettelheim, *The Informed Heart*, Macmillan (New York), 1960

Communists, Socialists, trade union leaders, Jews, homosexuals, gypsies, tramps and even priests and nuns were held there. They lived in tightly packed dormitory blocks under a system of rigid discipline. Men's heads were closely shaven and they were flogged if they infringed camp rules. Many died from epidemic diseases, ill-treatment, or were shot trying to escape. Horrific reports about the ill-treatment of prisoners and the sadism of the guards were amply reported in newspapers in Britain and elsewhere. No one who could read had any excuse for not knowing what was going on.

## The Blood Purge

One potential source of danger to the Nazi regime had yet to be dealt with – the possibility of armed revolt by the Army or the SA. Ernst Röhm commanded a ramshackle army of 2.5 million Brownshirts. Yet it served no useful purpose now that Hitler was Dictator. Röhm wanted the SA to form part of the Army with

himself as general but the German Army strongly objected. Hitler had to decide. If he backed Röhm, he offended the Army. If he backed the generals, could Röhm topple the regime? It was no secret that some SA leaders were unhappy and wanted to see more Socialism in the 'National Socialist' programme. Himmler and Göring despised Röhm and the SA. They plotted together. Statements made by Röhm – 'that ridiculous corporal' – 'Hitler is a traitor' – were passed on to the Führer. The prudish Hitler was told that many SA leaders (including Röhm) were homosexual.

Hitler's response was brutal. Senior SA leaders were pulled out of bed at dawn and shot. Ernst Röhm, one of Hitler's oldest supporters and hero of the Munich *Putsch*, was executed without trial. When the 'Blood Purge' or 'Night of the Long Knives' (29 June 1934) ended, a thousand people lay dead – most of them loyal Nazis. Over 150 SA leaders were executed in Berlin alone. Others murdered included General von Schleicher (page 80), Gustav von Kahr (page 74) and Gregor Strasser – a left-wing Nazi who wanted to nationalise the banks and major industries. Afterwards Hitler justified his actions (Source **O**).

**Source O** Adolf Hitler

I alone during those 24 hours was the supreme court of justice of the German people. I ordered the leaders of the guilty shot.

The power of the SA had been destroyed for good. 'Simply fizzled out,' was the verdict of one disillusioned SA officer. The news of the massacre appalled many people but it was accepted by the generals. President Hindenburg also approved while the outside world took the news calmly. 'The French are pleased,' wrote an American in Paris. 'They think this is the beginning of the end for the Nazis.'

*Q*uestions

1 Use Sources **I**, **J** and **K** to explain what Hitler was afraid of. Is there any reason to think he had cause for alarm?

2 Why did foreigners take the news of the Blood Purge with relative calm? What do you think it should have taught them?

3 Compare Source **J** with Source **K**. What bias, if any, can you detect in these reports? Which elements of each source are facts and which are opinions? What is their value as historical evidence?

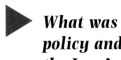

## Nazi racial policy

> ### What was the Nazi racial policy and how did it affect the Jews?

### The Master Race

The Nazis believed the Germans were a pure race of Aryan descent – the *Herrenvolk* or 'Master Race'. They were portrayed in art as blond, blue-eyed, tall, lean and athletic – a fit people to master the world. Accordingly, the Nazis took steps to increase their numbers. 'The German woman brings children into the world,' screamed the slogans. Birth control clinics were closed and laws against abortion rigidly enforced. Parents got tax benefits and generous interest-free marriage loans if the wife promised not to take a job until the loan had been paid off. Women with eight children got the Mother's Gold Cross. The policy worked! The birthrate rose by 40% in 1933-39.

### The Untermenschen

Jews and Slavs, by contrast, were *Untermenschen* – 'subhumans'. Both Hitler and Goebbels were especially virulent in denouncing 'the Jew' (Sources **B** and **C**).

**Source B**  Adolf Hitler in *Mein Kampf* in 1924

> The Jew is and remains a parasite, a sponger, who, like a germ, spreads over wider and wider areas according as some favourable area attracts him.

**Source C**  Dr Josef Goebbels in 1930

> The Jew is the real cause for our loss of the Great War. The Jew is responsible for our misery and he lives on it. He has corrupted our race, fouled our morals, undermined our customs, and broken our power.

Josef Goebbels, propaganda leaflet printed in Louis L. Snyder, *The Weimar Republic*, van Nostrand, 1966

**Source A**  Nazi propaganda against the Jews. Young children are shown reading *Der Stürmer*, the vicious anti-Jewish newspaper edited by Julius Streicher.

Cartoonists drew grotesque pictures of Jewish moneylenders in children's story books. Jewish schoolchildren were made to stand in front of a blackboard slogan – 'The Jew is our greatest enemy!' Even feature films at the cinema were used for anti-Semitic propaganda. Yet it wasn't as if Jews were a substantial or threatening minority. There were no more than half a million Jews in Germany in 1933 – fewer than one person in every hundred. They were only seen as a threat because they played a prominent role in certain spheres of German daily life. Over 17% of bankers, 16% of lawyers, 10% of doctors and dentists and about 5% of writers, journalists, lecturers and university students were Jews. They were almost always perceived as being rich despite the fact that most were no more affluent than other Germans and one Jew in four in Berlin was in receipt of charity. 'All of them rich. I hardly knew poor Jews,' recalled a German woman after the war.

### Boycotting Jewish shops

Many shops and most large department stores were also owned by Jews. The Nazis urged Germans to boycott these premises (Sources **D** and **E**).

> 'If you buy from a Jew, you are a traitor to your country. German women remember – Boycott the Jews.'

Shopkeepers made sure there was no mistake. They displayed signs reading *Deutsches Geschäft* – 'German Business'.

**Source D** Boycott of Jewish shops

**Source E** Boycott proclamation 1933

We appeal to you, German men and women, to observe this boycott. Don't buy in Jewish shops or warehouses! Don't engage Jewish lawyers, avoid Jewish doctors! Those who ignore this appeal prove that they sympathize with Germany's enemies.

Adapted from a translation in the *Official Handbook to Dachau Concentration Camp*, International Dachau Committee, 1978

Hatred of Jews extended to their role in German culture. The works of Jewish writers and composers were banned, such as the music of Felix Mendelssohn. Leading scientists, like Albert Einstein, and other distinguished Germans fled or were forced to leave Germany because of their race. Nearly 40,000 Jews left Germany in 1933, over 20,000 each year between 1934 and 1937, 40,000 again in 1938 and double that number in 1939. They were the lucky ones.

## The Nuremberg Laws

The Nazis wanted a law to ensure the purity of the German blood. They got it in September 1935. The edict: 'Marriage between Jews and German citizens is forbidden,' caused great distress and confusion to Jews and non-Jewish Germans alike. People were often uncertain whether the laws applied to them, to their boyfriends or girlfriends, or to their neighbours and colleagues. The Nazis tried to hide the more obvious signs of persecution during the 1936 Olympic Games but a 24-year-old Englishwoman saw abundant evidence of racism at this time (Source **F**).

**Source F** By a British teacher in Germany in August 1936

KASSEL: Fine shops – nearly all with sign *Deutsches Geschäft*. *Der Stürmer* newsstands at all the important corners.
*MUNDEN*: One shop with notice 'Jews not welcome'. We were in the town-hall when a band of youths marched past. They wore shorts and open shirts. It was raining hard but they marched with spirit and sang loudly rejoicing in their physical fitness. Their song was: 'Germany is awaking. Death to the Jews!'

## Kristalnacht

The persecution of Jews so far was as nothing compared to the horrors to come (page 130). The turning point came on 9 November 1938 when the Nazis launched a terrorist campaign after a German diplomat was murdered by a young Jew in Paris (Source **G**).

**Source G** Newspaper report, Berlin, 10 November 1938

The death of party member vom Rath by the Jewish murderer has aroused spontaneous anti-Jewish demonstrations throughout the Reich. In many places Jewish shop windows have been smashed and the show-cases of Jewish shopkeepers wrecked. The synagogues from which teachings hostile to the State and People are spread, have been set on fire and the furnishings destroyed.

*Deutsche Allgemaine Zeitung*, 10 November 1938. Adapted from a translation in the *Official Handbook to Dachau Concentration Camp*, International Dachau Committee, 1978

An eyewitness recalled that in Wiesbaden,

'It was the SA that did it all. I saw how they pushed the Jews together and how they threw stones through the panes of glass.'

**Questions**

1  Why was *Kristalnacht* so called? Use Source **G** to explain why it was later seen as a turning point in the treatment of the Jews in Germany.

2  Use the sources here and elsewhere (such as on pages 73, 74, 76, 79, 80, 82) to write an account explaining how and why Jews were persecuted in Germany in 1933–39. What evidence is there that the German people as a whole were guilty as well as the Nazis?

## Tackling unemployment: Strength Through Joy

**What was Nazi policy towards workers and to what extent did they and the German people benefit from Nazi rule in the 1930s? Why was Hitler successful in reducing unemployment at a time when it remained high elsewhere?**

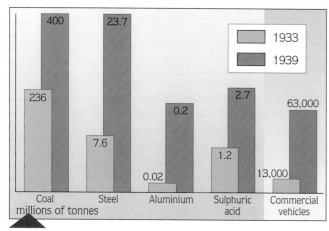

**Source A** Growth of heavy industry in Germany

### The German Labour Front

Trade unions were banned in May 1933. It was inconceivable to the Nazis that workers could be allowed to strike or put pressure on their employers. In future, German workers should have one aim above all others – to work to the best of their ability for the good of the State. Trade unionists and workers who disagreed were rounded up and sent to concentration camps for 're-education'. In place of the trade unions, the Nazis created a German Labour Front run by Dr Robert Ley. This looked after workers' interests by improving working conditions instead of fighting for higher pay. As the unemployment rate fell (Source **E**), it was easy for workers who had been on the dole to make the most of what State control could offer and forget the reminders of a police state, such as the sudden disappearance of a shop steward with left-wing views.

Robert Ley set up two enterprises to implement Hitler's policies. The 'Beauty of Labour' organisation put pressure on manufacturers and industrialists to improve factory working conditions by installing better lighting and ventilation, providing works canteens serving hot meals, and by planting trees and grassland to create garden factories. Slogans such as 'FIGHT AGAINST NOISE!' and 'CLEAN WORKERS IN A CLEAN WORKS!' exhorted the works manager to maintain high standards.

Ley also set up the 'Strength Through Joy' (*Kraft durch Freude* or *KdF*) organisation in 1933 to provide opportunities to improve the leisure time activities of lower paid workers. The *KdF* organisation was very popular in Germany and mushroomed into a vast business enterprise. It subsidised sea cruises, holidays abroad and at home, built health resorts and spas, ran coach tours, sponsored concerts, booked blocks of seats for workers at the theatre and opera, provided cheap sports facilities – such as sailing and skiing – and even manufactured a 'people's car' – the *Volkswagen* – to give everyone the chance to own a car.

**Source B** Two German women – teenagers in the 1930s – interviewed after the war

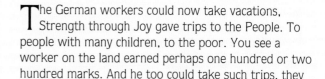

The German workers could now take vacations, Strength through Joy gave trips to the People. To people with many children, to the poor. You see a worker on the land earned perhaps one hundred or two hundred marks. And he too could take such trips, they were so cheap. It was a completely wonderful privilege.

Quoted in *Frauen*, by Alison Owings, Rutgers University Press, 1993; Penguin Books, 1995

### The Labour Service Corps

The Nazis also set up a scheme which gave every young man a compulsory six months period of service in the Labour Service Corps, the *Arbeitsdienst*, (Sources **C** and **D**).

**Source C** By an Australian visitor in 1938

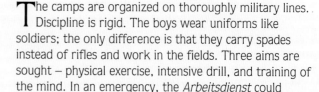

The camps are organized on thoroughly military lines. Discipline is rigid. The boys wear uniforms like soldiers; the only difference is that they carry spades instead of rifles and work in the fields. Three aims are sought – physical exercise, intensive drill, and training of the mind. In an emergency, the *Arbeitsdienst* could immediately put 200,000 drilled and well-organized infantrymen into the field.

*The House that Hitler Built*, by Stephen Roberts, Methuen, 1938

Source D The Arbeitsdienst on parade with shovels instead of rifles

world (Source **F**). Rearmament kept the iron and steel works busy as well as factories making weapons and munitions (Source **A**). Even the splendid new motorways, or *autobahns*, were designed with a view to rushing armed forces to the frontier in time of war.

## Everyday life in Germany

Despite their lack of freedom, most Germans benefited from Nazi rule before 1939 (Source **G**) – provided they were not members of one of the persecuted minority groups and provided they had no existing commitment to trade unionism or to left-wing political parties or policies.

**Source G**  By a German historian writing in 1961

Young people in Germany often receive contradictory information about the true conditions of life in the Third Reich. History books, documents, films and magazines describe it as ugly and horrible. Their elders, on the other hand, often tell them that most people lived well then, that people had jobs and earned good money, and that those were the best years in memory, at least up to the war.

Extract from *The Burden of Guilt*, by Hannah Vogt, translated by Herbert Strauss, Oxford, 1964

## Tackling Unemployment

As you can see from Source **E**, the number of people unemployed in Germany had already fallen before Hitler took office. But there is no denying the fact that Nazi methods, however unscrupulous, were highly successful in lowering unemployment in the 1930s.

**Source E**  Unemployment in Germany, 1928–39

| 1928 | 1929 | 1930 | 1931 | 1932 | 1933 |
|------|------|------|------|------|------|
| 8.4% | 13.1% | 15.3% | 23.3% | 30.1% | 26.3% |
| **1934** | **1935** | **1936** | **1937** | **1938** | **1939** |
| 14.9% | 11.6% | 8.3% | 4.6% | 2.1% | 0.6% |

This dramatic fall in unemployment contrasted strikingly with comparable figures for Britain (page 48) and the USA (page 99). Much of Hitler's success derived from policies condemned by the rest of the

**Source F**  Why unemployment fell in Germany

Conscription was introduced in 1935. Millions of young men had to serve in the armed forces instead of joining dole queues

Rearmament provided thousands of jobs in arms factories making guns, tanks, planes, ships

The Nazis created jobs by giving government money to farmers and manufacturers in an effort to make the country self–sufficient in food, raw materials and manufactures

Wages and prices were strictly controlled, so factory owners could keep down their costs

The flight of thousands of Jews from Germany, the concentration camps, the recruitment of a large secret police force and the establishment of thousands of government jobs also cut down the numbers of the unemployed

**FALLING UNEMPLOYMENT IN GERMANY**

Workers could be sent to work wherever there was a shortage of labour

The Nazis encouraged industrialists to use artificial methods to manufacture goods in short supply from Germany's raw materials, such as making petrol from coal and synthetic fibres from wood

Factory owners could be directed to make the products the government needed.

Large public building works were started, such as vast new government buildings and fast motorways (autobahns)

**Questions**

1 What were the advantages and disadvantages of Nazi policy towards workers?

2 Use Source **E** to draw a graph showing unemployment in Germany 1928–39.

3 Why and how was Hitler successful in reducing unemployment in Germany when it remained high in other countries?

4 On balance, did the average German family benefit or suffer from the effects of Nazi rule in the 1930s? Quote evidence to support your answer from the sources printed here and on pages 80–5.

## Propaganda, education and the mass media

▶ **How did the Nazis use propaganda, education, culture and the mass media to control the people?**

### Propaganda

Goebbels used all the different types of media to whip up support for the Nazis and incite hatred against their enemies. Goebbels thought it his duty to distort or falsify facts. Nazi maps showed airfields in tiny Czechoslovakia menacing German cities and towns! Goebbels also made effective use of the radio to inform and misinform the German people. He made sure Germans heard only praise, never criticism. He said:

'If you tell a lie, tell a big lie. If you tell a big lie often enough people will believe it.'

Everyone was urged to buy the 'People's Receiver' – a small black wireless set – which could only receive the Nazi radio station. People called it the 'Goebbelsschnauze' (Goebbels Snout)!

### The Cult of the Führer

Goebbels also played a leading part in developing the semi-mystical 'cult of the Führer'. A newspaper reader said:

'Just as in my youth the dear Lord used to appear in my dreams, so now the Führer appears'.

Dr Robert Ley told an audience in 1937,

'Everything comes from Adolf Hitler. His faith is our faith, and therefore our daily prayer is: "I believe in Adolf Hitler alone!"'

Rudolf Hess went even further on 24 December 1940:

'On this Christmas, our prayer is: "Lord Almighty, Thou hast given us the Führer: Thou hast blessed his struggle by a mighty victory."'

### The Nuremberg Rallies

The high spot of the Nazi year was the Nuremberg Rally in the Autumn. The American journalist, William L. Shirer, first saw Hitler there in 1934 and watched spellbound for 'seven days of almost ceaseless goose-stepping, speech-making, and pageantry' (Sources **A** and **B**).

**Source A**  Parade of swastikas on Party Day at the Nuremberg Rally in 1934

**Source B**  By William L. Shirer at the 1934 Nuremberg Rally

*S*eptember 7th: Another great pageant tonight. Two hundred thousand party officials packed in the Zeppelin Meadow with their twenty-one thousand flags unfurled in the searchlights like a forest of weird trees. Hitler shouted at them through the microphone, his words echoing across the hushed field from the loud-speakers.

*Berlin Diary*, by William L. Shirer, Hamish Hamilton, 1941

**Source C**  By Virginia Cowles, an eyewitness at the 1938 Nuremberg Rally

*A*s the time for the Führer's arrival drew near, the crowd grew restless. Suddenly the beat of the drums increased and a fleet of black cars rolled into the arena. The stadium looked like a shimmering sea of swastikas. Hitler began to speak. The crowd hushed into silence, but the drums continued their steady beat. Hitler's voice rasped into the night and every now and then the multitude broke into a roar of cheers. Some began swaying back and forth, chanting 'Sieg Heil' over and over again. I looked at the faces around me and saw tears streaming down people's cheeks. The drums had grown louder and I suddenly felt frightened.

*Looking for Trouble*, by Virginia Cowles, Hamish Hamilton, 1941. Quoted in *Eyewitness: the 20th Century*, edited by Jon E. Lewis, Robinson Publishing, 1994

**Source D** Young children giving the Nazi salute in 1936

**Source E** Hitler Youth poster

Hitler told journalists that the parades, military bands and speeches would send the rank and file members of the party back to their towns and villages full of fire and enthusiasm to preach the Nazi gospel with renewed zest and determination.

## Indoctrinating the Young

The Nazis taught children to believe implicitly in the Führer (Sources **D** and **F**). On Hitler's birthday (20 April) they put flowers beside his picture at home and at school. At morning assembly they sang a song to the Führer, heard a speech by a pupil praising his achievements and ended the ceremony with 'Sieg-Heil'. Children were not educated to think for themselves. The Nazis did not want criticism or doubt. One-sided education like this is called indoctrination. Children were also encouraged (and later compelled) to join the various Nazi Youth Organisations. Boys joined the *Deutsches Jungvolk* (German Young People) at the age of 10 and the *Hitler-Jugend* or Hitler Youth (Source **E**) when they reached 14. The equivalent organisations for girls were the *Jungmädelbund* (League of Young Girls) at 10 and the *Bund deutscher Mädchen BdM* (League of German Girls) at 14.

## Nazi culture

Nazi culture was very different from that of the Weimar Republic. Artists painted realistic-looking scenes of heroism or ordinary people working for the Fatherland (Source **G**). Music had to be tuneful – something everyone could enjoy. Jazz was frowned on since it originated in Black America. Hitler himself worshipped the music of Richard Wagner – a great composer but a man of prejudice who detested Jews. Many German writers, composers, musicians and artists couldn't stomach the prejudices of the Nazis and followed the example of George Grosz (page 73) who fled from Germany in 1933.

**Source F** By an Australian visitor in 1938

In every case the children wanted to join the Hitler *Jugend*. The brown shirt or drab blouse of Hitler won every time. To be outside Hitler's organization was the worst form of punishment. Hitler has captured the children heart and soul. Time out of number they answered my queries why they believed or did so-and-so by the reply: 'Because the Führer wills it!'

*The House that Hitler Built*, by Stephen Roberts, Methuen, 1938

**Source G** Painting from *Art for Everyone* published in Munich in 1939

Nazi leaders, like Hitler and Goebbels, wanted paintings and sculptures to be realistic and patriotic – portraying ideal German men or women in heroic poses.

## Questions

1 Why did the Nazis place such emphasis on education and the various youth organisations? What did they hope to achieve?

2 Use Sources **D**, **E** and **F** to explain why children were keen to join the Hitler Youth organisations.

3 Use the sources to explain how the Nazis used propaganda, education, culture and the mass media to control the people.

# 8 Boom, depression and New Deal in the USA

## The Roaring Twenties

▶ **What was isolationism and what effect did it have on the United States in the 1920s?**
**What were the Roaring Twenties and how did they affect the lives of ordinary people?**

### Isolationism

As you have seen, President Woodrow Wilson led the United States into the First World War in 1917 (page 34) and later played a leading part in the peace negotiations which followed. But his ambitious plans for a League of Nations (page 40) went ahead without him because Congress refused to ratify the Treaty of Versailles and let the USA join the League. Many Americans were opposed to the idea of joining the League, since it could mean sending American troops to fight in foreign disputes. They wanted the USA to isolate itself from world problems. This is why many Americans voted for Warren Harding, the Republican Presidential candidate, in 1920. Harding was an isolationist who campaigned with the slogan 'America First'. He wanted a return to normalcy, meaning an America which would lead a normal life and behave in a normal manner. Isolationism led the President and Congress (the American Parliament) to:

- restrict immigration into the USA;

- raise tariffs (duties) on imports to make it more difficult for foreign goods to compete with those made in America (page 92);

- lower taxes to give people more spending money to buy American goods (page 92).

Despite isolationism, the USA could not ignore world problems entirely (Source **A**). As you have seen, American bankers played a large part in helping Germany to solve her financial problems in 1924 (page 76). The USA also helped to organise the Kellogg Pact in 1928 (page 43).

### Restricting immigration

Between 1901 and 1910, over nine million immigrants entered the United States. This number fell by more than a half to four million between 1921 and 1930, after Congress approved measures restricting the number of immigrants allowed into the country.

**Source A** US battleship in the Brooklyn Navy Yard in New York. The United States had a continuing interest in seeking worldwide peace. In 1922, a naval disarmament conference held in Washington, DC, limited the size of the world's navies. The USA had to get rid of 30 warships like this one while the Royal Navy disposed of 19 and the Japanese 17.

Most Americans were themselves members of immigrant families but approved of these restrictions because many US workers were unemployed in the years immediately after the war.

Restrictions in 1917 banned Asian immigrants other than Japanese and required all immigrants to pass a literacy test. In 1921, Congress passed the Emergency Quota Act to limit the number of new immigrants from each country to 3 per cent of the number of people born there who were resident in the USA in 1910. For instance, the Russian quota was fixed at 34,284 (3 per cent) immigrants because there were 1,142,800 Russian-born US citizens in 1910. Even more stringent measures were introduced in 1924 (Source **C**) when Japanese immigrants were banned completely (page 104). You can see the difference this made and some of the reasons why in Sources **D** and **E**.

**Source B**  Immigrant family on Ellis Island in New York harbour. Poor immigrants were examined here before being allowed to enter the USA.

**Source E**  From an American school history textbook published in 1961

The First World War revealed some alarming facts in regard to our foreign population. (1) Many immigrants neglected to become naturalized American citizens. They retained their real allegiance to the lands from which they had come. (2) Radical labor agitators were suspected of 'taking their orders from Moscow'. (3) Over one thousand newspapers in the United States were printed in foreign languages. (4) Over 10 per cent of the people here could not speak English. (5) American labor leaders [*trade unionists*] were disturbed over the hordes of incoming foreigners who were accustomed to work for low wages. (6) Patriotic citizens generally were alarmed at the number of newcomers who had no knowledge of American institutions or ideals.

Extract from *Our Country's History*, by David Saville Muzzey, Ginn, 1961

**Source C**  The 1924 Johnson-Reed Immigration Act

The annual quota of any nationality shall be two per cent of the number of foreign-born individuals of such nationality resident in continental United States as determined by the United States census of 1890, but the minimum quota of any nationality shall be 100.

Extract from *The Immigration Act of 1924*, quoted in *Documents of American History*, edited by Henry Steele Commager, F. S. Crofts, 1941

**Source D**  Quota levels of immigrants to USA

|  | EFFECTS | |
|---|---|---|
|  | 1921 | 1924 |
| Number of immigrants restricted to: | 3% of 1910 population | 2% of 1890 population |
| EUROPE | | |
| UK/Ireland | 77,342 | 62,574 |
| Germany/Austria | 75,510 | 52,012 |
| Eastern Europe | 63,191 | 10,902 |
| Italy | 42,957 | 3,845 |
| Scandinavia | 41,859 | 19,274 |
| Russia | 34,284 | 2,248 |
| Rest of Europe | 20,263 | 10,691 |
| ASIA | 1,043 | 1,300 |
| AFRICA | 122 | 1,200 |
| REST OF WORLD | 424 | 621 |

From 1929 onwards these quotas were further adjusted but made little difference since the USA in the Depression years was no longer attractive to immigrants except Jews escaping from Nazi Germany.

*Questions*

1  Draw two bar charts to illustrate the statistics presented in Source **D**, one representing the figures for 1921 and the other the 1924 figures. Plot the countries along the x-axes and the numbers of immigrants along the y-axes.

2  Did the 1924 Act allow more, or fewer, immigrants to enter the USA compared with 1921?

3  Make a list of the countries from which potential US immigrants were: **a)** better off, **b)** worse off, **c)** much worse off, in 1924 compared with 1921.

4  How did the American Government try to encourage emigration from some countries at the expense of others? Use Sources **D** and **E** to explain why they did this.

5  Imagine you are an opponent of isolationism in the 1920s. Write a speech for a US Senator to try to make members of Congress change their minds.

Source F Picture postcards from America during the boom years. Oil wells in California (top left), iron and steel works in Cleveland, Ohio (top right), small-town bank in New England (bottom right).

## The boom years

The American economy prospered in 1919 and then fell sharply. By 1921, over 12 per cent of the workforce was unemployed. Measures taken by the government to boost the economy soon created new jobs and in 1927 the unemployment rate fell to under 3 per cent. This period of great prosperity is often called the 'Boom Years', 'Roaring Twenties' or 'Jazz Age'. The USA was now the richest country in the world (Source **F**). President Coolidge said, 'The business of America is business'. His successor, Herbert Hoover, claimed, 'The poor man is vanishing from among us' while the Republican Party boasted, 'a chicken in every pot' and 'two cars in every garage'. There were several reasons for this:

## Reasons for the boom years

**1** American manufacturers prospered during the war because there was little competition from British and German manufacturers who were busy making weapons, munitions and uniforms to fight the war instead of exporting goods to America. Some US firms made huge profits selling weapons to the Allies. Britain and France both got huge loans from the US Government to help buy them.
**2** American manufacturers could sell everything they made after the war. Foreign manufacturers found it hard to compete when Congress passed the Fordney-McCumber tariff on foreign imports in 1922. This was followed in 1929 by the Hawley-Smoot Tariff Act which raised import duties even higher. Tariffs 'protected' American products by making them cheaper than foreign goods (which had to pay the extra tax). When foreign governments retaliated by putting high tariffs on American exports, US businesses dependent on foreign trade suffered. This is why US foreign trade had been cut in half by 1931.
**3** Demand for goods was stimulated by a flood of advertising. Mail order catalogues, posters, radio and cinema commercials urged customers to buy, buy, buy! If you didn't have the cash, you could always borrow the money you needed on hire purchase. Many people began to live on credit, owing money to banks and finance houses and paying it back in instalments.
**4** People even borrowed money from banks to buy shares on the New York Stock Exchange. They thought they couldn't lose since industries were making big profits and share prices were rising fast. This provided extra finance for industry and helped big business to expand. In 1928 alone, some shares rose to five times their original value.
**5** Workers in industry got high wages yet the taxes they paid actually fell to help them buy more American goods. Many more people could afford to buy cars, domestic appliances, stocks, shares and cinema tickets.
**6** Newer products did very well. Six million cars were sold in 1929 compared with two million in 1919 (Source **G**). Car manufacturers used 80 per cent of America's rubber (for tyre manufacture), half of the sheet glass produced and a tenth of the steel. The road-building industry prospered in turn. The radio industry sold sets worth $60 million in 1922 and worth $800 million in 1929. Washing machines, electric shavers, vacuum cleaners, gramophones, gramophone records and many other luxuries and non-essential goods all saw similar sales increases.
**7** Mass production methods, pioneered by car-maker Henry Ford, made it cheaper and much easier to manufacture goods than by hand. Ford trained each worker to perform a specific task as a vehicle or engine passed by on an assembly line.

**Source G**  The fifteen millionth Ford automobile in 1927

**Source G**  The fifteen millionth Ford automobile in 1927

## The motor industry

In 1909 the Model T Ford motor car cost $950. By 1924, its price was only $290 and the Ford motor company was making 7500 cars a day. Everyone wanted one. Some put a car ahead of all other purchases for the home (Sources **H** and **I**). Motoring became a popular leisure-time activity for millions of Americans. The number of vehicles more than tripled between 1919 and 1932.

**Source H**  Mother of nine children

> We'd rather do without clothes than give up the car.

**Source I**  American woman in the 1920s

> I'll go without food before I'll see us give up the car.

There were soon many complaints about traffic jams. One man said he didn't use his car as much as he used to (Source **J**).

**Source J**  Complaints about traffic in the 1920s

> The heavy traffic makes it less fun. But I spend seven nights a week on my radio.

## The leisure industry

Radio changed everyday life almost as much as the automobile. It brought entertainment into the home. Cinema managers complained that customers were staying at home instead of going to the movies. Film producers responded by bringing in the first 'talkies' in 1927. Radio, cars and the telephone made people more mobile, making it possible for them to seek their fortunes elsewhere, such as in the cities or on the Pacific coast. Young people found freedom in jazz, ragtime, dancing, smoking, motoring and the cinema. Hollywood film stars influenced the way people dressed, the perfume the women used, and the way in which men combed their hair or wore a moustache.

*Questions*

1  Why did the economic activities illustrated in Source **F** prosper during the Boom Years?

2  Draw a diagram like the one on page 104 to explain the reasons for the boom years in America between 1924 and 1929.

3  Why do you think the radio and the automobile became so important to people living in the United States in the 1920s?

4  Which of the reasons given above for the boom years were isolationist (putting America first at the expense of foreign interests)?

5  Look at Source **F**. Are there any drawbacks to using picture postcards as sources of information about the past?

## Farmers

Despite the boom, many Americans did not share in the general prosperity. Farmers formed 25 per cent of the population but their share of the national income was only 10 per cent. About one million people left the land in the 1920s. Some left voluntarily. Others were evicted from their farms and smallholdings after failing to pay the rent. Many could not keep up the payments on machinery and buildings bought during the war years when demand for food was high. Prices tumbled after the war but rents, mortgage repayments, machinery and fertiliser costs rose by 30 per cent.

Farmers might have prospered had they been able to sell their surpluses overseas. But the introduction of the Fordney-McCumber tariff in 1922 penalised foreign manufacturers (page 92) and meant that foreign countries earning fewer US dollars from exports, had less to spend on American cotton, meat and corn. The Hawley-Smoot Tariff which raised duties higher still in 1929 made matters worse. Wheat prices fell from 233 cents a bushel in 1920 to 32 cents in 1932. Farm incomes fell by two-thirds. The small and less efficient farmers went bankrupt.

## Black Americans

The poorest families in America in the 1920s and 1930s lived in southern states such as Alabama, Louisiana and Mississippi (Sources **K** and **L**).

**Source L**   US Government report in 1938

Southeastern farms are the smallest in the Nation. Family incomes are exceptionally low, the sickness and death rates are unusually high. Even in southern cities from 60 to 88 per cent of the families on low incomes are not spending enough on food to purchase an adequate diet.

Extract from *National Emergency Council Report, 25 July 1938*, quoted in *Documents of American History*, edited by Henry Steele Commager, F. S. Crofts, 1941

Many were Black Americans, the descendants of former slaves who had only been freed some 60 years or so earlier. They lived in rural slums and worked long hours on cotton and tobacco plantations for low pay. Racial intolerance and discrimination against Black Americans was widespread throughout America. The cities of the North were segregated with Black Americans living mainly in the city slums, such as Harlem in New York City. Sometimes there were clashes. Race riots broke out in Chicago in 1919 after a Black American strayed into a 'FOR WHITES ONLY' area by the lake. Conditions were even worse in the South where the law was used to enforce racial discrimination. Blacks were expected to 'know their place'. Those who didn't were punished by the Ku Klux Klan. Lynchings, brandings, tarrings and beatings were carried out at night under a flaming cross. The Ku Klux Klan was a secret society of Whites, drawn largely from the poorest sectors of the community, such as the poor farmers who had been hit hard by the slump in farm prices after the war. But the Ku Klux Klan also had the support in some southern states, of members of the police force and even of judges, state senators and congressmen. Victims of the Klan included Jews, Catholics, foreign immigrants and other minority groups as well as Black Americans. By 1926, the Ku Klux Klan was at its peak but a scandal involving a well-known Klan leader – and the increasing prosperity brought by the Boom – began to lessen its appeal.

**Source K**   Picture postcard – 'picking cotton in the sunny South'.

D-16  PICKING COTTON IN THE SUNNY SOUTH

# Gangsters

The Boom Years also saw another unpleasant side to the American way of life – the rise of the gangster. The boom in crime coincided with rising prosperity and the passing of the Volstead Act in 1919 which prohibited the manufacture and/or sale of intoxicating liquor. Many supporters of Prohibition came from the small towns of Middle America. They put pressure on their congressmen to vote for the Bill. By banning alcohol completely they thought they could abolish organised crime.

Far from making the United States free from drink and free from crime, however, it had entirely the opposite effect. Millions of respectable Americans who liked to drink beer, wine or spirits, were forced to use 'speakeasies' – illegal bars or taverns where illicit liquor was sold. Some of this liquor was smuggled across the Canadian and Mexican frontiers but much of it was distilled illegally inside the USA itself. The suppliers of liquor were called bootleggers and because this lucrative trade was against the law, it was soon organised by large-scale gangsters, such as 'Scarface' Al Capone of Chicago. Capone bribed police and even put city officials on to his pay roll. Gangland killings multiplied, giving cities like Chicago and New York a terrible reputation for violence and crime. Prohibition was eventually repealed in 1933, forcing gangsters to turn to other rackets such as drugs and prostitution.

**Source M**
This painting in 1930 was called 'City Life'. At the bottom left you can see a bootlegger's illegal equipment which was used to make liquor.

1 Explain, in a few sentences, each of the following and why they were important in the USA in the 1920s:
**a)** the Fordney-McCumber and Hawley-Smoot Tariff Acts, **b)** the Volstead Act, **c)** the Ku Klux Klan.

2 Why do you think the quota system (page 91) might have been welcomed by many Americans in the Mid West and in the Deep South?

3 What reasons help to explain why the Ku Klux Klan flourished in America in the 1920s and early 1930s?

4 Use the information in this chapter to write a caption for Source **M** explaining to a foreigner what the painting 'Still Life' tells you about the United States in the late 1920s.

# The Wall Street Crash and its impact

▶ **What were the causes and consequences of the Wall Street Crash and the Depression?**
**How did the American Government respond to the Depression?**

## The Great Depression

In October 1929 a dramatic fall in share prices on the New York Stock Exchange (in Wall Street) caused thousands of American businesses to collapse. The consequences were felt all over the world:

- American banks hard hit by the Crash called in the huge loans they had earlier made to industries overseas, such as in Germany, causing them to collapse as well.

- The USA imposed higher tariffs on foreign imports, as you have seen, to protect America's farms and industries. Other world governments did likewise, causing a catastrophic fall in world trade.

- Businesses had to shut down, or sack workers, because of the fall in demand, making millions unemployed all over the world.

This was the Great Depression. The worst years were from 1930 to 1933. You have seen how it affected Britain (page 48) and Germany (page 78), but it started in America with the Wall Street Crash.

**Source A** Rise and fall in share prices 1925–33.

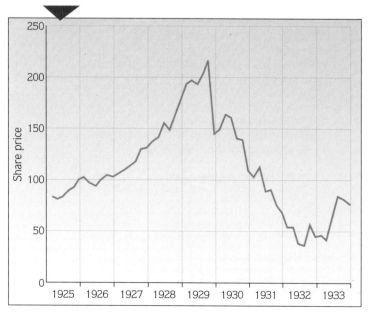

## Causes of the Crash

The peak boom years came in 1928–9 – a time when millions of Americans were feverishly buying shares (or stock) in companies and selling them on at a later date when the value had risen. They thought they couldn't lose. Everyone knew someone who had made a fortune. By the summer of 1929, some experts could see that the boom years were coming to an end. Yet prices on the stock market continued to rise. Some people even mortgaged their houses or their businesses to buy shares. On trains and buses, you could see people reading the lists of stock market prices instead of the headlines or sports pages. Nurses, window cleaners, film stars, widows, cowboys and grocers all 'played the market' (Sources **A** and **B**).

**Source B** The Crash – by John Hersch (a former stockbroker's clerk)

> The Crash – it didn't happen in one day. There were a great many warnings. The country was crazy. Everybody was in the stock market, whether he could afford it or not. Shoeshine boys and waiters and capitalists.
>
> Quoted in *Hard Times: An Oral History of the Depression*, by Studs Terkel, Pantheon Books, 1986

As a result many companies were over-valued by the stock market. Their factories, resources and profits were not worth as much as the investors seemed to think they were. What was worse, American industry was producing more manufactured goods than people could buy. Some experts said as much and forecast that share prices would go down. But so long as investors were confident their money was safe and likely to make a profit, there seemed little cause for alarm. It was only when some people began to sell their shares – and others started to follow – that the unthinkable happened. In late October 1929, prices fell so sharply that hundreds of thousands of people were ruined (Sources **C** to **F**).

## The Crash

**Source C**  Shareholders in Wall Street wait anxiously for news

**Source D**  Headlines in *The Philadelphia Inquirer*, THURSDAY: 24 October 1929

STOCK VALUES CRASH IN RECORD STAMPEDE

CURIOUS JAM WALL STREET TO SEE THE 'SHOW'
Huge Crowd Throngs 'Money Lane' Seeking Thrill
Butcher, Baker and Candlestick Maker
Rush to View 'World Series' of Finance

After a few weeks the stock market quietened down. John D. Rockefeller and other multi-millionaires used their money to buy shares and this prevented any further panic. Nonetheless, the value of shares continued to plunge downwards. As you can see from the graph, the events of October 1929 merely started a trend which was to continue off and on for another 3½ years.

**Source E**  Headlines in *The New York Times*, TUESDAY: 29 October 1929

STOCKS COLLAPSE IN 16,410,030 – SHARE DAY, 240 Issues Lose $15,894,818,894 in Month

**Source F**  Arthur A. Robertson, a businessman, remembers the Crash

Suicides, left and right, made a terrific impression on me, of course. People I knew. It was heartbreaking. One day you saw the prices at a hundred, the next day at $20, at $15. On Wall Street, the people walked around like zombies. You saw people who yesterday rode around in Cadillacs lucky now to have carfare [*bus fare*]. One of my friends said to me, 'If things keep on as they are, we'll all have to go begging.' I asked, 'Who from?'

Quoted in *Hard Times: An Oral History of the Depression*

## Questions

1  Why was the New York stock market booming in 1929? Why did John Hersch say 'the country was crazy' (Source **B**)? What should a sensible investor have done with his or her shares at that time?

2  Sources **B** and **F** are taken from an oral history of the Depression years in the USA. What is oral history? Can you suggest the advantages and disadvantages of using historical evidence like this?

3  Look at the graph in Source **A**: **a)** when were share prices at their highest, **b)** when were they at their lowest, **c)** when did they begin to climb upwards again?

4  In your own words, write a brief account describing what happened to the average value of shares before and after the Wall Street Crash in October 1929.

5  Draw or paint a 1929 poster warning Americans about the risks they will run if they continue to borrow money to invest in shares on the stock market.

**Source G**  Dole line in the Bowery

## Impact of the Depression

The Wall Street Crash had a knock-on effect. Businesses could not borrow money because their share value had fallen. People who lost money when share prices fell had less to spend in shops or on cars. Many people were unable to repay the money they had borrowed from the banks. By 1932, nearly half of America's banks had gone bust. People tightened their belts and bought fewer luxuries – so even more factories shut down or sacked workers. Being unemployed, they, in turn, had less to spend, so many more factories closed down and many more workers lost their jobs. And so it went on.

By 1932, 14 million Americans were out of work but there was no unemployment pay. In every large American city you could see men queuing for a lump of bread and a bowl of soup. The YMCA in New York's Bowery (Source **G**) gave away 12,000 free meals a day. There were many evictions. The homeless poor slept in the parks, under bridges, in the doorways of shops and public buildings, or in empty railway waggons. You can see some of these effects of the Depression in Sources **H** to **L**.

**Source H**  Signs in the streets

A great many shops were empty, with dusty plate-glass windows and signs indicating that they were for rent. Few factory chimneys were smoking. The streets were not so crowded with trucks as in earlier years. There was no mechanical hammering from building work to damage the ear. Beggars were on the pavements in much larger numbers than ever before.

*Since Yesterday*, by Frederick Lewis Allen, Harper and Brothers, 1939. Quoted in *The American Reader*, by Paul M. Angle, Rand McNally, 1958

**Source I**  Salary cuts

Among the well-to-do salary cuts had been widespread. These people were sacking servants. In many homes, wives who had never before done housework were cooking and scrubbing. Husbands were wearing the old suit longer, resigning from the golf club, paying seventy five cents for lunch instead of a dollar.

From *Since Yesterday*

**Source J**  Hoovervilles

On the outskirts of the cities and on vacant plots there were groups of makeshift shacks made out of packing boxes, scrap iron, anything that could be picked up free from the city dumps. Men and sometimes whole families of evicted people were sleeping on automobile seats carried from scrapyards, warming themselves before fires of rubbish in grease drums.

From *Since Yesterday*

**Source K**  Fighting for scraps

One vivid, gruesome moment of those dark days we shall never forget. We saw a crowd of some fifty men fighting over a barrel of garbage outside the backdoor of a restaurant. American citizens fighting for scraps of food like animals!

*We Too Are the People*, by Louise V. Armstrong, in *Since Yesterday*

## Self-help

Critics laid the blame on President Hoover and the ruling Republican Party, who they said had done nothing, and were doing nothing. 'They got us into this mess, they should get us out again,' they said. But Hoover believed, like his fellow Republicans and many people in Britain, that the problem of high unemployment would solve itself. Employers should be able to cut wages because unemployed workers were desperate to get a job. This would enable the employers to slash their prices – making it much easier for people to buy their products – creating extra jobs – and causing unemployment levels to fall.

Hoover saw no reason to spend public money on creating new jobs. Self-help was all the working man needed. Hoover called it 'the American system of rugged individualism'. He regarded government help as a step on the way to socialism. To alleviate the problems of the farmers, Hoover told them to grow less – even though many Americans were starving. The Government hoped this would make wheat scarce, causing the price to rise. But desperate farmers did the opposite, thinking that if they grew more, they would have more to sell. In 1931, wheat prices in Chicago dropped to their lowest in eighty years. Many farmers went bankrupt and were evicted from their homes. Some took the law into their own hands.

The position of many farmers worsened in the 1930s when drought and poor farming methods caused crop failure and widespread soil erosion. In Oklahoma, thousands of poor tenant farmers abandoned their homes and holdings and emigrated to California. 'The roads of the West and Southwest teem with hungry hitchhikers. The campfires of the homeless are seen along every railroad track' wrote one observer.

In the end, Hoover had to spend some Government money on projects to put the unemployed to work but it was not enough. By 1932 the average American income had fallen by a third in only three years. In June 1932, Hoover belatedly introduced a much bigger relief scheme to provide loans to railways, insurance companies and banks in danger of collapsing. But it was too late. The American people had decided to vote for Franklin Delano Roosevelt – a Democrat who offered them hope.

**Source L** Hooverville on the outskirts of Los Angeles in 1932

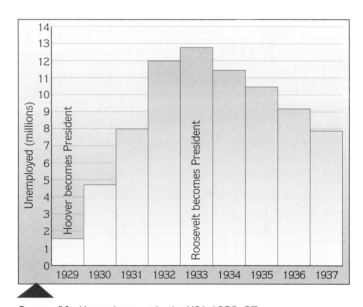

**Source M** Unemployment in the USA 1929–37

1 Use Sources **J** and **L** to explain what Hoovervilles were. How do you think they got this name?

2 Use Source **M** and the graph on page 96 (Source **A**) to say when you think the Depression affected the USA most.

3 How would your impression of the effects of the Depression on America change if your studies were restricted to, **a)** Sources **H** and **I**, **b)** Sources **G, J, K** and **L**? Why do these differences matter?

## The New Deal

▶ ***How far was the New Deal successful in ending the depression in the USA?***

### The New Deal

When President Roosevelt (Source **A**) took office in March 1933, he called for a 'new deal' for the people of America. He said he was going to demand from Congress powers as great as those needed in wartime to deal with the crisis.

### The hundred days

Roosevelt had three main aims (Source **C**). One of his first actions was to close the banks for a few days while his advisers dealt with the financial problems facing America. In the next hundred days, he sent fifteen important new laws to Congress for approval, such as the Agricultural Adjustment Act (AAA). Farmers agreed to plough up growing crops and kill off young livestock in return for cash. This forced up prices and helped to double farm incomes in only three years. Roosevelt used public money to give relief to the unemployed. This increased demand in the shops and helped create new jobs. At last, Americans thought, the country is on the move again.

The most lasting and most memorable achievements of the New Deal were the imaginative and far-reaching projects instigated by the Federal Government under the so-called Alphabet Laws (such as the AAA). Government agencies and organisations were specifically designed to create new jobs. Millions of Americans were employed under these schemes (Source **B**) and millions more regained confidence in America and the American dream.

### FRANKLIN DELANO ROOSEVELT (1882-1945)

Franklin Delano Roosevelt, a wealthy lawyer, was struck down with polio in 1921 and spent the rest of his life handicapped. This did not stop him becoming President in 1933 – a position he held for the rest of his life. Roosevelt was determined to do something positive to end the Depression. His first 100 days in office in 1933 gave despairing Americans hope. Something was being done at last to help their country out of its difficulties.

**Source A**
President Roosevelt

**CCC** CIVILIAN CONSERVATION CORPS **1933:** recruited two million jobless youths and sent them to camps to care for the American countryside. They were paid a small wage and given clothing, accommodation and meals. In return they built forest roads, sprayed pests and planted trees. Most enjoyed the experience and were fitter and healthier as a result. Many trade union leaders disapproved. They said it was similar to the activities of the Hitler Youth.

**CWA** CIVIL WORKS ADMINISTRATION **1933:** gave work to about 4 million of the unemployed on public works, such as new dams, roads and schools.

**FERA** FEDERAL EMERGENCY RELIEF ADMINISTRATION **1933:** temporary measure providing unemployment benefit or dole money. It wasn't much but it helped to bring some comfort to people suffering deprivation and poverty.

**FHA** FEDERAL HOUSING ADMINISTRATION **1934:** provided Government loans to help householders buy, repair or improve their homes.

**FSA** FARM SECURITY ADMINISTRATION **1937:** system through which the Government made loans to help farmworkers and tenant farmers.

**NLRB** NATIONAL LABOR RELATIONS BOARD **1935:** dealt with strikes and disputes between workers (labor) and employers. In its first two years it successfully resolved 75 per cent of the disputes it reviewed.

**NRA** NATIONAL RECOVERY ADMINISTRATION **1933:** a popular scheme to improve working conditions in factories and to encourage employers to set minimum wages, eliminate cheap labour and recognise trade unions. Firms signed up, agreeing to a common code of behaviour. In return they could display the NRA Blue Eagle badge with its slogan 'We Do Our Part'. Met hostility from employers reluctant to bargain with trade unions.

**PWA** PUBLIC WORKS ADMINISTRATION **1933:** completed 34,000 PWA projects, such as building new schools, dams and slum clearance.

**REA** RURAL ELECTRIFICATION ADMINISTRATION **1935:** built power lines to cover the many parts of rural America which were not already served by the private electricity companies.

**TVA** TENNESSEE VALLEY AUTHORITY **1933:** vastly improved a poor area of the American South, controlling flooding, building hydro-electric dams, improving river navigation and controlling soil erosion by planting trees.

**WPA** WORKS PROGRESS ADMINISTRATION **1935:** took over much of the work of the CWA and PWA. It built thousands of new projects, such as hydro-electric dams (including the Grand Coulee Dam), bridges, airports, power stations, sewers, waterworks and many public buildings (including 70 per cent of all new schools built in this period). These public works improved America, at the same time employing millions of workers, who would otherwise have been unemployed.

**Source C** Roosevelt's three aims

ROOSEVELT'S THREE MAIN AIMS

1. Alleviate distress

2. Create new jobs

3. Ensure the Wall Street Crash could not happen again

*Questions*

1 Name an Alphabet Law or organisation designed to help:
**a)** poor people living in Tennessee,
**b)** young men without a job, **c)** factory workers, **d)** farmers, **e)** farmworkers, **f)** people living in remote areas, **g)** people who were unemployed.

2 How far was the action taken by Roosevelt to help the USA out of the Depression similar to the action taken by: **a)** President Hoover in 1929-32 (page 99), **b)** the National Government in Britain (page 50), **c)** Adolf Hitler in Germany (page 87)? How was the New Deal different?

3 How do you account for the fact that despite all the heavy physical exercise they got, the average young person put on over a stone (7 kg) in weight when working for the Civilian Conservation Corps? What does this tell you about America in 1933?

## Verdicts on Roosevelt's New Deal

**Source D**   Thomas L Stokes (a junior member of the government)

They were exciting, exhilarating days. It was one of the most joyous periods of my life. We came alive, we were eager. We were infected with a gay spirit of adventure, for something concrete and constructive finally was being done about the chaos which confronted the nation.

Extract from *Chip Off My Shoulder*, by Thomas L. Stokes, Princeton University Press, 1940

**Source E**   By an American historian

The CCC left its monuments in the preservation and purification of the land, the water, the forests, and the young men of America.

Quoted in *Historical Atlas of the United States*, National Geographic Society, 1988

**Source F**   Republican policy statement: *The New York Times*, 12 June 1936

The New Deal administration has been guilty of frightful waste and extravagance, created a vast number of new offices and sent out swarms of inspectors to harass our people. It has destroyed the morale of many of our people and made them dependent upon the government.

**Source G**   1936 Presidential Election: *The New York Times*, 4 November 1936

ROOSEVELT SWEEPS THE NATION
POLL SETS RECORD
America yesterday gave Franklin Delano Roosevelt the most overwhelming testimonial of approval ever received by a national candidate in the history of the nation. The President was the choice of an overwhelming majority of the voters in all parts of the country.

Despite the obvious signs of success, many critics denounced the New Deal (Source **F**). A cartoonist showed Roosevelt carrying away a shed labelled 'Private Rights'. Republicans said he was taking over the powers of Congress. Roosevelt spoke out against these critics in a broadcast to the people (Source **H**).

**Source H**   One of Roosevelt's 'fireside chats' on the radio

It is true that the toes of some people are being stepped on and are going to be stepped on. But these toes belong to the comparative few. A few timid people who fear progress will try to give new and strange names for what we are doing. Sometimes they will call it Fascism and sometimes Communism and sometimes Socialism. But in so doing they are trying to make very complex something that is really very simple and very practical.

## Achievements and Failures

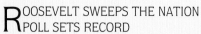

**Source I**   WPA poster in 1938. Work relief for millions of unemployed Americans was provided by the WPA – the Works Progress Administration.

Roosevelt persuaded Congress to pass other laws to improve living conditions, eliminate injustices and help Americans unable to help themselves. The Social Security Act of 1935 set up a long-overdue unemployment insurance scheme for workers and provided social welfare benefits for the handicapped. It also introduced a compulsory retirement pension scheme.

But he did not always get his way. In 1936, the Supreme Court ruled that the Agricultural Adjustment Act was unconstitutional. Although he got round this later, Roosevelt was disturbed that the Supreme Court could overrule laws which the elected President and Congress had passed. After his landslide re-election in 1936, he put forward proposals to make Supreme Court judges retire at 70 and enlarge their numbers so he could appoint judges sympathetic to the New Deal (Source **J**).

**Source J** Radio broadcast by President Roosevelt, 9 March 1937

By bringing into the judicial system a steady and continuing stream of new and younger blood, I hope, first, to make the administration of all Federal justice speedier and therefore less costly; secondly, to bring to the decision of social and economic problems younger men who have had personal experience and contact with modern facts and circumstances under which average men have to live and work.

Quoted in *Documents of American History*, edited by Henry Steele Commager, F. S. Crofts, 1941

But Congress, sympathetic to the New Deal, turned his proposals down. For all its faults, they preferred a Supreme Court which could curb the power of the President if he tried to go above the law.

## Isolationism in the 1930s

Isolationism continued to play an important part in American politics in the 1930s even under a forward-looking President like Roosevelt. As a result, it delayed American entry into the Second World War until December 1941. America preferred to stay neutral (Source **K**) even though Roosevelt criticised the actions of the dictators (Source **L**).

**Source K** The Neutrality Act: 1 May 1937

Whenever there exists a state of war between, or among, two or more foreign states it shall thereafter be unlawful to export arms, ammunition, or implements of war from the United States to any belligerent state.

After Hitler's aggressive acts of 1938 and March 1939, Roosevelt tried to get Congress to amend the Neutrality Law but was rebuffed. It was only when Hitler invaded Poland in September 1939 that Americans began to see where their interests really lay (Source **M**).

**Source L** Cartoon in *Punch*, 13 October 1937. WILL HE COME RIGHT OUT?

WILL HE COME RIGHT OUT?

**Source M** Broadcast by Roosevelt, September 1939

Passionately though we may desire detachment, we are forced to realise that every word that comes through the air, every ship that sails the sea, every battle that is fought, does affect the American future.

Quoted in *Historical Atlas of the United States*

Congress finally agreed to repeal the ban on arms sales to countries at war – much to the relief of the British and French governments. But even after the fall of France in 1940 (page 121), isolationism was still a vote-winning policy (Source **N**).

**Source N** *The New York Times*, 18 July 1940

ROOSEVELT RENOMINATED
STRICT ANTI-WAR PLATFORM IS ADOPTED
NO ARMY ABROAD UNLESS U.S. IS ATTACKED

**Q**uestions

1 Why did many Americans regard Roosevelt's first hundred days as 'exciting and exhilarating'?

2 Use Sources **D**, **E**, **G**, **I** and **J** and the graph on page 99 to make a list of Roosevelt's main achievements. Did he solve the problem of unemployment?

3 Look at Sources **F** and **H** and make a list of the main objections to Roosevelt's policies. How did he deal with these criticisms? What was the view of the American people?

4 What was the point of the cartoon (Source **L**)? How and why did the US Government stay neutral for so long?

# 9 Peace for our time: 1931–9

## Failure of the League of Nations

▶ **How and why did the League of Nations fail to resolve the crises in Manchuria (1931) and Abyssinia (1934–6)?**
**How far did the Depression make the work of the League more difficult?**

## The Manchurian Crisis 1931

Although the League of Nations had some early successes (page 42), it was powerless when the major powers put it to the test in Manchuria in 1931 and Abyssinia in 1935.

Japan had been badly hit by the Depression (Source **A**). Her industrial strength depended on exports and these fell by 50% between 1929 and 1931. Without exports, she could not afford to buy the imports she needed. The country was overcrowded. Japan's militarists – right-wing extremists and many army officers – thought the Japanese needed more living space. This is why they targeted the semi-independent Chinese province of Manchuria. China at this time was split in two by a civil war between Nationalists and Communists. The Japanese already had some business interests in Manchuria. They ran the South Manchuria Railway, for instance. The militarists hoped that by controlling Manchuria's natural resources, they could help Japan become self-sufficient in raw materials at a time when the Depression was hitting overseas trade hard. You can see how they accomplished this in Sources **B**, **C** and **D**.

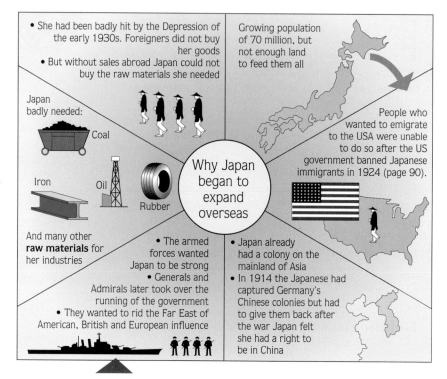

**Source A** Why Japan began to expand overseas

**Source B** Report by Tsang Shih-yi, Chairman of the Provincial Government, 19 September 1931

At 10 o'clock last night, (Japanese) railway guards picked a quarrel by blowing up a section of the railway at Huankutun, and subsequently accused the Chinese military of having done this. The Japanese immediately staged a surprise attack upon Peitaying. Many houses were burnt and many people shot dead. At 5.30 a.m. large groups of Japanese soldiers began entering the city of Shenyang [*Mukden*] and immediately occupied all Government buildings.

Quoted in *Source Materials in Chinese History*, edited by Charles Meyer and Ian Allen, Frederick Warne, 1970

**Source C** Japanese Government statement, dated 24 September 1931

A detachment of Chinese troops destroyed the track of the South Manchuria Railway in the vicinity of Mukden and attacked our railway guards at midnight on September 18. A clash between Japanese and Chinese troops then took place. In order to forestall an imminent disaster, the Japanese army had to act swiftly. The Chinese soldiers garrisoned in the neighbouring localities were disarmed, and the duty of maintaining peace and order was left in the hands of the local Chinese organisations under supervision of the Japanese troops. The Japanese Government harbours no territorial designs in Manchuria.

*The China Yearbook 1931–32*, quoted in Source Materials in Chinese History

**Source D** C. T. Wang, Foreign Minister of the Chinese Government

Appropriate steps are being taken to inform the League of Nations and the powers who signed the Kellogg pact of the unwarranted actions of Japanese troops.

Article by Hallett Abend in *The New York Times*, Monday, 21 September, 1931

## The League of Nations

The Japanese army used the Mukden incident to occupy the whole of Manchuria and installed the former Chinese Emperor, Pu Yi, as puppet (figurehead) ruler of the newly created 'independent' state of Manchukuo. This was done to make it look as if the Manchurians were seeking independence from China. The League of Nations sent a team to investigate the Chinese complaint of Japanese aggression. But although Japan was roundly condemned in October 1932 and again in February 1933, none of the member nations of the League seemed prepared to back words with force. Japan left the League

undeterred. The success of the militarists later helped to turn Japan into a military state and paved the way for further invasions of China in 1935 and 1937.

## The Abyssinian Crisis 1934–6

A second test of the resolve of the League of Nations came in 1935 when Mussolini, Fascist dictator of Italy, invaded Abyssinia (Ethiopia). Italy, like Japan, had been disappointed at Versailles not to have been given a League of Nations mandate to administer a former German colony in Africa. Mussolini wanted a 'place in the sun' where Italian colonists could plant tropical crops and utilise local raw materials to help Italy prosper during the Depression. Like Hitler and the Japanese militarists, he was obsessed with the idea of self-sufficiency – producing all the raw materials needed by a modern society from resources under his control.

Mussolini's chance came in December 1934 when an incident at Wal Wal on the Abyssinian border with Italian Somaliland led to a clash in which 100 soldiers were killed. The Italians demanded compensation and the dispute was put to the League of Nations for settlement. Abyssinia, ruled by the Emperor Haile Selasse, had been a member of the League of Nations since 1923 and signed the Kellogg Pact. She was fully entitled to seek the protection the League provided for its members under the policy of 'collective security'. This did not deter Mussolini. Italian troops were sent by troop-ship through the Suez Canal to growing international disquiet in the summer of 1935.

**Source E** German cartoon on the Manchurian Crisis

**Questions**

1 Use Sources **B**, **C** and **D** to explain how the Manchurian Crisis began according to, **a)** Chinese, and **b)** Japanese sources.

2 What actions should the Members of the League have taken according to their Covenant (Source **D** on page 40)? Why was it hard to prove that Japan was the aggressor in Manchuria?

3 How did the German cartoonist (Source **E**) interpret the actions of the League of Nations in dealing with the Manchurian Crisis?

4 Design a poster justifying the seizure of Manchuria to the Japanese people.

5 What effect do you think the League's handling of this dispute had on Mussolini and Hitler?

## Mussolini invades Abyssinia

The League's solution to the Wal Wal incident proved unacceptable to Italy and in October 1935 Mussolini took action (Sources **F** and **G**).

**Source F** By an American journalist in Asmara, capital of the Italian colony of Eritrea

At five o'clock on the morning of October 2, the thunderous roar of a column of motor trucks awakened me. The procession continued hour after hour, manned by drivers sunburned to the colour of old leather, dusty, begoggled, with their mouths and noses swathed in handkerchiefs to keep them from breathing the clouds of talcum-like dust. On some of the trucks was chalked the inscription, 'Rome to Addis Ababa'.

Extract from *I Found No Peace*, Webb Miller, Gollancz, 1937

**Source G** Map of Abyssinia and the adjacent Italian colonies of Eritrea and Somaliland

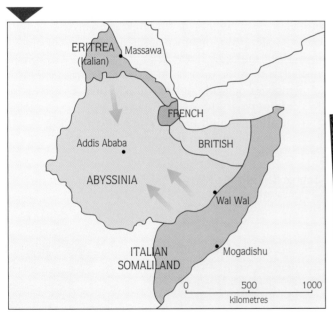

THE AWFUL WARNING

FRANCE AND ENGLAND *(together ?)*. "WE DON'T WANT YOU TO FIGHT, BUT, BY JINGO, IF YOU DO, WE SHALL PROBABLY ISSUE A JOINT MEMORANDUM SUGGESTING A MILD DISAPPROVAL OF YOU."

**Source H** Cartoon in *Punch* in August 1935

**Source I** Emperor Haile Selassie on the front cover of *Weekly Illustrated* magazine, 15 June 1935. Although there was much sympathy in Britain for Abyssinia, little pressure was put on the Government to use force to deter Mussolini

Despite the bravery of the Abyssinian soldiers, the result was never in doubt. Four days after the invasion, the League of Nations branded Italy the aggressor and agreed to impose economic sanctions prohibiting trade with the Italians but failed to include a ban on oil. Mussolini later admitted to Hitler that if oil had been banned he would have had to call off the invasion. In December, British and French ministers – Sir Samuel Hoare and Pierre Laval – prepared a secret plan to give Italy much of the territory it had already taken. When the news leaked out, people were scandalised at the way Western governments seemed to be caving in to force.

## Abyssinia at the League of Nations

The Italians completed their conquest in May 1936. Shortly afterwards the crisis was debated at the Assembly of the League of Nations on 30 June–4 July 1936 (Sources **J** and **K**). But instead of taking effective action against Mussolini, the League voted to end trade sanctions against Italy.

**Source J** Speech by the Emperor Haile Selassie to the League of Nations

The issue before the Assembly today is a question of collective security; of the very existence of the League; of the trust placed by States in international treaties; of the value of promises made to small States that their integrity and their independence shall be respected and assured. I ask the fifty-two nations. What measures do they intend to take?

Quoted in *Speeches and Documents on International Affairs*, edited by Arthur Berriedale Keith, Oxford, 1938

The British Foreign Minister, Anthony Eden, who was later better known as an opponent of appeasement, assured the Emperor of his sympathy but stated the reality of the situation as he saw it by then (Source **K**).

**Source K** Speech by Anthony Eden to the League of Nations

The facts should be squarely faced. The course of military events and the local situation in Ethiopia have brought us to a point at which the sanctions at present in force are incapable of reversing the order of events in that country. In our view only military action could do this now. I cannot believe that, in present world conditions, such military action could be considered a possibility. So far as His Majesty's Government is concerned, our policy has been based on the principles for which the League stands.

Quoted in *Speeches and Documents on International Affairs*

## Why the League Failed

The League of Nations failed in Manchuria and in Abyssinia largely because trade sanctions were of little use since the League could not control the trade of non-League nations, such as the United States. The alternative – military force – was equally useless since member nations were not willing to contribute troops to a League of Nations army. In other words, the

**Source L** By Webb Miller – an American journalist

I felt that the Italian invasion was in fact no less and no more reprehensible than the series of unprovoked aggressions and land grabs by which England, France, Belgium, Spain, Portugal, and Germany had gobbled up the entire continent of Africa, excepting Ethiopia and Liberia, previous to the World War. I had seen how the other Allies after the World War cheated Italy out of her share. I found Ethiopia savage, uncivilised, and unknown. Not one person in ten thousand could read or write; punishments involved cruel mutilations; unchecked disease was rapidly killing off the population, and the vast majority lived in filth, poverty, and degradation.

Extract from *I Found No Peace*

doctrine of collective security was a failure. The League had no effective way of compelling other countries to accept its decisions.

The League also failed to represent the views of four of the most powerful nations in the 1930s. The United States never became a member of the League, Japan left in 1933, Germany only joined in 1926 and left in 1933, while the Soviet Union, not admitted for political reasons until 1934, left in 1939.

Questions

1 Quote evidence from Source **F** to support Mussolini's claim that an oil ban would have forced him to call off the invasion.

2 What does Source **H** tell you about the attitude of *Punch* magazine to British and French attempts to resolve the Abyssinian Crisis?

3 List Webb Miller's reasons for backing Mussolini in Abyssinia (Source **L**). Write a reply to each argument on your list.

4 What action should the League of Nations have taken under the terms of the Covenant (page 40)? Argue the case for or against taking such action.

5 Write a short speech for the Emperor Haile Selassie attacking Anthony Eden's claim (Source **K**) that 'our policy has been based on the principles for which the League stands.'

6 How did the Abyssinian Crisis put an end to the League of Nations as an influential world body?

## Hitler's expansionist policies

**How and why was Hitler allowed to overturn the terms of the Treaty of Versailles?**
**What was appeasement?**

### Setting aside the Treaty of Versailles

Hitler's first priority on coming to power was rearmament despite the restrictions imposed on Germany at Versailles (page 38). It was always clear that he would do this – from his speeches and even from the first policy statement of the infant Nazi Party in 1920 (page 74).

Officially, the German army was restricted to only 100,000 men, even though neighbouring Czechoslovakia had 140,000 soldiers and Poland 270,000. Conscription, U-boats and a German air force were also banned. This was intolerable to any German, let alone Hitler. In October 1933, he left the League of Nations and withdrew from the Disarmament Conference – a clear indication that Germany was about to rearm regardless of the League.

On 16 March 1935, Hitler shocked the world by announcing plans to create an army of over half a million men by reintroducing conscription (compulsory military service). At the same time, Göring proudly unveiled his Luftwaffe which had been formed in secret after thousands of Germans had been urged to 'learn to fly'. Nine days later – on 25 March

**Source A** German armed forces on parade at the Nuremberg Rally 1935

1935 – Hitler met two British Cabinet Ministers, Sir John Simon and Anthony Eden, in Berlin. He told them why he had decided to rearm (Source **B**).

**Source B** By Hitler's interpreter

We have experienced Bolshevism in our own country. We are only safe against the Bolsheviks if we have armaments which they respect.

Extract from *Hitler's Interpreter*, by Dr Paul Schmidt, edited by R. H. C. Steed, Heinemann, 1951

When Sir John Simon argued that the rearmament clauses of the Treaty of Versailles could not be broken by a decision of Germany on its own, Hitler said that the other Powers had first broken the Treaty 'by failing to disarm themselves' (Source **D** on page 40). Hitler said he was prepared to negotiate (Source **C**). He wanted to increase the size of the German Navy until it was 35 per cent the size of the Royal Navy. German diplomats said 'Hitler did all the talking, Simon all the listening.'

**Source C**

We shall not let conscription be touched but we are prepared to negotiate regarding the strength of armed forces. Our only condition is parity [*equality*] on land and in the air with our most strongly armed neighbour.

Extract from *Hitler's Interpreter*

On 11 April 1935, the British and French prime ministers (Ramsay MacDonald and Pierre Laval) met Mussolini at Stresa to discuss the crisis. They agreed to 'oppose with all suitable means any unilateral denunciation of treaties.' This was called the Stresa Front. Hitler's actions were further condemned by the Council of the League of Nations on 17 April 1935.

# The Anglo-German Naval Agreement

It was all the more shocking then, when Britain signed the Anglo-German Naval Agreement in June. This made it clear that Germany could build a navy up to 35 per cent of the size of the Royal Navy, as Hitler had earlier demanded. It looked to many observers as if Britain was accepting that Hitler had a right to rearm. The French Prime Minister, Pierre Laval, sent a strong note to London (Source **D**), a Paris newspaper added further weight to the protest (Source **E**) and an American journalist made a note in his diary (Source **F**).

**Source D**   French Prime Minister Laval

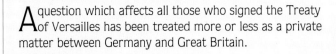

A question which affects all those who signed the Treaty of Versailles has been treated more or less as a private matter between Germany and Great Britain.

**Source E**   Paris newspaper

Does London imagine that Hitler has renounced any of the projects indicated in his book *Mein Kampf*? If so, the illusion of our friends across the Channel is complete.

Quoted in *Chronicle of the Twentieth Century*, edited by Derrik Mercer, Longman, 1988

**Source F**   William L. Shirer

Germany gets a U-boat tonnage equal to Britain's. Why the British have agreed to this is beyond me. German submarines almost beat them in the last war, and may in the next.

Extract from *Berlin Diary*, by William L. Shirer, Hamish Hamilton, 1941

However, France itself had already gone against the spirit of the Treaty on 2 May 1935 when Laval signed a pact of mutual assistance with the Soviet Union. When Göring saw Laval later that month, he greeted him with the sarcastic words, 'I trust you got on well at Moscow with the Bolsheviks, Monsieur Laval'. These breaches, however, were as nothing compared with the actions of the third partner in the Stresa Front – Mussolini – when he invaded Abyssinia in October 1935 (page 106). You can see from Sources **A**, **G** and **H** how German rearmament developed in the years before 1939.

**Source G**   Warning by Sir Nevile Henderson, British Ambassador in Berlin

The rearmament of Germany, if it has been less spectacular because it is no longer news, has been pushed on with the same energy as in previous years. The air force continues to expand at an alarming rate, and one can at present [1938] see no indication of a halt. We may well soon be faced with a strength of between 4000 and 5000 firstline aircraft. It is not an army, but the whole German nation which is being prepared for war.

Extract from *Failure of a Mission: Berlin 1937-1939*, by Sir Nevile Henderson, Hodder and Houghton, 1940

**Source H**   Chart showing the extent of German rearmament 1933–39

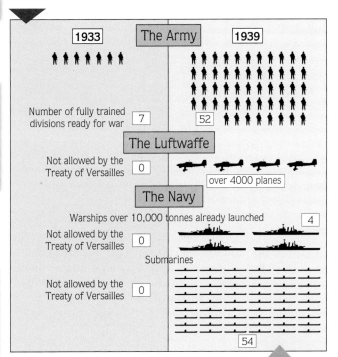

## Questions

1 Use Sources **B** and **C** to make a list of the reasons given by Hitler for German rearmament.

2 Since Hitler's actions were in direct breach of the Treaty of Versailles, why was he allowed to go ahead? What were the reactions of Britain, France and Italy to his reasons?

3 Use Sources **D**, **E** and **F** to explain why the signing of the Anglo-German Naval Agreement made the French so annoyed. How was it a breach of the terms of the Treaty of Versailles (page 38)?

Source I  Militarism and appeasement in the 1930s

| BELIEFS | **Germany: Fascism: Militarism**<br>There is glory for the people in war<br>Rearmament is essential to make the country strong<br>The terms of the Treaty of Versailles must be rejected<br>It is every man's duty to die for the Fatherland if necessary<br>The German people need extra living space, or colonies overseas<br>Interests of State must always come before those of the individual |
|---|---|

1. Rearmament 1933–5
2. Re-occupation of the Rhineland, 1936
3. Anschluss (Union) with Austria, 1938
4. Czech Sudetenland, 1938
5. Bohemia and Moravia (Czechoslovakia), 1939
6. Memel, 1939
7. Poland, 1939

Source J  Conservative Party Election Manifesto in 1935

| BELIEFS | **Britain: France: Appeasement**<br>Fascism can be used to keep Communism at bay<br>Better to give way a little than risk another war<br>The terms of the Treaty of Versailles were too harsh<br>Collective security – nations acting together – can halt aggressors<br>The pointless slaughter of the First World War must not be repeated<br>World problems can be solved by discussion around the conference table<br>Disarmament is essential; rearmament was a main cause of World War One |
|---|---|

| **United States** | **Soviet Union** |
|---|---|
| Strongest / richest country in world<br>Not a member of League of Nations<br>Isolationist – America First<br>Not interested in Europe | Growing stronger and more powerful<br>Not trusted – Communist / totalitarian<br>Not trusted – sought peace in 1917<br>Not trusted – Purges in 1936–8 |

The National Government's Policy
PEACE
The National Government has led the world in the pursuit of Peace. As an example to other countries it has disarmed to the verge of risk. It has refused to embark on a race in armaments.
FOR A REAL PEACE POLICY SUPPORT THE NATIONAL GOVERNMENT

## Appeasement

On 3 September 1939, Neville Chamberlain, the British Prime Minister declared war on Germany. He said what a blow it had been, to him personally, to know that his 'long struggle to win peace' had failed. This chapter is about that long struggle to win peace. British policy, and that of French leaders in the 1930s, is called *appeasement* – trying to buy off dictators by negotiating agreements which give in, bit by bit, to their demands under threat of war.

Hitler, like Mussolini and the Japanese militarists, had a very different view of war from that of the British and French governments (Source **I**). Anthony Eden (Source **K**) told the League of Nations: 'There is in our judgement, no dispute between nations that cannot be settled by peaceful means'. But this was not Hitler's view.

There is little doubt, however, that the attitude of many ordinary people in Britain at that time was in favour of appeasement (Source **J**). No one wanted to fight another world war so soon after the last. Many people were ashamed of the Paris Peace Treaties and could see that the German-speaking peoples had many genuine grievances. Germany had been forced to disarm but other countries had not done likewise. German-speakers living in countries like Czechoslovakia were not always fairly treated. In particular, East Germans were separated from the rest

of Germany by a narrow strip of Poland called the Polish Corridor. Lloyd George had tried to get this particular proposal omitted from the Treaty of Versailles (Source **D** on page 37). As early as March 1919 (four months into the peace), he said that imposing it on the Germans 'will simply mean another war'. He was right. It was this issue which sparked off the Second World War in 1939 (page 120).

THE AUTOGRAPH COLLECTOR

**Source K**  1937 cartoon showing Eden trying to stop Hitler and Mussolini marching forward

## Communism

Another factor was the attitude of many people in Britain and France to Soviet Communism. Trotsky had wanted to make Russia the centre of worldwide Bolshevik revolution (page 62). Communism had great appeal to desperate working people hit hard by the effects of the Depression. This is why affluent people in the West saw Hitler and Mussolini as allies in the struggle against the spread of Communism. There were no strikes in Hitler's Germany. Mussolini's trains ran on time. The politician Harold Nicolson met the Conservative MP Sir Henry Channon and his wife in 1936 and reported 'they think we should let gallant little Germany glut her fill of the reds in the East. Otherwise we shall have not only reds in the West but bombs in London and Southend.'

## Entering the Rhineland

Hitler's next action after rearmament was just as provocative. He deliberately sent a small contingent of soldiers into the demilitarised Rhineland to test Allied reaction (Source **L**). This, too, was a blatant breach of the Treaty of Versailles (and of the Locarno Pact). But, as Hitler hoped and expected, the Allies did nothing, even though many German generals warned him it would mean certain war (Sources **M** and **N**).

**Source L**  German troops march into Cologne in the Rhineland: March 1936

**Source M**  From the diary of newspaper correspondent William L. Shirer

Berlin. 8 March 1936: Hitler has got away with it! France is not marching. Instead it is appealing to the League! No wonder the faces of Hitler and Göring and Blomberg and Fritsch [*top German commanders*] were all smiles this noon. Oh, the stupidity (or is it paralysis?) of the French! I learned today on absolute authority that the German troops had strict orders to beat a hasty retreat if the French army opposed them in any way. They were not prepared or equipped to fight a regular army. Apparently Fritsch and most of the generals opposed the move.

Extract from *Berlin Diary*

**Source N**  Hitler's admission to his interpreter

The forty-eight hours after the march into the Rhineland were the most nerve-racking in my life. If the French had then marched into the Rhineland, we would have had to withdraw with our tails between our legs, for the military resources at our disposal would have been wholly inadequate for even a moderate resistance.

Extract from *Hitler's Interpreter*

Questions

1 How did the Germans in Cologne (Source **L**) greet the soldiers marching into the Rhineland?

2 What was the point of the cartoon in Source **K**?

3 Look at the Party Political Manifesto (Source **J**). Can you see any basic difference between a policy of PEACE and a policy of appeasement?

4 Use Sources **M** and **N** to explain why Hitler was not yet ready for war with Britain and France. What did he propose to do if the French Army intervened?

5 What reasons help to explain why Britain and France did nothing to stop Hitler dismantling the Treaty of Versailles step by step?

## Fascism against Communism

The Abyssinian Crisis moved Mussolini closer to Hitler. In October 1936, he agreed an anti-Communist pact with Hitler, claiming the link between Berlin and Rome would be 'an axis, around which can revolve all those states of Europe with a will towards cooperation and peace'.

The following month, Japan and Germany signed the Anti-Comintern Pact directed at preventing the spread of Communism. Ribbentrop, the German Foreign Minister, said Germany and Italy would keep Communism at bay in Europe, while Japan would do the same in the Far East.

That same year, Germany and Italy both intervened in the Spanish Civil War, sending troops ('volunteers'), weapons and aircraft to aid the Spanish Fascist leader, General Franco, in his rebellion against the lawful, elected, left-wing Republican Government of Spain. This caused a worldwide outcry but there was little the other powers could, or wanted, to do about it. Stalin supplied Russian arms, weapons and troops to help the Republicans and many Western volunteers went to Spain to fight there as well. But France and Britain kept out of the conflict, forming a Non-Intervention Committee which weakened the Republicans, while doing little to curb Hitler and Mussolini.

## Hitler's Secret Plans

Hitler, meanwhile, made his future plans known to his top military commanders. The only solution for Germany, he said, lay in acquiring extra *lebensraum* ['living space'] in Europe. Germany needed land and raw materials close to the Reich. Her problem could only be solved by force. Any delay in going to war after 1943–5 would mean risking war with other nations better armed and equipped with more up-to-date weapons. A senior officer, Colonel Friedrich Hossbach, took notes (Source **O**).

**Source O** The Hossbach Memorandum – Notes on Hitler's speech, 5 November 1937

Our first objective must be to overthrow Czechoslovakia and Austria. The Führer believed that almost certainly Britain, and probably France as well, had already written off the Czechs. Problems with the Empire and reluctance to enter a protracted European war were decisive reasons why Britain would not take part in a war against Germany. An attack by France without Britain was hardly likely. The annexation of Czechoslovakia and Austria would mean extra foodstuffs for 5 to 6 million people, shorter and better frontiers and the freeing of armed forces for other tasks.

Quoted in *Documents on German Foreign Policy*, Washington DC, 1949

**Source P** French cartoon

## Anschluss

Hitler's plans for Austria and Czechoslovakia (Source **O**) had been expressly forbidden by the Paris Peace Treaties. Remarkably, both were achieved without bloodshed inside a year. Union with Austria (*Anschluss*) had been a long-standing Nazi aim (page 74). In fact, several Austrian Nazis had been imprisoned after trying to seize power in 1934. When Hitler met the Austrian Chancellor, Kurt von Schuschnigg, in February 1938, he demanded their release. He also threatened to invade Austria if von Schuschnigg failed to bring Nazis into his goverment.

Von Schuschnigg gave in, but later announced (9 March 1938) that Austrians would be asked to vote yes or no to a simple question: 'Are you in favour of an independent, social, Christian, German, united Austria?' Two days later, American journalist William L. Shirer was swept along a Viennese street by 'a shouting hysterical Nazi mob shrieking "Sieg Heil!, Heil Hitler!"' Hitler had issued an ultimatum – cancel the vote or face invasion. Von Schuschnigg made a radio broadcast later the same evening (Source **Q**).

**Source Q** Radio announcement by the Austrian Chancellor, 11 March 1938

The German Government today handed to the President an ultimatum, with a time limit, ordering him to nominate as chancellor a person designated by the German Government and to appoint members of a cabinet on the orders of the German Government; otherwise German troops would invade Austria.

Extract from *Berlin Diary*

The Austrians gave way yet again and Dr Arthur Seyss-Inquart, an Austrian Nazi, became Chancellor. Exuberant crowds filled Vienna's main streets, singing Nazi songs and flaunting the Swastika. Shirer saw thugs 'heaving paving blocks into the windows of Jewish shops'. Seyss-Inquart immediately invited in German armed forces 'to help preserve the peace'. The following morning (12 March 1938), German troops crossed the Austrian border (Source **R**).

**Source R** Report in 1938

Cheers greeted German troops as they arrived over the frontier and came into Austrian towns. Swastikas hung from windows, crowds gave the Nazi salute; buttonholes, not bullets, greeted the marching men as they penetrated further into the land where Hitler was born.

*These Tremendous Years*, Daily Express Publications, 1938

LITTER

*Peace.* "I had hoped—and I still hope—for a better task than this."

**Source T** *Punch* cartoon, 8 June 1938

(April 1938) Hitler asked Austrians and Germans to vote together on whether they wanted *Anschluss* or not. Stormtroopers supervised the referendum and Hitler's actions were approved – by 99.75 per cent of the vote!

**Source S** Buttonhole for a German soldier after the Anschluss, March 1938

On 13 March 1938, Seyss-Inquart went even further. He declared Austria to be a province of the Third Reich. Three days later Hitler drove through Vienna. A British reporter said older men and women in the crowds had 'tears of joy in their eyes.' A month later

**Questions**

1 Does the Hossbach Memorandum (Source **O**) prove that Hitler started the Second World War? What reasons did Hitler give for concluding that neither Britain nor France would defend Austria and Czechoslovakia?

2 Use Source **Q** to help explain how Hitler brought about *Anschluss* without using troops. What effective action, if any, could Britain and France have taken to prevent this?

3 How far do Sources **R** and **S** provide convincing evidence that the Austrians wanted *Anschluss* with Germany?

4 What was the point of the two cartoons (Sources **P** and **T**)? In what ways were they similar?

## The Munich Crisis

**Source A** Sudeten Nazis in 1938. Henlein's followers formed a 'Free Corps' armed with rifles in 1938 to defend their homeland against the Czechs

▶ **What was the Munich Crisis and why was it important?**

### The Czech Sudetenland

The Czech Sudetenland was a long strip of land close to the Czech frontier where most of the people were German rather than Czech or Slovak. They complained they were at a disadvantage compared with Czechs (Source **B**).

**Source B** From a biography of Neville Chamberlain

Neither Germans nor Slovaks could count on receiving justice, in their own tongue, in the law courts. Unemployment was chronic in the German region, about twice the rate of the country at large, but unemployment benefit for Germans was wholly inadequate, and much lower than for Czechs.

Extract from *The Life of Neville Chamberlain*, by K. Feiling, Macmillan, 1946

The German minority wanted to become part of Hitler's Germany, where unemployment was rapidly declining. This is why their leader, Konrad Henlein, formed the Sudeten German Homeland Party (Source **A**). At a conference in Berlin, on 29 March 1938, the German Foreign Minister, Joachim von Ribbentrop, told them the Nazis would 'not tolerate a continued suppression of the Sudeten Germans by the Czechoslovak Government'.

### First reactions

The Czechs reacted to the Nazi threat by stationing extra troops in the Sudetenland. Tension grew during the summer. France said she would come to Czechoslovakia's aid in the event of an invasion. Britain also warned Germany that she too might be forced to take action if France went to war. But it was a bluff. Chamberlain had already made his real position clear (Source **C**). According to the French Foreign Minister, he confirmed this at a conference in London on 28 April 1938 (Source **D**).

**Source C** Letter from Chamberlain to his sisters, 20 March 1938

You have only to look at the map to see that nothing France or we could do could possibly save Czechoslovakia from being overrun by the Germans, if they wanted to do it. She would simply be a pretext for going to war with Germany. That we could not think of unless we had a reasonable prospect of being able to beat her to her knees in a reasonable time, and of that I see no sign. I have therefore abandoned any idea of giving guarantees to Czechoslovakia, or the French, in connection with her obligations to that country.

Extract from *The Life of Neville Chamberlain*

**Source D** By George Bonnet, French Foreign Minister

If Germany wanted Czechoslovakia then the Prime Minister quite frankly could not see how she was to be prevented. The Prime Minister had witnessed a war and had seen how impossible it is for anyone to emerge from it stronger or happier.

George Bonnet, French Foreign Minister in 1938, quoted in *Defense de la Paix, De Washington au Quai d'Orsay*, Geneva, 1946

The Soviet Union proposed collective action to support the Czechs but neither Britain nor France trusted Stalin. The Soviet Union was not a democracy. The main news from Moscow in 1938 was of the Purges not freedom.

## The tension mounts

In August, Germany started large scale military exercises near the Czech border. People began to think that there might really be a war. But voices were already being heard in France and Britain advising caution and recommending the partition of Czechoslovakia instead. In early September, the Czech Government announced far-reaching concessions to the Sudeten Germans but too late to mollify Hitler. The Czech proposals were rejected. On 12 September 1938 Hitler whipped up German support for the Sudeten Germans with a vitriolic speech in Nuremberg.

Two days later Chamberlain made an unsuccessful trip to Bavaria to try to make Hitler see sense. On his return, the British and French drew up a plan conceding the Sudetenland to Germany and got the Czech government reluctantly to agree. Chamberlain made another trip to Germany – Godesberg – on 22 September 1938 (Source **E**).

**Source E**  Chamberlain leaves Godesberg after meeting Hitler

Once again, he was bitterly disappointed. Hitler had new demands to make which were rejected by the Czechs. Troops massed on the borders. The atmosphere in Europe was electric. Air raid shelters were constructed. Children were evacuated from London. Meanwhile, Chamberlain told the Czechs that Bohemia would be 'overrun and nothing that any other Power can do will prevent this fate for your country and people'. Despite this, he mobilized the Royal Navy on 27 September. Hitler later told Göring, 'Do you know why I finally yielded at Munich? I thought the Home Fleet might open fire.'

At the last minute, Hitler was persuaded to call a final conference at Munich. Chamberlain told a packed House of Commons the news (Source **F**). The four great powers met in Munich (Source **G**) on 29–30 September and signed the agreement. Russia was not invited, nor was Czechoslovakia!

**Source F**  By Sir Henry Channon, a Conservative MP

We stood on our benches, waved our order papers, shouted – until we were hoarse – a scene of indescribable enthusiasm – Peace must now be saved, and with it the world.

Extract from *Chips: The Diaries of Sir Henry Channon*, edited by Robert Rhodes James, Weidenfeld and Nicolson, 1967

**Source G**  The Führerhaus in Munich where Hitler met Chamberlain in September 1938

1 Using Source **E**, explain what Chamberlain's body language tells you about the Godesberg meeting on 22 September 1938. ['Body language' is when you can tell what someone is thinking from their actions, facial expressions or the position of their body.]

2 Which sources provide early evidence that Chamberlain did not intend to defend Czechoslovakia? What were his reasons? Were they convincing reasons or the words of an appeaser?

3 Make a list of the arguments which were, or could have been, used to: **a)** justify, and **b)** deny, Hitler's claims to the Czech Sudetenland.

*Questions*

## The joint declaration

After signing the Munich Agreement, Chamberlain met Hitler again in the Führer's private flat and got him to sign a joint declaration (Source **H**).

Afterwards, there was disagreement about the circumstances which led to the signing of the Declaration (Sources **I** and **J**).

We, the German Führer and Chancellor and the British Prime Minister, have had a further meeting today and are agreed in recognising that the question of Anglo-German relations is of the first importance for the two countries and for Europe.

We regard the agreement signed last night and the Anglo-German Naval Agreement as symbolic of the desire of our two peoples never to go to war with one another again.

We are resolved that the method of consultation shall be the method adopted to deal with any other questions that may concern our two countries, and we are determined to continue our efforts to remove possible sources of difference and thus to contribute to assure the peace of Europe.

*September 30, 1938.*

**Source H** The Joint Declaration

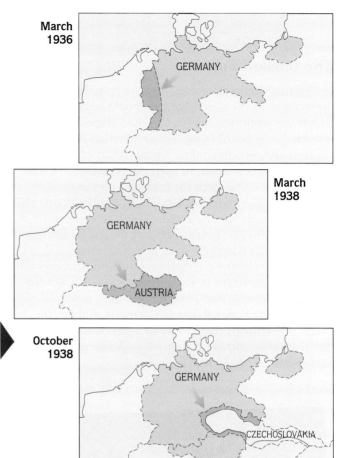

**Source K** (1) How Hitler dismantled the Treaty of Versailles between 1936 and 1938

March 1936 — GERMANY

March 1938 — GERMANY / AUSTRIA

October 1938 — GERMANY / CZECHOSLOVAKIA

**Source I** Letter from Neville Chamberlain to his sisters, October 1938

I had a very friendly and pleasant talk. At the end I pulled out the declaration, which I had prepared beforehand, and asked if he would sign it. As the interpreter translated the words into German, Hitler frequently ejaculated 'Ja, Ja,' ['Yes, Yes'] and at the end said 'Yes, I will certainly sign it; when shall we do it?' I said 'Now'.

*The Life of Neville Chamberlain*

**Source J** By Hitler's interpreter, Dr Paul Schmidt, 1951

Hitler listened absent-mindedly to Chamberlain's remarks, contributing little to the conversation. Towards the end, Chamberlain drew the famous Anglo-German Declaration from his pocket. Slowly, emphasising each word, I translated this statement to Hitler. I did not share Chamberlain's impression, expressed in a private letter of his now published, that Hitler eagerly assented to this declaration. My own feeling was that he agreed to the wording with a certain reluctance, and I believe he added his signature only to please Chamberlain, without promising himself any too much from the effects of the declaration.

*Extract from Hitler's Interpreter*

## The Results of Munich

Once again, Hitler had got his way without using force. Czechoslovakia lost most of her heavy industries, coal mines and fortifications, together with 3 million Sudeten Germans and 700,000 Czechs. Had Germany's opponents taken collective action (as Stalin wanted), their combined forces would have easily outnumbered the Germans. France and Czechoslovakia together had over twice as many troops, Russia had four times as many and the Royal Navy was much more powerful than the German navy.

Munich encouraged both Hitler and Stalin to believe that when the crunch came neither Britain nor France would back their words with action. But it did give them time to accelerate their existing rearmament programmes (Source **L**).

**Source L** Neville Chamberlain at a Cabinet meeting, October 1938

It would be madness for the country to stop rearming until we are convinced that other countries will act in the same way. For the time being, therefore, we should relax no particle of effort until our deficiencies have been made good.

Quoted by D. B. Adams *History of the 20th Century*, Purnell, 1969

# World reactions to Munich

World reaction to the Munich Agreement was either for or against – as you can see from these sources.

**Source M**  French newspaper – *L'Époque*

We have lost an ally. If we were incapable of resisting the formidable German menace in the past when we were stronger, how will we resist the next time when we will be less strong?

**Source N**  French newspaper – *L'Oeuvre*

The Munich agreement has done better than put aside war. It has brought back into the hearts of all the love of peace and has shown in a striking fashion that the most difficult problems can henceforward be resolved round a table.

**Source O**  *New York Times*

Let no man say too high a price has been paid for peace in Europe until he has searched his soul and found himself willing to risk in war the lives of those who are nearest and dearest to him.

**Source P**  *Chicago Tribune*

There is little now to prevent Hitler from dominating and organising Middle and Eastern Europe.

**Source Q**  *Sydney Morning Herald*

Britain and France have consented under a threat of war to give Germany control of important and strategic industrial areas.

**Source R**  Clement Attlee – Labour Party – Leader of the Opposition

Hitler has successfully divided and reduced to impotence the forces which might have stood against the rule of violence. Today we are in a dangerous position. We are left isolated. All potential allies have gone.

Keesing's Contemporary Archives 1937–40

**Source S**  Sir Samuel Hoare – Home Secretary

Owing to her geographical position, if war had come, whoever won or lost, Czechoslovakia would have been inevitably destroyed with immense slaughter and devastation.

**Source T**  Report of speech by Sir John Simon – Chancellor of the Exchequer

There were, he maintained four hopeful features. For the first time a dictator had made some concession. Again, dictators had learned that hatred of war prevailed among their own well-drilled peoples. Thirdly, in spite of Dr.Goebbels, the German people now knew that Britain too wanted peace; and lastly, there was a great awakening in this country to the need that conciliation must be backed by strength.

Keesing's Contemporary Archives 1937–40

**Source U**  Front page of the *Daily Herald*, 30 September 1938

Questions

1  List the Sources **M** to **T** in two columns headed **a)** arguments FOR, and **b)** arguments AGAINST, the Munich Agreement. For each argument, say whether you think it is weak or convincing.

2  There are many different views about the Munich Agreement. Some German historians have even argued that Hitler gave way at Munich, not Chamberlain. For each of the interpretations A, B and C (below), say which facts and sources: **a)** support, and **b)** contradict, the interpretation in question.

A)  Chamberlain was a spineless appeaser who simply gave in at the first threat of force

B)  Chamberlain was a realist who took the practical view there was nothing anyone could do to stop Hitler marching into Czechoslovakia

C)  Chamberlain wanted to buy time so Britain could build up her strength through rearmament and the mobilisation of her armed forces.

3  The two accounts (Sources **I** and **J**) differ widely in their interpretation of the private meeting between Hitler and Chamberlain. How do you think these differences arose? Is it possible to say which is the correct interpretation?

## Poland – the Last Year of Peace

 ### Why did appeasement fail to prevent the outbreak of war in 1939?

### Heightened tension

The following March, Hitler forced the Czech Government to agree to turn Bohemia and Moravia into German Protectorates. Nazi soldiers marched into Prague and were greeted by angry, weeping crowds. Czechoslovakia had ceased to exist as an independent state. For the first time, Hitler had seized control of a country inhabited by non-Germans. Chamberlain argued that this was not aggression, and did not call for a British military response. But within a week Hitler also took the Memel, a predominantly German region of Nazi sympathisers, away from Lithuania.

People who had cheered Chamberlain the previous September now set their teeth against appeasement. It was clear that Hitler's next victim would be Poland and that he could only be stopped by force. France and Britain could not help but the Soviet Union could. Yet, on 26 March 1939, Neville Chamberlain wrote that he profoundly distrusted Russia and had no faith in Stalin's willingness or ability to act as an effective ally. In any case, the Poles (ruled by a right-wing dictatorship) hated the Russians as much as they hated the Germans. By this time, however, Chamberlain had to do something, so on 31 March 1938, he gave Hitler a last warning (Source **B**).

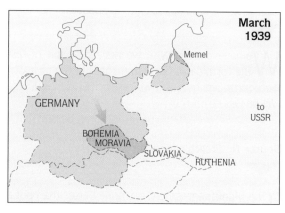

**Source A**  How Hitler dismantled the Treaty of Versailles in 1939

**Source B**  Chamberlain's warning to Hitler: 31 March 1939

Any action which clearly threatened Polish independence, and which the Polish government accordingly considered it vital to resist with their national forces, His Majesty's Government would feel themselves bound at once to lend the Polish government all support in their power.

Extract from *The Life of Neville Chamberlain*

France offered a similar guarantee the same day. In the circumstances, however, it is hardly surprising that Hitler treated these promises with disbelief (Source **C**).

**Source C**  Cartoon in *Punch*, 5 April 1939

118

Ironically, Hitler had sounder reasons for overturning Versailles in Poland than in Czechoslovakia or Austria. East Prussia (see map on page 38) had been forcibly separated from the rest of Germany by a strip of what had once been Prussia – the Polish Corridor – so that Poland could have access to the free city and port of Danzig (Gdansk). Danzig was 96 per cent German and by 1939 had a Nazi Government and wanted to return to Germany. Hitler, as we have seen (Source **O** on page 112), had other motives as well for attacking Poland, such as Germany's need for *lebensraum* (living space), extra farmland, fuel and raw materials.

When Poland rejected German demands, tension began to mount. Hitler renounced his 1934 Non-Aggression Treaty with Poland and the 1935 Naval Agreement with Britain. The Soviet Union, Britain and France began talks to try to form a common front against Nazi aggression. But the two Western Powers were still suspicious of Russia and reluctant to accept the demands made by Stalin. They delayed making a decision about an alliance until it was too late.

On 22 May 1939 Mussolini and Hitler agreed the Pact of Steel – a military alliance – which guaranteed immediate aid from the other partner in the event of war and in August Count Ciano, Mussolini's Foreign Minister, learned at first hand (Sources **D** and **E**) there would be no last-minute solution to the Polish problem.

**Source D** From Count Ciano's diary

August 11,1939. 'Well Ribbentrop,' I asked, 'what do you want? The Corridor or Danzig?' 'Not that any more,' he said, gazing at me with his cold metallic eyes. 'We want war!'

*Ciano's Diary*, edited by Malcolm Muggeridge, Heinemann, 1947

**Source E** From Count Ciano's diary

AUGUST 12, 1939. Hitler is very cordial, but he, too, is impassive and implacable in his decision. I realize immediately that there is no longer anything that can be done. He has decided to strike, and strike he will. All our arguments will not avail in the least to stop him. He continues to repeat that he will localize the conflict with Poland.

Extract from *Ciano's Diary*

**Source F** Cartoon dated 20 September 1939. This cartoon was published after Germany and the Soviet Union had agreed to divide Poland between them

Ciano said later that Hitler and Ribbentrop were sure that both France and Great Britain would not want to go to war, while Mussolini was equally sure they would. On the 23rd of the month, the world heard the startling and ominous news that the Soviet Union and Germany had signed a Non-Aggression pact. It was obvious now to anyone, that Hitler could strike at Poland whenever he wanted without inviting retaliation from the Red Army, the only armed force in Eastern Europe capable of pushing back the German Army. What the world wasn't told, however, was that secretly both powers had also agreed to divide Poland between them (Source **F**).

*Q*uestions

1 Why were Britain and France reluctant to ally themselves with Stalin?

2 What was the point of the BARKING DOG cartoon (Source **C**)? What private path was Hitler proposing to cross? Who was the barking dog and why was there some doubt as to whether the dog would bite?

3 What evidence tells us that the Nazi leaders had already made up their minds to invade Poland before the signing of the pact with Stalin?

4 What was the point of the RENDEZVOUS cartoon (Source **F**)?

# 10 A modern world at war

## Blitzkrieg

▶ **How and why did the war begin in September 1939?**
**Why was Germany successful in launching attacks on**
**Poland and Western Europe in 1939–40?**

## Poland

On Friday, 1 September 1939, German forces began a
rapid invasion of Poland using tanks, mechanised
infantry, dive bombers and fighter aircraft to surprise
and shock the enemy. The speed and savagery of the
German attack was so effective and its impact on the
Poles so deadly, it was called *Blitzkrieg* ('lightning-
war'). On Sunday, 3 September 1939 the German
Foreign Office received an ultimatum from Britain
giving Germany two hours to agree to withdraw her
troops from Poland. Hitler's interpreter took it to the
Führer (Sources **A** and **B**). At 11 a.m. Britain was at
war with Germany.

**Source A** By Dr Paul Schmidt,
Hitler's interpreter

I slowly translated the
ultimatum. When I finished
there was complete silence.
Hitler sat completely silent
and unmoving. After an
interval which seemed an
age, he turned to
Ribbentrop. 'What now?'
asked Hitler with a savage
look, as though implying that
his Foreign Minister had
misled him about England's
probable reaction.

Extract from *Hitler's Interpreter*

France declared war on
Germany later in the day. But
there was nothing they could
do to halt Hitler (Source **C**).

**Source B** By Albert Speer, one of Hitler's leading Ministers

Hitler was initially stunned, but quickly reassured
himself and us by saying that England and France had
obviously declared war merely as a sham, in order not to
lose face before the whole world. There would be no
fighting; he was convinced of that, he said. I do not think
that in those early days of September, Hitler was fully
aware that he had irrevocably unleashed a world war. He
had merely meant to move one step further.

Extract from *Inside the Third Reich*, by Albert Speer, translated by
Richard and Clara Winston, Weidenfeld and Nicolson, 1970

**Source C** Map of the war: ▶
1939–41

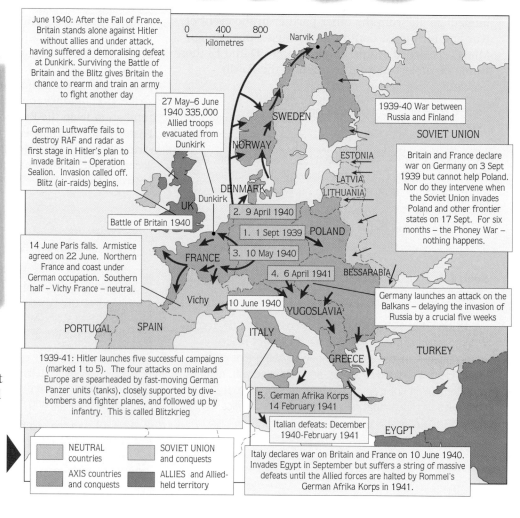

June 1940: After the Fall of France, Britain stands alone against Hitler without allies and under attack, having suffered a demoralising defeat at Dunkirk. Surviving the Battle of Britain and the Blitz gives Britain the chance to rearm and train an army to fight another day

27 May–6 June 1940 335,000 Allied troops evacuated from Dunkirk

German Luftwaffe fails to destroy RAF and radar as first stage in Hitler's plan to invade Britain – Operation Sealion. Invasion called off. Blitz (air-raids) begins.

Battle of Britain 1940

14 June Paris falls. Armistice agreed on 22 June. Northern France and coast under German occupation. Southern half – Vichy France – neutral.

1939-40 War between Russia and Finland

Britain and France declare war on Germany on 3 Sept 1939 but cannot help Poland. Nor do they intervene when the Soviet Union invades Poland and other frontier states on 17 Sept. For six months – the Phoney War – nothing happens.

2. 9 April 1940

1. 1 Sept 1939

3. 10 May 1940

4. 6 April 1941

10 June 1940

Germany launches an attack on the Balkans – delaying the invasion of Russia by a crucial five weeks

1939-41: Hitler launches five successful campaigns (marked 1 to 5). The four attacks on mainland Europe are spearheaded by fast-moving German Panzer units (tanks), closely supported by dive-bombers and fighter planes, and followed up by infantry. This is called Blitzkrieg

5. German Afrika Korps 14 February 1941

Italian defeats: December 1940-February 1941

Italy declares war on Britain and France on 10 June 1940. Invades Egypt in September but suffers a string of massive defeats until the Allied forces are halted by Rommel's German Afrika Korps in 1941.

NEUTRAL countries

AXIS countries and conquests

SOVIET UNION and conquests

ALLIES and Allied-held territory

0  400  800 kilometres

Narvik

SWEDEN

NORWAY

SOVIET UNION

ESTONIA

LATVIA

LITHUANIA

DENMARK

Dunkirk

UK

POLAND

FRANCE

BESSARABIA

Vichy

YUGOSLAVIA

PORTUGAL  SPAIN

ITALY

GREECE

TURKEY

EYGPT

After Poland had been partitioned between Germany and the Soviet Union, Hitler expected Britain and France to agree peace terms. The Nazi newspaper, *Volkischer Beobachter*, carried the headline,

'GERMANY'S WILL FOR PEACE – NO WAR AIMS AGAINST FRANCE AND ENGLAND'.

But this time Hitler was ignored. Britain's war aims had changed – as Winston Churchill made plain in Parliament on 3 September 1939: 'This is not a question of fighting for Poland,' he said. 'We are fighting to save the whole world from the pestilence of Nazi tyranny'. In practice, however, very little happened for six months (Source **C**). This is why this period was called 'the Phoney War'.

## Norway and the Fall of France

The land war in Europe erupted again in April 1940, when German forces attacked Denmark and Norway after British ships tried to lay mines in the seas off Norway to stop Swedish iron ore reaching Germany. The failure of the expedition helped to bring down Chamberlain. His successor was Winston Churchill (page 127).

In May and June 1940, for the second time in 26 years, Belgium and France felt the full impact of an advancing German army. This time the attack came through the Ardennes, a hilly area which the French had thought unsuitable for tank warfare. The German tanks proved them wrong as the Panzer units raced to the Channel coast, cutting off the French and Belgian armies in Flanders as well as a British Expeditionary Force (BEF) of about a quarter of a million men. The main German armies drove on towards Paris, leaving the BEF time enough to escape by sea from Dunkirk (Source **D**). It was a massive and demoralising defeat.

**Source D**  Troops waiting at Dunkirk

Most of the British Army's vehicles and equipment were left behind but there were relatively few casualties and the soldiers lived on to fight another day.

Churchill had promised, 'I have nothing to offer but blood, toil, tears and sweat'. Now he rose to the occasion with yet another stirring speech telling the British people and the world, 'We shall never surrender'. This was of little use to the French. On 10 June Mussolini declared war and four days later German troops goose-stepped into Paris. France surrendered on 22 June, leaving Britain on her own.

## The Battle of Britain

Churchill, once again, urged his fellow countrymen to stand firm (Source **E**).

**Source E**  Winston Churchill, 18 June 1940

> Let us therefore brace ourselves to our duty and so bear ourselves that if the British Commonwealth and Empire last for a thousand years men will still say, 'This was their finest hour'.

Hitler's plan to invade Britain – 'Operation Sealion' – was put into effect. The first requirement was control of the air. Göring's Luftwaffe successfully destroyed many RAF airfields and radar installations (page 128) but when they were directed to bomb London instead, the RAF had time to recover and won a great victory, forcing Hitler to call off the invasion for good. Churchill paid tribute to the bravery of the RAF pilots:

'Never in the field of human conflict was so much owed by so many to so few'.

*Q*uestions

1 What conclusion does the writer draw from Hitler's body language in Source **A**? To what extent does Source **E** on page 119 support this conclusion?

2 Using Sources **A** and **B**, describe Hitler's reaction to the Allied declaration of war in your own words.

3 Why was *Blitzkrieg* so effective?

4 Look at Source **D**. How does a painting like this differ from a photograph as a record of an historical event, such as Dunkirk?

## Operation Barbarossa

Hitler, like Churchill, knew that Britain would never be able to invade mainland Europe without the backing of a powerful ally – either the Soviet Union or the United States. In July 1940, he told his generals his plans (Source **F**).

**Source F**  Hitler talks to his generals

The sooner we smash Russia the better. Britain's last hopes will be shattered. Germany will then be master of Europe and the Balkans.

**Source I**  Grand parade in Moscow's Red Square in November 1941. Few of the soldiers depicted here lived to see the end of the war.

Hitler had other war aims as well. He had a lifelong hatred of Communism. Only in European Russia and the Ukraine could Germany find the abundant *lebensraum* ('living space') and raw materials he thought she needed for her growing population. The Soviet Union would become part of the German Empire (Source **G**).

**Source G**  Hitler talking in 1941

The Russian space is our India. Like the English, we shall rule this empire with a handful of men. We'll supply grain to all in Europe who need it. The Crimea will give us its citrus fruits, cotton and rubber.

Extract from *Hitler's Table-Talk*, translated by Norman Cameron and R. H. Stevens, Weidenfeld and Nicolson, 1953

The attack on the Soviet Union – codenamed 'Operation Barbarossa' – began on 22 June 1941. It took Stalin by surprise, even though it was common knowledge in Germany that an attack was due. As the German tanks drove deep into Russia, they encountered problems (Source **H**).

The onset of the Russian winter also caught the German army unprepared. Their soldiers had inadequate winter clothing and their tanks and vehicles ran into difficulties, first in the autumn muds and later in the intense cold of the Russian winter. No such problems hindered the Russians fighting on their native soil. In December, white-uniformed Russian soldiers, some on skis, drove the Russians back in front of Moscow (Source **I**).

## The agony of Russia

The war brought prolonged suffering and tragedy to most Russian families. Nearly 14 million soldiers were killed and over seven million Russian civilians also died, many of them Jews. Both sides committed many cruelties. A German soldier described some of these barbarities when on leave from the Russian Front (Source **J**).

**Source H**  By German General Guenther Blumentritt

It was appallingly difficult country for tank movement – great virgin forests, widespread swamps, terrible roads, and bridges not strong enough to bear the weight of tanks. The resistance also became stiffer, and the Russians began to cover their front with minefields. It was easier for them to block the way because there were so few roads.

German General Guenther Blumentritt, quoted in *The War 1939-1945*, edited by Desmond Flower and James Reeves, Cassell, 1960

**Source J**  German cruelty

We shoot the prisoners on the slightest excuse. Just stick them up against the wall and shoot the lot. We order the whole village out to look while we do it, too. They do as terrible things as we do to them.

Extract from *Hausfrau at War*, by Else Wendel, Odhams Press, 1947. Quoted in *The Faber Book of Reportage*, edited by John Carey, 1987

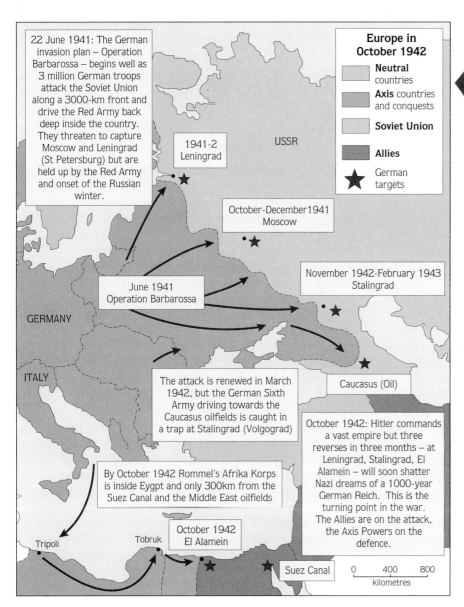

22 June 1941: The German invasion plan – Operation Barbarossa – begins well as 3 million German troops attack the Soviet Union along a 3000-km front and drive the Red Army back deep inside the country. They threaten to capture Moscow and Leningrad (St Petersburg) but are held up by the Red Army and onset of the Russian winter.

**Europe in October 1942**

Neutral countries

Axis countries and conquests

Soviet Union

Allies

★ German targets

1941-2 Leningrad

USSR

October-December 1941 Moscow

June 1941 Operation Barbarossa

November 1942-February 1943 Stalingrad

GERMANY

ITALY

The attack is renewed in March 1942, but the German Sixth Army driving towards the Caucasus oilfields is caught in a trap at Stalingrad (Volgograd)

Caucasus (Oil)

October 1942: Hitler commands a vast empire but three reverses in three months – at Leningrad, Stalingrad, El Alamein – will soon shatter Nazi dreams of a 1000-year German Reich. This is the turning point in the war. The Allies are on the attack, the Axis Powers on the defence.

By October 1942 Rommel's Afrika Korps is inside Eygpt and only 300km from the Suez Canal and the Middle East oilfields

Tripoli  Tobruk  October 1942 El Alamein

Suez Canal

0    400    800
kilometres

## The German campaign in 1942

The following spring the German army renewed the offensive but with a change of plan. Hitler ordered them to take the oilfields of the Caucasus in the south-east. A large German army laid siege to Stalingrad (Volgograd) but once again the Russian winter intervened. Top Soviet general, Marshal Zhukov, led them into a trap. He encircled the German Sixth Army and forced it to surrender on 31 January 1943. That same month another Russian army partially relieved Leningrad, after a devastating siege in which hundreds of thousands of Russians died.

From this time onward the Russians were on the offensive. The war had turned. The immense size and much greater population of the Soviet Union began to tell. In July 1943 the Red Army inflicted a devastating defeat on the Germans at Kursk. More tanks were engaged here than in any other battle in history. The Germans were outnumbered by 1.3 million men to 900,000 and by 3600 tanks and heavy guns to 2700. One year later, near Minsk, Soviet commander

**Source K**  Hitler attacks the Soviet Union: June 1941–October 1942

Marshal Rokossovsky's army of 1.2 million men, 5200 tanks and guns and 6000 aircraft overwhelmed the German army of 400,000 men, 900 tanks and guns and 1300 aircraft facing them. From now on, the defeat of Germany was only a matter of time.

## North Africa

The first real turning point in the war, however, came in Egypt. The war in North Africa had originally been fought between Italian and British troops but a crushing defeat for Italy was avenged by Rommel's crack Afrika Korps who drove the British Eighth Army back inside Egypt, threatening the Middle East and even India. Churchill appointed Montgomery to lead the Eighth Army (the Desert Rats). 'Monty' led his army from the front, using a tank as his battle headquarters. He launched a massive attack against Rommel's heavily fortified positions on 23 October 1942. The battle at El Alamein lasted a fortnight but ended on 4 November with the Afrika Korps in full and final retreat.

*Questions*

1  Look at Source **K**. Write a radio news item summing up the progress made by the Axis powers to October 1942.

2  Draw or paint a Russian or German propaganda poster for use in December 1941.

3  What reasons explain why the Soviet Union fought back so successfully against the Germans in 1942–3?

4  Why were the victories at Stalingrad and El Alamein so important?

5  What does the painting (Source **I**) add to your understanding of the Soviet Union during the war?

6  Write down some of the reasons why Hitler attacked the Soviet Union in 1941. Which were consistent with the war aims in the Hossbach Memorandum (Source **O** on page 112)?

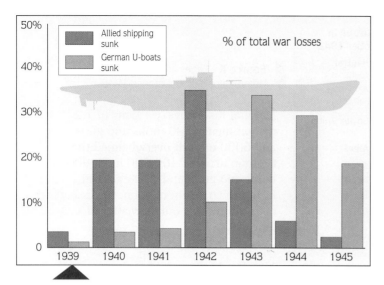

Source L  The U-boat war

## The war in the Atlantic

The crucial conflict at sea was in the Atlantic where over 2700 Allied merchant ships and more than a hundred warships were torpedoed by German U-boats. The convoy system (page 27) helped keep losses down but disruption to food supplies was serious. Allied losses reached a peak in 1942 (Source **L**). The turning point came in 1943, when new technology was used to search for, and destroy, the U-boats. Radar, the *Huff Duff* electronic system and the use of *Ultra* to decode German U-boat messages (see Source **C** on page 129), helped long-range aircraft and convoy escort ships locate the U-boat packs. Once located, the enemy submarines were destroyed by depth charges or underwater missiles launched from sophisticated *Hedgehog* and *Squid* launchers (page 129).

The anti-submarine campaign was so successful, the German U-boat fleet was temporarily withdrawn from the North Atlantic in the summer of 1943. Seven out of 51 U-boats had been sunk in one encounter alone and total U-boat losses for May 1943 were 37, followed by another 34 in July. When the U-boats returned in the Autumn, they sank four Allied ships in October but lost 22 U-boats in doing so. To all intents and purposes, the Battle of the Atlantic was over.

## Strategic bombing

By 1943, too, Allied bombers were daily causing immense human suffering over Germany itself (Source **M**). Earlier raids targeting specific factories had failed because the bombers couldn't locate their targets through smoking chimneys, low clouds and ferocious anti-aircraft fire. Air Chief Marshal Harris, newly-appointed head of RAF Bomber Command, was told to destroy German morale with massive air raids which would cut industrial production by 'dehousing' the workers. If people didn't turn up for work, factory output would fall (Sources **R**, **S** and **T**).

Sources **N** to **Q** show what happened when Allied bombers bombed Hamburg almost continuously for ten days in July–August 1943. The city was targeted because of its huge number of war industries, including a giant U-boat works. The Americans bombed by day, the British by night. The Allies used 'Window' (metal foil strips) to confuse German radar, making it impossible to locate the bombers at night. Vast numbers of incendiary bombs set fire to timber buildings and warehouses by the docks. The immense heat generated by the fires sucked in oxygen, causing a terrible firestorm (Source **O**). Three out of every five homes were destroyed or made uninhabitable, and some 600 factories were destroyed. A million people fled from the city, while over 40,000 were killed and another 40,000 badly injured.

Source M  Ruins of Cologne in 1945

Source N  By Albert Speer, one of Hitler's Ministers

Huge conflagrations created cyclone-like firestorms. The asphalt of the streets began to blaze. People were suffocated in their cellars or burned to death in the streets. Gauleiter Kaufmann repeatedly begged Hitler to visit the stricken city.

Extract from *Inside the Third Reich*, by Albert Speer, translated by Richard and Clara Winston, Weidenfeld and Nicolson, 1970

Source O  Firestorm in Hamburg: from Hausfrau at War by Else Wendel

Tuesday night, 27 July: Out in the square it was like a furnace. A great flame was shooting straight out towards them. A flame as high as the houses and nearly as wide as the whole street.

Extract from *Hausfrau at War*

**Source P**  From the diary of a Hamburg woman: Wednesday, 28 July 1943

There was no gas, no electricity, not a drop of water, neither the lift nor the telephone was working, no trams, no Underground. Most people loaded some belongings on carts, bicycles, prams, just to get away, to escape. People wearing Nazi party badges had them torn off their coats and there were screams of 'Let's get that murderer'.

*On the Other Side*, by Mathilde Wolff-Monckeberg, translated and edited by Ruth Evans, Peter Owen, 1979

**Source Q**  From the diary kept by Josef Goebbels

*July 25th 1943*: The letters addressed to me are disturbing; they contain an unusual amount of criticism. Above all, they keep asking why the Führer does not visit the bombed areas, why Göring is nowhere to be seen, and especially why the Führer doesn't talk to the German people and explain the present situation.

*The Goebbels Diaries [1942–43]*, translated and edited by Louis P. Lochner, Hamish Hamilton, 1948

**Source R**  By Albert Speer, one of Hitler's Ministers

In spite of the losses of factories we were producing more, not less. From my contacts with the man in the street I carried away the impression of growing toughness. Our heaviest expense was in defence. Ten thousand anti-aircraft guns pointed towards the sky could well have been employed in Russia against tanks. Half our electronics industry was engaged in producing radar for defence against bombing.

Extract from *Inside the Third Reich*

**Source S**  From a history of the Second World War published in 1994

This was the only major way in which Britain could directly assist the Soviet Union.
[*The raids*] forced the Germans to disperse their aircraft factories, a process that cost them months of production. Seeing the overflight of British bombers headed for Germany showed the people [*of occupied Europe*] that liberation, however distant, was at least a possibility.

*A World at Arms*, by Gerhard L. Weinberg, Cambridge, 1994

**Source T**  From a history of the Second World War published in 1986

Hamburg recovered with astonishing speed. Overall manufacturing output recovered to some 70 percent of the pre-raid effort within six weeks.

*The Illustrated History of World War II*, Consultant Editor Barrie Pitt, Temple Press Aerospace, 1986

**Source U**  Bomber crew returning from a mission. Over 55,000 men – two-thirds of all those in the RAF who died in the war – were killed during Bomber Command operations.

*Questions*

1  Use Source **L** to explain when and why Germany lost the Battle of the Atlantic.

2  How reliable do you think Sources **N, O, P, Q** and **R** are as evidence about the air raids on Hamburg? Is there any reason to suspect the writers of being biased?

3  Which sources show that the raids, **a)** did, and **b)** did not, damage the German war effort?

4  Which sources show that the raids, **a)** did, and **b)** did not, have a serious effect on the morale of the German people?

5  Write down the evidence which a lawyer could use to: **a)** accuse, and **b)** defend, Air Chief Marshal Harris of committing a war crime by bombing Hamburg. In your own words, say what you think history's verdict on the Hamburg raids should be.

Source V Monument in Warsaw to the victims of the Warsaw Uprising in August 1944

## Resistance movements in occupied Europe

As they advanced towards Germany, the Allied forces were assisted by resistance workers or partisans in occupied Europe who sabotaged railway trains and blew up lorries carrying vital supplies. Members of the French Resistance, for instance, destroyed telephone cables, railways and bridges behind the lines to hamper German troops rushing to repel the Allies after the D-Day landings. Soviet partisans did the same before the battle at Minsk in June 1944 (page 123).

The Germans had ruled by terror in the lands they conquered, using public executions, torture and starvation to subdue the people. Many workers were rounded up and sent as labourers to work in German mines and factories. Many of those left at home joined the resistance movements, risking their lives to shelter Allied pilots and pass on vital information to the Allies. Sometimes their activities endangered other people as well. When Reinhard Heydrich, the hated Nazi Protector of Czechoslovakia, was assassinated by the Czech resistance in May 1942, the Nazis destroyed the village of Lidice, shot every man in the village and sent the women to concentration camps. SS soldiers carried out a similar crime on 10 June 1944, when they massacred the 648 inhabitants of the French village of Oradour-sur-Glane.

## Victory in Europe

After January 1943, the Allies suffered no major defeats of any consequence. The Axis Powers were on the retreat (Source **W**). People everywhere followed the progress of the Russian armies as they advanced through Eastern Europe towards Berlin. Even after D-Day most of Hitler's soldiers faced east not west. There were temporary setbacks but on 25 April 1945, the pincer movement from East and West snapped shut when American and Russian soldiers met at last by the river Elbe. Three days later, Mussolini was killed by Italian partisans and two days after that Hitler committed suicide. Berlin fell on 2 May and Germany itself surrendered on 8 May 1945, VE Day.

**Source W**  Victory in Europe: October 1942–May 1945

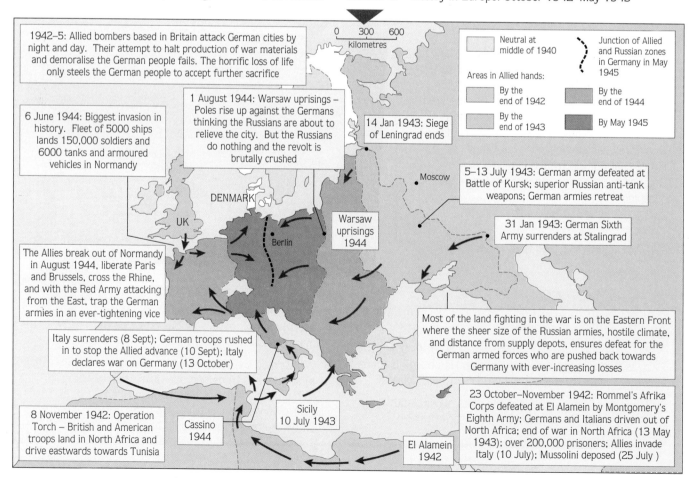

1942–5: Allied bombers based in Britain attack German cities by night and day. Their attempt to halt production of war materials and demoralise the German people fails. The horrific loss of life only steels the German people to accept further sacrifice

1 August 1944: Warsaw uprisings – Poles rise up against the Germans thinking the Russians are about to relieve the city. But the Russians do nothing and the revolt is brutally crushed

6 June 1944: Biggest invasion in history. Fleet of 5000 ships lands 150,000 soldiers and 6000 tanks and armoured vehicles in Normandy

14 Jan 1943: Siege of Leningrad ends

5–13 July 1943: German army defeated at Battle of Kursk; superior Russian anti-tank weapons; German armies retreat

31 Jan 1943: German Sixth Army surrenders at Stalingrad

The Allies break out of Normandy in August 1944, liberate Paris and Brussels, cross the Rhine, and with the Red Army attacking from the East, trap the German armies in an ever-tightening vice

Most of the land fighting in the war is on the Eastern Front where the sheer size of the Russian armies, hostile climate, and distance from supply depots, ensures defeat for the German armed forces who are pushed back towards Germany with ever-increasing losses

Italy surrenders (8 Sept); German troops rushed in to stop the Allied advance (10 Sept); Italy declares war on Germany (13 October)

23 October–November 1942: Rommel's Afrika Corps defeated at El Alamein by Montgomery's Eighth Army; Germans and Italians driven out of North Africa; end of war in North Africa (13 May 1943); over 200,000 prisoners; Allies invade Italy (10 July); Mussolini deposed (25 July )

8 November 1942: Operation Torch – British and American troops land in North Africa and drive eastwards towards Tunisia

Cassino 1944

Sicily 10 July 1943

El Alamein 1942

Warsaw uprisings 1944

DENMARK

UK

Berlin

Moscow

0  300  600
kilometres

Neutral at middle of 1940

Junction of Allied and Russian zones in Germany in May 1945

Areas in Allied hands:

By the end of 1942

By the end of 1944

By the end of 1943

By May 1945

## Wartime diplomacy

As the prospect of an imminent Allied victory became ever more certain, the politicians made haste to sort out the postwar arrangements they thought Europe would need. The immediate cause of the Second World War had been the German invasion of Poland on 1 September 1939. Yet, when the war ended in May 1945, much of Poland became part of the Soviet Union, and Poland itself became a dependent Communist satellite (page 147). As in all great wars, the main belligerents had changed their war aims. Although the United States and Soviet Union stayed neutral when Churchill and Britain faced Hitler alone, their armies did most of the fighting later on.

## The wartime conferences

Only Churchill and Roosevelt attended the Casablanca Conference in January 1943 when Britain and the USA decided to invade Italy and demand the unconditional surrender of the Axis Powers. At three further conferences at Teheran (28 November–1 December 1943), Yalta (February 1945) and Potsdam (July–August 1945) the Allied leaders made a number of key decisions – as you can see from the short summary in Source Y.

---

**WINSTON CHURCHILL (1874–1965)**

When war broke out in 1939, Winston Churchill was put in charge of the Royal Navy, the same job that he had held in 1914. He became Prime Minister in May 1940. Churchill was in his element as a war leader. He took an active but sometimes ill-informed part in military decisions, such as when he sacked or demoted an outstanding general he disagreed with. His most important role in the war was as a symbol – a pugnacious British Bulldog defying Hitler to do his worst. His aggression and his oratory fired audiences who listened to him and gave a huge boost to the war effort at home and abroad. He even managed to make Dunkirk seem like a victory.

**Source X** Winston Churchill on a wartime poster

"LET US GO FORWARD TOGETHER"

---

**Source Y** Key decisions at the wartime conferences

**TEHERAN CONFERENCE (28 November–1 December 1943)**

- D-Day landings in May or June 1944
- A new World Organisation after the war to replace the League of Nations
- Polish frontiers to be redrawn to give Russia a buffer zone
- Poland to be given part of Germany in compensation

**YALTA CONFERENCE (4–11 February 1945)**

- Eastern Polish frontier to follow partition line agreed with Hitler in 1939
- Western Polish frontier to follow the rivers Oder and Neisse
- Free elections to be held in countries liberated by the Allies
- United Nations to go ahead on lines drawn up at Dumbarton Oaks (page 162)
- Four Occupation Zones in Germany after the war (US, UK, USSR, France)
- Germany to pay war reparations, mainly to the Soviet Union
- USSR to declare war on Japan three months after defeating Hitler; in return, USSR to get back territory lost to Japan in 1904–5

**POTSDAM CONFERENCE (16 July–2 August 1945)**

- Council of Foreign Ministers to draw up peace treaties with Axis powers
- Prosecution of Nazi war criminals
- Reparations by Germany to include dismantled factories and machinery

**Questions**

1 Use the information on the map (Source **W**) to write an explanatory summary of the latter stages of the war.

2 How did the Resistance movements assist the Allied armies?

3 The Allies attacked from the East, South and West. Which of these was the most decisive Allied thrust? Why?

4 Use Source **Y** to explain how the Allied war aims at the end of the war differed from those of Britain and France in September 1939.

## Technology and warfare

▶ **How did technological developments change the nature of warfare in the period 1939–45?**

### Designing weapons for a purpose

Technology played a very important part in the Second World War. Weapons were speedily developed to suit the strategy and tactics of the commanders. Since the war effort took precedence over everything else, technology advanced at a far faster rate than in peacetime. Aircraft, tank and munitions factories were stretched to their capacity, often working 24 hours a day, seven days a week (Source **A**).

The types of weapon employed depended on the use to which they were going to be put. The German *Panzer* Mark II tanks spearheading the *Blitzkrieg* attacks of 1939–40 needed speed and manoeuvrability and were only 10 tonnes in weight and armed with 20 mm guns. Four years later, the Germans were using Tiger Mark II tanks weighing 68 tonnes and armed with 88 mm guns. They needed tanks with thick armour plating and powerful guns to fight against the Red Army in Russia.

Similar considerations changed the design of aircraft (Source **B**). The American B-29 Superfortress introduced in 1943 could carry 10 tonnes of bombs at a speed of 600 kph and attack targets 4000 km away. It was used to attack Japan from airbases deep inside mainland China. By contrast, the twin-engined, German Heinkel HE-111 bombers which bombed Britain in 1940–1 had a range of less than 1000 km, carried no more than 2.5 tonnes of bombs and flew at only 330 kph. The Heinkels were protected by Messerschmitt ME109 fighters which were evenly matched against the British Spitfires opposing them during the Battle of Britain. The Spitfire was marginally faster (about 550–600 kph) and more manoeuvrable but the ME109 could dive or climb more rapidly and its guns fired further than the British plane.

### New inventions and technical developments

The most important technological development in conventional air warfare came in 1944 with the world's first jet aircraft. The British Gloster Meteor (top speed 660–800 kph) was not quite as fast as the

**Source A**  Soviet poster: 'Follow this worker's example. Produce more for the front.'

German Messerschmitt ME262 (top speed 870 kph). Neither made any real impact on the war although they pioneered the almost universal switch to jet aircraft after 1945.

At sea, aircraft carriers replaced battleships as the most effective type of warship in the Pacific after the landmark naval battles of the Coral Sea and Midway in 1942 (page 133) were fought by aircraft launched from carriers a hundred kilometres or so apart.

Finding effective weapons of defence was as important as developing weapons of attack. This is why British, American and German scientists developed radar (RAdio Direction And Range) systems using radio beams to provide early warning of advancing enemy aircraft. Using *Ultra* to unravel the secret of the German *Enigma* codes (Source **C**) made another substantial contribution to the Allied victory.

Source B  British Typhoon fighter-bombers in action in Normandy in 1944

Some of the sophisticated weapons systems used in the war

AIRBORNE CIGAR (ABC) – electronic device carried by bombers which jammed radio messages sent to Luftwaffe night fighters from the ground

CHURCHILL CROCODILE – flamethrower which fired burning fuel

CRAB – flail tank using rotating chains to detonate mines in a minefield

ENIGMA – German machine used to transmit secret radio messages in code

FIDO (Fog, Intensive, Dispersal Of) – system using burning fuel to clear away fog from RAF runways so aircraft could land in all weathers

HEDGEHOG and SQUID launchers firing depth charges ahead of a warship

HUFF DUFF (High Frequency Direction Finding) – pinpointing a U-boat's position from its radio transmissions

KATYUSHA – Russian launcher system firing 36 rockets at targets 5 km away

KNICKEBEIN – German navigation system for bombers using two radio beams

OBOE, G-H, H2S, MICKEY, MICRO-H – navigation aids for bombers using radar

PANZERFAUST – German anti-tank missile fired from a hand-held gun

PLUTO (Pipe Line Under The Ocean) – carrying fuel for D-Day tanks/vehicles

ULTRA British system used to decode Enigma messages

## Secret weapons

The most significant and far-reaching technological developments of the Second World War, however, had a profound effect on the development of the Cold War after 1945. The atomic bomb was developed in the United States between 1942 and 1945 by a team of scientists working on the *Manhattan Engineer District* project at Los Alamos in New Mexico. German nuclear scientists were working on a similar project but this was sabotaged by the Allies. When the American bomb was tested on 16 July 1945, some of the scientists involved were horrified at what they had done. Three weeks later it was dropped on Hiroshima (page 134).

Meanwhile German scientists had developed Hitler's secret V-weapons. The V1 'flying bomb' had stubby wings, was jet-powered, filled with a tonne of high explosives, and flew a set distance before the engine cut out and it dived towards the ground. The first V1s landed on London on 13 June 1944. Five days later, a single V1 killed 119 people and injured 102 others. The RAF soon devised ways of dealing with it (page 139) but there was no stopping the V2 rocket which carried a tonne of explosives at 6000 kph giving little warning of its approach (page 139).

Questions

1  Name **a)** three weapons which made it easier to locate the enemy, **b)** two weapons for which there was no defence, and **c)** one weapon which was used to confuse the enemy.

2  In what ways is the Soviet poster (Source **A**) similar/dissimilar to the British poster (Source **D**) on page 137?

3  How did the course of the war affect the development of new weapons?

4  How did new weapons affect the course of the war?

## The Holocaust

▶ *What was the Final Solution and what was its significance?*

### The Final Solution

The reasons why the Second World War was fought can seem insignificant and of little consequence now when set against the horrors and cruelties of the war, such as the Allied fire raids on Hamburg (page 124), Dresden and Tokyo, the atom bombs on Hiroshima and Nagasaki (page 134), the Russian massacre of 4500 captured Polish officers in Katyn forest and the *SS* reprisals at Lidice and Oradour-sur-Glane (page 126). But even these pale in comparison with the horrors of the Holocaust.

The cold-blooded extermination of human beings by the Nazis began in 1939 when selected mentally ill patients were put to death so their hospital beds could be taken by wounded soldiers in the war. Workers in the gas chambers of Austria were told to keep quiet or face death themselves. In 1944–5, the Allied armies were horrified to discover similar installations when they liberated the Nazi concentration camps. Six million Jews had been put

to death, one-third of them at Auschwitz in Poland. The Nazis called it the *Final Solution*.

It began in March 1941, when Rudolf Hoess, the Commandant of Auschwitz, a concentration camp in Poland, received orders from Heinrich Himmler, Head of the Gestapo, to turn Auschwitz into an extermination camp (Source **B**).

When the trains crowded with Jews arrived at Auschwitz, they were surrounded by *SS* guards. The barbed wire which sealed the sliding doors to the waggons was released and the prisoners were separated into two groups – those fit for work and those unfit. The unfit prisoners were taken to a block labelled 'Shower'. They could see the shower roses in the ceiling above. An eyewitness after the War said that the prisoners were told they were going to have a bath after their long journey. Sometimes they were promised a drink of hot coffee. Packed inside the gas chambers they realised the truth too late. Within minutes they were dead.

**Source A**  Caring for the survivors at Bergen-Belsen concentration camp in 1945. Bergen-Belsen was liberated in April 1945. British soldiers discovered 10,000 unburied corpses there while another 13,000 former prisoners died later.

**Source B**  Himmler's orders
▼

The Führer has ordered the final solution of the Jewish question and we – the *SS* – have to carry out this order. I have chosen Auschwitz for this task both because of its good transport links and because the area can be easily sealed off and camouflaged. You will maintain the strictest silence concerning this order.

The victorious Allies put many of the people held responsible on trial for war crimes. Almost without exception, they claimed they were 'only obeying orders.'

Source F   Dachau Camp Commandant, Obersturmbannführer Martin Gottfried Weiss, December 1945

I was absolutely powerless in the face of the experiments of Dr Rascher and Prof Dr Schilling. On 10 November 1942, Himmler told me: 'Rascher and Schilling are responsible to me personally for their experiments and you must obey their orders.'

From *Concentration Camp Dachau 1933–1945*

## Human experiments

Not only were the Nazis guilty of genocide (the extermination of a race or people), they also conducted unspeakable experiments on live human beings.

Source D   Letter from Dr Sigmund Rascher at Dachau Concentration Camp to Heinrich Himmler

9 August 1942 Esteemed Reichsfuhrer! I wondered if it would be possible to test the effects of our different combat gases using the persons who are destined for these chambers anyway. The only reports which are available so far are of experiments on animals or of accidents which occurred in the manufacture of the gases. Because of this paragraph I am marking this letter 'Secret'.

From *Concentration Camp Dachau 1933–1945*, the official handbook to the museum, published by the international Dachau Committee, 1978

The Munich newspaper *Suddeutsche Zeitung* headed its report of the Dachau trial with the headline,

'EACH ONE BLAMES THE OTHER, ALL WERE INNOCENT'.

Some Germans committed suicide on learning what had been done in their name. Ever since, the fact of the holocaust has remained uppermost in the minds of all those who have tried to understand the actions of Nazi Germany, both before and during the War.

## Taking the blame

After the war, the Allies made German civilians walk round the camps to show them what had been happening under their noses (Source E).

Source E   By an American serviceman

When the people saw what the camp was like and were led through the torture chambers and past the ovens, men and women screamed out and fainted. Others were led away crying hysterically. All swore that during the past years they had no idea of what had been going on in the camp just outside their town.

Lester Atwell. Quoted in The War 1939–1945, edited by Desmond Flower and James Reeves, Cassell, 1960

Questions

1   How did the artist (Source **A**) and the sculptor (Source **C**) portray the Nazi concentration camps?

2   Which sources suggest that the Nazis knew what they were doing was evil?

3   When a British officer refused to order an attack on Le Havre in 1944 because it would harm civilians, he was sent to prison for 'disobeying orders'. Were German officials accused of war crimes entitled, therefore, to claim that they had had to obey orders? Was this true of Dr Rascher (Source **D**)?

4   How would you distinguish between war crimes and legitimate acts of war? Who is responsible for a war crime – the soldiers or officials who carry it out or the people who give the orders, or both?

## The war against Japan

▶ **How, why and where was the war against Japan fought? Why did the Allies win?**

### Causes of the war in the Pacific

In the Far East, Japan and China (backed by the USA) had been at war since 1937. After Dunkirk and the fall of France and the Netherlands in 1940, the British, French and Dutch Far Eastern empires were vulnerable to attack by the third Axis Power, Japan. Japanese militarists were actively seeking to expand overseas (page 104). When their troops took over airfields and naval bases in French-held Vietnam and Cambodia in July 1941, Roosevelt suspected rightly they were planning to seize oilfields in the Dutch East Indies and attack the British colonies of Burma and Malaya.

The United States retaliated by cutting off 80 per cent of Japan's oil. This greatly inflamed the situation and both sides made preparations for war. US and Japanese officials tried to resolve the problem but, as they talked, the Japanese Navy drew up plans to destroy the US Pacific Fleet at Pearl Harbor. When the final decision to go to war against the USA was made on 1 December 1941, six Japanese aircraft carriers, supported by battleships, cruisers and destroyers, were already at sea. Roosevelt knew a Japanese attack was imminent – but didn't know when or where.

### Pearl Harbor

At 6.0 a.m. on 7 December 1941, warplanes on board the Japanese carriers close to Hawaii began to take off. When they swept over Pearl Harbor two hours later, they were picked up on American radar but reports of a massive formation of planes were instantly dismissed as being 'nothing to worry about'. By the end of the raid, nearly 200 American warplanes had been destroyed on the ground, four battleships had been sunk and four others badly damaged (Source **A**). Luckily, the US aircraft carriers 'Lexington', 'Saratoga' and 'Enterprise' were all at sea. But over 2300 Americans died and Roosevelt called it 'a date that shall live in infamy'. Four days later, Germany and Italy declared war on the United States as well. By then Japanese forces were attacking Western outposts across a wide part of South-East Asia (Source **C**), including many islands, Hong Kong, Burma and Malaya.

**Source A**  The West Virginia ablaze at Pearl Harbor

### Jungle warfare

Many of the places where the Pacific war was fought were areas of jungle. This was unfamiliar territory for most Allied troops and the Japanese were far better equipped and trained to fight there than their opponents. The Japanese soldiers who captured Malaya and Singapore, for instance, wore light clothes, carried little equipment, and used bicycles and river boats to move swiftly through the jungle. An American general later described what it was like to fight in areas like this (Source **B**).

**Source B**  By US General Eichelberger

> The men were more frightened by the jungle than by the Japanese. There is nothing pleasant about sinking into a foul-smelling bog up to your knees or lying in a slit trench, half submerged, while a tropical rain turns it into a river. Jungle night noises were strange to Americans – and in the moist hot darkness the rustling of small animals in the bush was easily misinterpreted as the stealthy approach of the enemy.
>
> Quoted in *The War 1939–1945* edited by Desmond Flower and James Reeves, Cassell, 1960

By the beginning of June 1942, the Japanese controlled a vast Far Eastern empire (Source **C**). They called it the Greater East Asia Co-Prosperity Sphere.

**Source C** Maps of the war in the Pacific: **a)** Maximum extent of the Japanese conquests to May 1942; **b)** The succession of battles and events which led to the Japanese surrender in August 1945.

## The war at sea

So far the tide of battle had been in favour of Japan. But now they paid the price for failing to sink the American aircraft carrier fleet. Their own attack on Pearl Harbor had shown only too clearly the effect that an aircraft carrier fleet could have in the Pacific. Now it was the turn of the Americans.

In May 1942, American and Japanese aircraft carriers fought the first battle in the history of naval warfare without even seeing each other. This was the battle of the Coral Sea, near Australia and the Solomon Islands. Although the Americans lost one of their biggest carriers, the 'Lexington', they severely damaged a Japanese carrier, sank another, and prevented the Japanese from taking Port Moresby in Papua – which would have been an effective base from which to invade Australia.

One month later, on 4 June 1942, they avenged Pearl Harbor at the Battle of Midway, sinking four Japanese aircraft carriers together with 332 Japanese planes. This was the turning point of the war, only six months after it had begun. In August 1942, American marines landed on Guadalcanal – the first step in a strategy called island-hopping. By the summer of 1945, US marines had captured Okinawa and Iwo Jima, two islands close to Japan and were making plans to invade Japan itself. You can see the main events of the war in the maps (Source **C**).

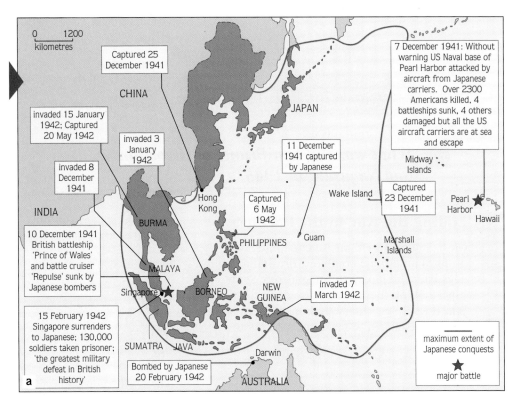

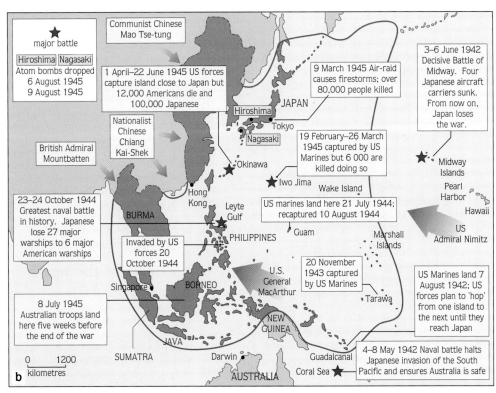

1 Why is it hard to understand why the Americans defending Pearl Harbor (Source **A**) were caught napping by the Japanese?

2 Use the information on the maps (Source **C**) to explain what was meant by:
**a)** the Greater East Asia Co-Prosperity Sphere, and **b)** island-hopping.

3 Using the information here and on pages 104–5 suggest reasons which help to explain: **a)** the causes of the Pacific War, **b)** why the Japanese were defeated.

Questions

## Hiroshima and Nagasaki

▶ **What was the significance of Hiroshima and Nagasaki in 1945?**

**Source B** *Punch* cartoon published on 18 April 1945

A CHANGE OF MASKS

### Ending the war in the Pacific

On 6 August 1945, an American bomber dropped an atomic bomb on Hiroshima. Eight days later the Japanese surrendered. Some experts think they would have done so anyway. Was it really necessary to drop an atom bomb? Use these sources to make up your mind.

**Source A**   Countdown to surrender

7 April 1945: Admiral Suzuki, a moderate, becomes Prime Minister of Japan. The Emperor tells him to seek a peaceful end to the war as soon as possible.

*22 June 1945*: Okinawa falls after a ferocious and fanatical campaign in which over 1000 kamikaze (suicide) pilots die and 100,000 Japanese soldiers (90% of those on the island) are killed. 12,000 US servicemen also die.

*June 1945*: US commanders make plans to invade Japan. They estimate as many as 500,000 Allied soldiers will die in the attempt.

*June–July 1945*: The Japanese ambassador in Moscow asks for Russian help in negotiating surrender but Stalin has already agreed to declare war on Japan by 8 August (Source **Y** on page 127). In any case, the Russians know the Allies are demanding unconditional surrender, so there is nothing to negotiate about.

*30 July 1945*: Suzuki rejects Allied terms for peace.

*6 August 1945*: Atom bomb on Hiroshima kills 80,000 people.

*8 August 1945*: Soviet Union declares war on Japan and invades Manchuria with 5000 tanks and 1.2 million soldiers.

*9 August 1945*: Atom bomb on Nagasaki kills 40,000 people.

*14 August 1945*: Japan surrenders.

**Source C**   Japanese telegram intercepted by US Intelligence

On the first of July, Sato [*Japanese ambassador in Moscow*] sent a long message to Tokyo. He strongly advised accepting any terms. The response of the Japanese Cabinet was that the war must be fought with all the vigour and bitterness of which the nation was capable so long as the only alternative was unconditional surrender.

*The Forrestal Diaries*, edited by Walter Millis, The Viking Press, New York, 1951

**Source D**   By President Truman's daughter

My father discussed the possibility of blockading and bombarding Japan into defeat with conventional weapons. General Marshall pointed out that [*despite intensive bombing*] the Germans remained in the war until their home territory was invaded and occupied by Allied troops. My father saw that conventional bombing, even if it worked, would cause more Japanese deaths than the use of one or two atomic bombs. The fire raid on Tokyo had killed 78,650 people.

From *Harry S. Truman*, by Margaret Truman, Hamish Hamilton, 1973

### Effects of the bomb

**Source E**   By a Japanese journalist

Thousands were scorched by a wave of searing heat. Many were killed instantly. Others lay writhing on the ground screaming in agony from the intolerable pain of their burns. Walls, houses, factories and other buildings were annihilated. Trees went up in flames. The grass burned on the ground like dry straw.

Quoted by Marcel Junod in *Warriors Without Weapons*, Cape, 1951. Reprinted in *The Faber Book of Reportage*, edited by John Carey, 1987

**Source F**   Relic of the atomic explosion at Hiroshima

**Source G**
Hiroshima after the bomb had fallen

**Source L**   Hiroshima bomb victims hear the Emperor's Proclamation in hospital: 15 August 1945

Silence reigned for a long time. By degrees people began to whisper. Someone shouted: 'How can we lose the war!' Following this outburst, expressions of anger were unleashed. 'Only a coward would back out now.' 'I would rather die than be defeated!' 'What have we been suffering for?' I began to feel the same way – fight to the bloody end and die. The one word – surrender – had produced a greater shock than the bombing of our city.

Quoted in *Hiroshima Diary*

**Source H**   Eyewitnesses at Hiroshima

The sight of the soldiers was more dreadful than the dead people in the river. Where the skin had peeled, their flesh was wet and mushy. Their eyes, noses and mouths had been burned away, and it looked like their ears had melted off.

I saw fire reservoirs filled to the brim with people who looked as though they had been boiled alive.

Quoted in *Hiroshima Diary*, by Michihiko Hachiya, translated and edited by Warner Wells, Gollancz, 1955

**Source M**   By President Truman's daughter

The final testimony for the rightness of Dad's decision on the atomic bomb comes from the Japanese themselves. Cabinet Secretary Sakomizu said the atomic bomb 'provided an excuse for surrender.' Hirohito's adviser, Marquis Kido said, 'The atomic bomb made it easier for us, the politicians, to negotiate peace.'

From *Harry S. Truman*, by Margaret Truman

## Should the bomb have been dropped?

**Source I**   Hirohito's Proclamation ending the war

The enemy has begun to employ a new and most cruel bomb, taking toll of many innocent lives. Should we continue to fight it would end in the ultimate collapse and obliteration of the Japanese nation.

**Source J**   President Truman in his autobiography

The atom bomb was no 'great decision'. It was merely another powerful weapon in the arsenal of righteousness. The dropping of the bombs stopped the war, saved millions of lives.

**Source K**   By Admiral Leahy, Truman's chief adviser

The use of this barbaric weapon at Hiroshima and Nagasaki was of no material assistance in our war against Japan. The Japanese were already defeated and ready to surrender because of the effective sea blockade and the successful bombing with ordinary weapons.

1  To which event does the cartoon (Source **B**) refer? What was the attitude of the cartoonist to the Japanese?

2  How do Sources **D** and **L** contribute to your understanding of the attack on Hiroshima in 1945?

3  What evidence is there to support or refute these statements about the dropping of the atom bomb: **a)** 'It gave the Japanese an excuse which would save their honour'; **b)** 'The Japanese were already defeated and ready to surrender'; **c)** 'It stopped the war, saved millions of lives'; **d)** 'Japan's soldiers would fight with total fanaticism to defend their sacred home soil'; **e)** 'It was of no material assistance in our war against Japan'?

4  Use the sources to argue the case *either* for *or* against the dropping of the atom bombs on Hiroshima and Nagasaki in August 1945.

5  A doctor from Hiroshima said: 'They ought to try the men who decided to use the atomic bomb and hang them all'. Put President Truman on trial for war crimes. Was he guilty or not guilty?

*Questions*

## The Home Front in Britain

### How did World War II change life in Britain in the period 1939–45?

### Evacuation

On 1–3 September 1939, as Hitler's tanks crossed into Poland, over 1.5 million people (mainly children) were evacuated from London and other industrial cities to the countryside where they were billeted in local homes. Many came from poor homes, products of the Depression (Source **A**).

**Source A**   Women's Institute report on evacuees in 1940

Except for a small number the children were filthy. They were unbathed for months. One child was suffering from scabies and the others had dirty septic sores all over their bodies. Their clothing was in a deplorable condition, some of the children being literally sewn into their ragged little garments.

Extract from *Town Children Through Country Eyes*, published by the Women's Institute, 1940. Printed in *The People's War*, by Angus Calder, Jonathan Cape, 1969

### Living standards

The evacuation focused attention on poverty in the slums. What had poor people to gain from winning the war? Sir William Beveridge chaired a Government committee in 1941–2 which prepared the way for the Welfare State eventually set up by Labour in 1945–51 (page 140). Beveridge identified 'Five Giant Social Evils' which would have to be tackled after the war – WANT, IDLENESS (mass unemployment), IGNORANCE (lack of education), DISEASE (ill health) and SQUALOR (the slums).

However, the war itself had a role to play in raising living standards as well. There was little unemployment after 1940. People not conscripted into the armed forces got jobs easily enough once the country was on a war footing. Two or more incomes went into many homes. The Government supplied free orange juice and vitamin tablets to pregnant mothers and milk and cod liver oil to children. Rationing, which cut the amount of fat, meat and sugar in people's diet, actually helped to keep them healthy despite the war.

**Source B**
Punch cartoon, 26 June 1940

### Home defence

At the start of the war, everyone was issued with a gas mask which they had to carry with them wherever they went. Many people volunteered to join vital home defence services, such as the ARP (Air Raid Precaution) wardens and the AFS (Auxiliary Fire Service). The threat of invasion in 1940 even led to the formation of a home army – the Local Defence Volunteers, or Home Guard ('Dad's Army'). Many were ex-soldiers from the First World War. They lacked weapons at first and had to train with wooden rifles or even broom handles. They manned local strongpoints, such as the concrete pillboxes erected at the sides of roads for use against enemy invaders.

Other precautions were also taken against a German invasion. Road signs were removed to confuse enemy parachutists. Motorists had to disable their vehicles when left unattended and maps and bicycles had to be hidden as well. Stakes were driven into the beds of the Norfolk Broads to stop enemy gliders or flying boats landing there. The novelist Evelyn Waugh described some of these precautions in his novel *Put Out More Flags* published in 1942 (Source **C**).

**Source C**   Seaside defences

The battalion was charged with the defence of seven miles of inviting coastline. They lined the sands with barbed wire and demolished the steps leading from the esplanade to the beach; they dug weapon pits in the corporation's gardens, sandbagged the bow-windows of private houses and with the cooperation of some neighbouring sappers [*army engineers*] blocked the roads with dragons'-teeth and pill boxes.

## Working for victory

Seven million women (40% of them married) worked in wartime factories making munitions and other essential products. Aircraft production expanded ten times in five years. The Minister of Labour, Ernest Bevin, recruited every tenth man to work in the coal mines instead of in the army.

Agriculture which had suffered in the Depression, prospered during the war. Permanent pasture was ploughed up. Even school playing fields were turned into vegetable gardens. By the end of the war, Britain was growing most of the food it needed and output of wheat, barley, oats and potatoes had all roughly doubled in only six years.

" *Nearly eight months this war's been on—and what have we got to show for it?* "

**Source E**   *Punch* cartoon, 1 May 1940

**Source D**   Government poster. Propaganda helped to change people's attitudes and spurred them on to do their best for the war effort. Information which could upset or frighten people was censored or withheld, such as the two-month ban on newspapers mentioning the V2 rocket in 1944.

WOMEN OF BRITAIN
# COME INTO THE FACTORIES
ASK AT ANY EMPLOYMENT EXCHANGE FOR ADVICE AND FULL DETAILS

## Conscription

Instead of relying on volunteers, the Government introduced conscription five months before the war began. By 1941, two million men had joined the armed services. Only men in reserved occupations (those vital to the war effort) were excused from service. Women, too, were conscripted into the armed services, the police force, fire service, or to work in factories. Many joined the Women's Land Army. Those who served in the WRNS (navy), WAAF (air force) or ATS (army) were often disappointed by the jobs they were given, such as cleaning, cooking and clerical work. None were given the opportunity to fire a gun or drop a bomb.

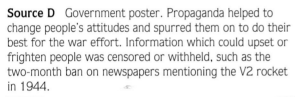

Questions

1  Look at the cartoons (Sources **B** and **E**). To which of the Government's various wartime precautions and activities does each cartoon refer?

2  Trace or copy the cartoon (Source **E**) and use arrows and labels to highlight the different ways in which this street scene had been changed by the war.

3  Look at Source **C**. Does it make any difference to the value of this source that it comes from a novel published in 1942?

137

## Rationing and economising

Two months after the war began, the first plans to ration foods were announced – beginning with butter and bacon. Seven weeks later sugar and meat were put on the ration as well. People had to register with shopkeepers in order to obtain their ration each week. It was inconvenient but it gave everyone the right to a certain amount of food, clothing, petrol and sweets. The Minister of Food said it was 'fair shares all round'.

The Government urged everyone to economise. 'Waste not, Want not!', 'Make Do and Mend', and 'Kill the Squanderbug' were slogans to be seen on posters. Families were asked to share hot baths to save fuel and to use no more than about 12 cm of water when they did so. 'Austerity' clothes saved cloth by doing away with men's trouser turn-ups and shortening women's skirts. Unwanted metal goods were melted down to make weapons, such as the iron railings around gardens and public parks. Two birds were shown on a cartoon drawing of a machine gun, saying: 'Why, we knew this when it was a pair of park gates!'.

## Air Raid Precautions

Air raid shelters made from corrugated iron and concrete were built in back gardens. In London, tube stations were used as shelters at night. Measures were also taken to protect towns against bombers. Anti-aircraft (*Ack-Ack*) guns ringed major cities while powerful searchlights searched the night sky for German bombers. Government blackout regulations laid down that every window had to be blacked-out at night – a law enforced by ARP wardens patrolling the streets. Motorists had to make do with only one headlight and none at all during an air raid.

**Source F**  Air raid precautions on cigarette cards issued just before the war

## The Blitz

The first major air raids began on London in September 1940. The main targets were the industrial areas and the docks. Since this was where many working people lived, they suffered most of the casualties. Other towns and cities were bombed as well as London. Coventry, Bristol, Liverpool and Southampton were all bombed in November 1940 and Birmingham, Manchester and Sheffield in December. By the end of the year, 22,000 people had been killed. The Government waited anxiously to see what effect the London Blitz would have on the people – especially since the capital was bombed night after night. Would the people panic (Sources **G** to **L**)?

**Source G**  *Evening Standard*, 13 January 1941

Seventeen women and children who were trapped in the basement of a London house damaged by a bomb last night shouted to wardens who went to their rescue. 'We're all right. Look after everybody else'. Then they started singing 'Tipperary' and shouting to the people in the road. 'Are we downhearted? No.'

*The London Blitz*, Maureen Hill, Chapmans, 1990

**Source H**  German radio: 18 September 1940

The legend of British self control and coolness under fire is being destroyed. All reports from London agree in stating that the people are seized by fear – hair-raising fear. The 7,000,000 Londoners have completely lost their self-control. They run aimlessly about in the streets and are the victims of bombs and bursting shells.

A GARDEN DUG-OUT

THE CIVILIAN RESPIRATOR—HOW TO ADJUST IT

A CHAIN OF BUCKETS

PROTECTING YOUR WINDOWS—A SANDBAG DEFENCE

AIR RAID WARDENS AND CIVILIAN VOLUNTEER DESPATCH-

ANTI-AIRCRAFT SEARCHLIGHT

**Source I** Wartime slogan chalked on a bombed-out building in London's East End

## The second London Blitz

Further terror from the air began in 1944 when the first V1 flying bombs appeared over London's skies (page 129). The *doodlebug* or *buzz bomb* as it was sometimes called could he heard approaching the city. When the engine cut out, people dived for cover. Since the Germans could launch their flying bombs at any time of night and day, air raid warnings were useless. Over a million people left London to escape them and 200,000 homes were damaged or destroyed. But, by the end of July, fighter aircraft, anti-aircraft guns and barrage balloons prevented most V1s reaching London. On 28 August 1944, only 4 out of 94 got through. But there was no answer to Hitler's second V-weapon. On 8 September 1944 a German V2 rocket carrying a tonne of high explosive was launched from Holland and landed in London three minutes later, killing three people. The only solution was to locate and destroy the launching sites in France and the Low Countries.

**Source J** From Hitler's war directive against England, 6 February 1941

The bombing campaign has had least effect of all, so far as we can see, on the morale and will to resist of the English people. No decisive success can be expected from terror attacks on residential areas.

Quoted in *Chronicle of the Second World War*, edited by Derrik Mercer, Longman, 1990

**Source K** From the diary of a British politician

Everybody is worried about the feeling in the East End, where there is much bitterness. It is said that even the King and Queen were booed the other day when they visited the destroyed areas.

*Harold Nicolson Diaries and letters 1939–45*, edited by Nigel Nicolson, Collins, 1967

**Source L** Queen Elizabeth (after Buckingham Palace suffered bomb damage in September 1940)

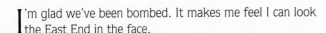

I'm glad we've been bombed. It makes me feel I can look the East End in the face.

**Questions**

1 List the various ways in which the war affected the lives of ordinary people. How and why did the Government take control of people's lives during the war?

2 For each of the Sources, **G** to **K**, say whether you think it is likely to be a reliable or unreliable source of information on the effects of the Blitz on morale in Britain. Give your reasons.

3 Use Sources **G** to **K** to write a balanced account of the effects of the Blitz on the people

4 What measures were taken to protect people against enemy attack from the air?

5 How does Source **J** contradict Source **H**? How do you account for this? Why is Source **J** more likely to be accurate than Source **H**?

# Britain and Europe: the postwar outlook

## The Second Welfare State

▶ *What features of British Society were changed as a result of the work of the Labour Government of 1945–51?*

### Labour's plans

The new Labour Government in 1945, led by Clement Attlee (Source **A**), promised the British people a Welfare State which would 'care for the individual from the cradle to the grave'. You can see the changes they made in Source **D**. Aneurin Bevan, Labour's Minister of Health, said the Government intended to bring in a National Health Service to give everyone an equal right to free medical care. He did his best to convince doctors and surgeons (Source **B**).

**Source B**   Report of Aneurin Bevan's speech in *The Times*, 6 September 1945

He knew he had to break down suspicions, but believed the new medical service would make Great Britain the envy of the world. He wanted to get rid of the atmosphere of suspicion which had been created in the last few months.

Yet by January 1948, only one in every 100 specialist doctors and surgeons in London was in favour of the scheme. They said they would lose their independence, spend valuable time filling in forms and have their earnings controlled by government. Bevan made concessions so they could treat private patients and gave them a guaranteed income each year – not just a payment each time they treated a patient. At the same time, he told people to choose their NHS doctor now. Doctors had to decide quickly whether to join since delay could mean patients going elsewhere. The opposition collapsed and the NHS came into being on 5 July 1948 (Source **C**).

**Source C**   Nurse interviewed on BBC TV in 1990

The great day came. It didn't only uplift us, it was the patients as well. It was just fantastic. It was something that you never believed could have happened – you know when you'd struggled and tried so long.

**Source A**   Clement Attlee on the front cover of *Illustrated* magazine, 24 July 1948

At first, the NHS was the envy of the world. Improvements in medical care were clear for all to see, such as a sharp decline in the infantile mortality rate. Older people got better-fitting false teeth, good quality spectacles and efficient hearing aids. Young mothers visited free ante-natal clinics and were paid maternity benefit. Twice as many people went to the dentist as before and spending on prescriptions doubled in twelve months. The cost of the NHS rose so steeply, charges had to be brought in for spectacles and false teeth in 1951 and for prescriptions as well in 1952.

### The National Insurance and National Assistance Acts

The second major social reform of the 1945–50 Labour Government was the National Insurance Act of 1946. In return for a compulsory weekly National Insurance contribution, a range of benefits were payable as of right (Source **D**). This was not charity nor was it based on the hated means test of the 1930s. Everyone could benefit and everyone contributed whether they made use of the benefit system or not.

The National Assistance Act of 1948 went even further (Source **D**). In future, everyone – no matter

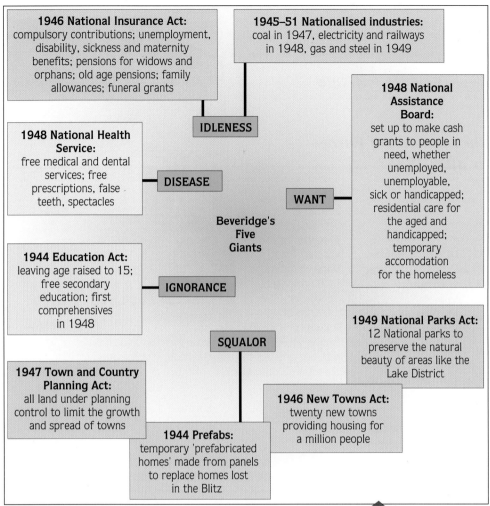

**1946 National Insurance Act:**
compulsory contributions; unemployment, disability, sickness and maternity benefits; pensions for widows and orphans; old age pensions; family allowances; funeral grants

**1945–51 Nationalised industries:**
coal in 1947, electricity and railways in 1948, gas and steel in 1949

**IDLENESS**

**1948 National Assistance Board:**
set up to make cash grants to people in need, whether unemployed, unemployable, sick or handicapped; residential care for the aged and handicapped; temporary accomodation for the homeless

**1948 National Health Service:**
free medical and dental services; free prescriptions, false teeth, spectacles

**DISEASE**

Beveridge's Five Giants

**WANT**

**1944 Education Act:**
leaving age raised to 15; free secondary education; first comprehensives in 1948

**IGNORANCE**

**SQUALOR**

**1949 National Parks Act:**
12 National parks to preserve the natural beauty of areas like the Lake District

**1947 Town and Country Planning Act:**
all land under planning control to limit the growth and spread of towns

**1946 New Towns Act:**
twenty new towns providing housing for a million people

**1944 Prefabs:**
temporary 'prefabricated homes' made from panels to replace homes lost in the Blitz

**Source D** The Welfare State: 1945–51

**Source E** *Punch* cartoon, 5 December 1945. 'Some people say I've got things in the wrong order'

**Source F** *Punch* cartoon, 8 August 1945. 'Britannia in Wonderland'

what their circumstances – could be certain of a minimum basic income. *The Times* said the National Assistance Board was now 'the citizen's last defence against destitution'. But it also gave a warning, asking whether the people of Britain could reap the benefits of the Welfare State 'while avoiding the perils of a Santa Claus State'.

## Nationalisation of industry

After 1945, shortages caused by the war gave a huge boost to industry and for many years there was almost full employment. But most industries were badly in need of modernisation, such as the coal mines (page 44). In 1945, Labour politicians believed the best way to achieve this was by putting key industries, such as mining, under state control. They did this by buying all the shares in those companies on behalf of the people. The coal-mining industry was nationalised in 1947 and run by the National Coal Board. Other industries were nationalised, too, such as gas, electricity and steel (Source **D**). Opposition to nationalisation was widespread (Source **E**). Some people thought the most pressing need in postwar Britain was reconstruction – building new homes (Source **F**) and making private industry profitable to enable the country to recover as soon as possible.

*Questions*

1 What problem was highlighted by the cartoon (Source **F**)? How did the Government try to deal with this problem?

2 What did *The Times* mean by a 'Santa Claus State'? What were the advantages and disadvantages of setting up a Welfare State 'caring for the individual from the cradle to the grave'?

3 What was the point of the cartoon (Source **E**)? How was it critical of Attlee and the Labour Party?

4 Write a short account of the Welfare State between 1905 and 1951. Explain how it began and how it developed.

## How and why did the countries of Europe draw closer together after 1945?

### The Council of Europe

During and after the Second World War, a number of organisations were created in which European states co-operated with one another, such as UNRRA (United Nations Relief and Rehabilitation Administration) to help refugees, NATO (North Atlantic Treaty Organisation) to defend Europe (page 150) and the OEEC which administered the $13 billion Marshall Aid programme (Source **A**). Some Europeans even began to dream of a United States of Europe to rival the USA.

In 1949, ten countries, including the UK, formed the Council of Europe. Others joined in the 1950s, and by 1994 the Council included most European countries. When it first met in 1949, a delegate said, 'We have started to co-operate; but we haven't even started to unite.' Some delegates simply wanted to share a common symbol, such as a European passport or European flag. Others wanted to put key industries, such as coal and steel, under European control. A handful wanted a common European currency to make it easier to do business and move from one country to another. In the end, the Council's main achievement was to establish certain basic human rights (such as freedom of speech) which every European country agreed to accept. To enforce these rights, a European Court of Human Rights was founded in 1959.

### The European Coal and Steel Community

In 1950, two Frenchmen, Robert Schuman and Jean Monnet, drew up a plan to make European industry more efficient by getting industrialists to follow the same policy on coal, iron and steel. Six countries (Belgium, France, Germany, Italy, Luxembourg and the Netherlands) accepted the plan and signed the Treaty of Paris which brought it into being on 18 April 1951. The new organisation was called the European Coal and Steel Community, or ECSC. Jean Monnet said it was the start of a 'united Europe' (Source **B**).

**Source A**
German poster: 'Freeway for the Marshall Plan'. Marshall Aid (page 147) not only helped the countries of Europe to recover after the war, it forced them to co-operate with one another through the OEEC (Organisation for European Economic Cooperation)

**Source B**  Jean Monnet at Strasbourg on 22 June 1953

We want other countries to join on an equal footing with us, to give up the divisions of the past and, by pooling their coal and steel production, to ensure the establishment of common bases for economic development as the first stage towards the European federation.

Quoted in *Twentieth-Century Europe*, edited by John W. Boyer and Jan Goldstein, University of Chicago Press, 1987

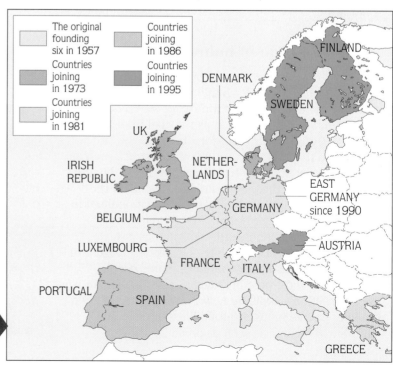

**Source C**  Map of Europe showing the growth of the EC since 1957

**President of the EC:**
post held by each country in turn for six months

**European Council:**
heads of government who meet twice
a year to decide overall policy

**Council of Ministers:**
Government ministers from each
member country who meet at
regular intervals to discuss
matters of importance to the EC

**European Commission:**
the civil servants who run the European Community –
headed by the President of the European Commission
together with the Commissioners from each country
who are responsible for carrying out EC policy and
drafting new laws and regulations

**European Parliament:**
assembly of MEPs (Members of the European
Parliament) elected by each country who discuss
the work of the EC and supervise its budget but do
not make new laws

**European Court of Justice:**
judges from each country who
decide on any legal cases which
involve EC laws and Treaties

# Founding the EEC

The ECSC was so successful, its member countries applied the same principles to every item of trade. They signed the Treaty of Rome on 25 March 1957, setting up the European Economic Community (EEC) to: **a)** promote unity, **b)** stimulate social and economic progress, **c)** preserve and maintain peace and liberty, and **d)** improve living standards and working conditions.

The EEC, or Common Market, was very successful (Source **D**). It made it much easier for the six member nations to trade with each other. Goods traded inside the Common Market were free from customs duties. Goods imported from outside the EEC had to pay a common import duty (tariff) of about 6per cent. Trade boomed and the industries of the EEC countries prospered.

Source D  *TIME* magazine, 28 January 1957

Out of the ashes and gutted cities of World War II, idealists tried to create a united Europe by means of a Council of Europe. They failed. Then came the hardheaded soldiers and diplomats who wanted to build Europe through a European army in a common uniform. Last week, Europeans found themselves being offered a third chance to build Europe. This time the approach was economic, and surprisingly enough, the chances were good.

## The Common Agricultural Policy

In 1962 the EEC brought in a new policy to help farmers, guaranteeing a minimum price for farm produce. Farmers were also given grants to help them modernise their farms. The Common Agricultural Policy (CAP) protected European farmers against foreign competition but created serious problems since it gave farmers an incentive to grow as much as possible without fear of falling farm prices. The EC piled up huge surpluses of food – popularly known as the butter, cheese and grain 'mountains' and the wine and milk 'lakes'.

Source F  Achievements of the European Community

- Bitter wartime enemies became friends
- Barriers to movement between countries were removed
- Trade increased, bringing prosperity to the members of the Community
- The Common Agricultural Policy kept food prices steady and prevented thousands of farmers from going out of business
- Common standards were adopted, such as the metric system, decimal currency and Value Added Tax
- Scientific and technological research was stimulated through joint projects
- The Community spoke out for Europe on major world issues, such as the Middle East
- EC regional policies provided grants to help build factories in areas with high levels of unemployment

Questions

1  What was Jean Monnet's aim for Europe in 1953 (Source **B**)? Is this the aim of the British Government today?

2  Why did the author of Source **D** think the future for the EEC was 'good'? How did he view NATO and the Council of Europe?

3  Critics of the EC would disagree that the points listed in the table (Source **F**) are 'achievements'. Find arguments for and against two or three of the statements on this list and compare your answers with those of your friends.

## Enlarging the Community

The UK was originally invited to join the ECSC, and later the EEC, but declined. British politicians at that time had no desire to see European laws come before British laws passed by Parliament. Many were worried, too, about the effect that membership of the Common Market could have on Britain's 'special' relationship with the English-speaking USA and English-speaking Commonwealth countries.

## The French veto

The success of the Common Market, however, and the growing independence of the Commonwealth nations, left the UK increasingly isolated. This is why Harold Macmillan's Conservative Government decided to apply for EEC membership in 1961 together with Ireland, Denmark and Norway. This change of heart was welcomed by five of the six members of the EEC but not by France. Talks broke down in 1963 when President de Gaulle of France vetoed the British application. Another unsuccessful attempt to join the EEC was made by Britain's Labour Government (led by Harold Wilson) in 1967 – the same year the organisation was renamed EC (European Community). You can see the points of view adopted by British and French politicians at that time in Sources **G** to **M**.

**Source G**  By the Reverend Sir Herbert Andrew, one of the British negotiators

The thing that really shook me about our negotiations to join the Common Market in 1961 was how little we counted in the thinking of the Community. We were not such a catch that they would go to very great lengths to catch us!

Extract from *The Price of Victory*, by Michael Charlton, BBC, 1983

**Source H**  By Edward Heath, who successfully negotiated Britain's entry into the EC in 1973

De Gaulle thought that Britain would look across the Atlantic all the time to the United States instead of to its friends in Europe, whereas de Gaulle was concerned with the unity of Europe and particularly of the Community.

Extract from *The Price of Victory*

**Source I**  From Harold Macmillan's diary

*January 1963*: What is the alternative to the European Community? If we are honest, we must say there is none.

Extract from *The Price of Victory*

**Source J**  Speech by Labour Prime Minister Harold Wilson, 20 March 1966

Given a fair wind, we will negotiate our way into the Common Market, head held high, not crawl in. Negotiations? Yes. Unconditional acceptance of whatever terms we are offered? No.

Extract from *Quotations in History*, by Alan and Veronica Palmer, Harvester Press, 1983

**Source K**  Report in the *Daily Telegraph*, 28 November 1967

President De Gaulle today suggested that Britain had discovered an interest in Europe only when she thought membership would help her to solve her economic problems and to go on playing a leading part in European affairs.

**Source L**  A cartoon on the attempt by Macmillan (right) to join the EEC. Adenauer of Germany (centre) says to De Gaulle (left): 'He says he wants to join – on his own terms.'

Source M  German cartoon on Macmillan's attempt to join the EEC. Macmillan is abandoning his sinking ship and being rowed to safety by the German economics minister Ludwig Erhard – a crewman on a ship called the 'Europa'.

When President de Gaulle retired in 1969, Britain, Denmark, the Irish Republic and Norway successfully renewed their applications to join the EC. Norway, however, voted against in a National Referendum, so in 1973, the Six became the Nine as the UK, Ireland and Denmark joined Europe.

## The National Referendum

There was still a lot of opposition to UK membership of the EC from both Left and Right (Source **N**). Harold Wilson, the Labour leader, decided to hold a National Referendum in 1975 to settle the matter once and for all. The British people voted to stay in by a majority of two to one.

## Expansion and development

Since 1973, the EC has continued to develop. In 1979, the first direct elections to the European Parliament were held. In the 1980s, right wing opinion in Britain began to swing away from Europe. The Prime Minister, Margaret Thatcher, argued with her European counterparts and gained the nickname 'The Iron Lady' by her refusal to accept majority opinion at EC meetings. Nonetheless, she signed the Single European Act which came into force in 1987, getting rid of many frontier controls and making it easier for

Source N  Labour and Conservative speakers jointly speak out against the EC in 1975

Europeans to see themselves as being one rather than apart.

Further steps towards this goal came in 1991 with the Maastricht Treaty which gave the European Parliament greater powers over EC legislation, brought in a Social Chapter to help workers and made plans for a single European currency by 1999. Britain refused to accept the Treaty as it stood and was allowed to stand aside from some of its provisions.

### Questions

1  Why was a National Referendum held in Britain in 1975? What are the arguments for and against giving everyone a vote on an important issue like this?

2  Ask your older friends and relatives if they can remember what their attitudes were to entering the Common Market in the early 1970s and how they voted in the National Referendum. Asking people to talk about the past is called oral history. What are the advantages and disadvantages of using historical evidence like this?

3  What was the point of the two cartoons (Sources **L** and **M**)? How far is the attitude of each cartoonist the same, and how do they differ? Were their views shared by any of the other writers quoted on these pages?

4  What were the main advantages and disadvantages to Britain of membership of the EC?

5  Use the sources to explain why De Gaulle vetoed the British applications to join the EEC. Was he justified in doing so?

# 12 The Cold War: 1945–63

## The Iron Curtain

> **What was the Cold War and how and why did it begin?**

## Superpower rivalry

When Churchill, Roosevelt and Stalin met at Yalta in February 1945 (page 127), they agreed that free elections should be held in all the nations liberated by their armies and that Germany should be divided after the war into four Occupation Zones, each controlled by one of the four great powers – the USA, the USSR, the UK and France. Because of the importance of Berlin as capital of Germany, this too was divided into four occupation zones after the war, even though it was well inside the Russian occupation zone. Access between Berlin and West Germany was controlled by the Soviets. A writer said 'it made Berlin into a potential time bomb'.

After 1945, it soon became clear there were really only two great powers, or superpowers – the USA and the USSR. Both had huge populations, vast conscript armies and the resources and technical expertise to develop and stockpile deadly nuclear weapons and the missiles to deliver them. Their disagreements about the future of the world led to the Cold War.

Only four days after the German surrender, Churchill sent a telegram to the new American President, Harry S. Truman, warning him that 'an Iron Curtain is drawn down upon' the Russian front. 'We do not know what is going on behind'.
This border between East and West became a barrier dividing Europe in two. The hostility between the two sides, one communist, one capitalist, led to a long war of nerves. An American friend of Churchill's, Bernard Baruch, said: 'Let us not be deceived – we are today in the midst of a cold war.' By this he meant a war of words between the Soviet Union and the West. It was not a 'hot' war, nor a 'shooting' war. But it was a war, nonetheless, in which there were enemies and friends, losers and winners, defeats and conquests. Coupled with Churchill's idea of an Iron Curtain, isolating the communist world from the West, these two ideas helped shape relations between East and West for the next forty years – as you can see from the diagram (Source **A**).

The Cold War should have come as no surprise. The Allies had been united in wanting to defeat Hitler. But this didn't mean they saw eye to eye.

---

Western statesmen could not forget that only six years earlier (1939), Stalin and Hitler had agreed a Non-Aggression pact – promising not to go to war with each other. This made it possible for Hitler to invade Poland and led later to Germany and Russia dividing the country between them. Stalin had also seized part of Romania, Lithuania, Latvia, Estonia and invaded Finland in 1939–40.

Communism and Capitalism were opposites. Churchill had pressed the West to intervene in the Russian Civil War only 25 years earlier. Churchill and Truman were known to be fierce enemies of Communism.

Germany was in chaos after the war, with her economy in ruins, and millions close to starvation. Massive aid was needed. But the Soviet Union too, had suffered terribly in the War. Millions of Russians had died. Stalin's priority was Russia, not Germany. Western concern and compassion for Germany – to ensure the return of democracy and stable government – was not shared by Stalin.

The United States had developed an atom bomb – a deadly new weapon kept secret from Stalin even though he was a wartime ally.

Stalin had promised that the people living in the Eastern European countries would be free to choose their own governments after the War. But it was already clear the Russians would only tolerate pro-Communist governments. There was nothing the Allies could do about this, short of going to war.

**Source A** Why the Cold War developed after 1945

---

Stalin feared the West might try to destroy Soviet communism, so he created a buffer zone of friendly East European countries separating the Soviet Union from the West. It gave Soviet forces time to react to an attack. To many Americans this was simply aggression, forgetting for the moment the colossal hardship the war had inflicted on the Soviet Union – over 20 million Russian dead and devastating damage to Soviet cities and industry which took years to reconstruct.

## The Iron Curtain countries

At first Stalin moved slowly in Eastern Europe. Opposition parties were permitted. At the first elections the voters were given a relatively free choice – provided the governments they chose were at least sympathetic to communist aims and ideals. But gradually East European communists took over. The West was kept in the dark until it was too late to insist on free elections (Source **B**).

**Source B** Eastern Europe, showing the Iron Curtain countries

Within the map:

**Soviet Union** Communist since 1917. Stalin, its hardline leader from the late 1920s to his death in 1953, had thousands of his opponents shot. His successors, such as Malenkov, Khruschev and Brezhnev, were more tolerant but still ruthless if they thought Russia's interests were threatened.

**East Germany** Soviet tanks suppressed disturbances in 1953. Berlin wall built 1961.

**Poland** Communist since 1947. Riots in 1956 put down with help of Russians.

**Czechoslovakia** Communist coup in 1948. Liberal reforms in 1968 suppressed by Warsaw Pact troops.

**Hungary** Hardline Communist in 1949 under Matyas Rakosi. Russians quelled uprising in 1956.

**Romania** Forced King Michael to abdicate in December 1947. More independent under Ceaucescu after 1967. Refused to invade Czechoslovakia in 1968

**Yugoslavia** Marshal Tito independent of Stalin. Broke with the USSR in 1948. Communist but traded with the West.

**Bulgaria** Communist since 1946

**Albania** Hardline Communist. Left Warsaw Pact in 1968 after Czech invasion

The West

IRON CURTAIN

## The Truman Doctrine

Only one Balkan country remained outside the Iron Curtain. This was Greece. Communist guerrillas (soldiers who harass an enemy behind the lines) had fought the Germans in Greece with some success in the war. They called themselves the National People's Liberation Army (ELAS). When the Germans withdrew, ELAS tried to take over the government of Greece. They were resisted by the British. By 1947, however, Britain could no longer afford to keep forces there, so President Truman stepped in, determined to resist communist aggression at all costs. On 12 March 1947 he spelled out his policy in a statement called the Truman Doctrine (Source **C**).

Truman immediately put his Doctrine into practice by supplying the Greeks with advisers and arms. As a result the attempted communist take-over of Greece was resisted.

**Source C** The Truman Doctrine

I believe that it must be the policy of the United States to support free peoples who are resisting attempted subjugation by armed minorities or by outside pressures.

## The Marshall Plan

The Truman Doctrine marked a major change in American foreign policy – from one of co-operation with Soviet Communism to one of confrontation. Truman was not going to stand by and watch Stalin take over the countries of Europe one by one. But what if a freely elected communist government came to power? What would America do then? This was a distinct possibility. Europe was still suffering the after-effects of the war. There were severe food shortages. Lack of money prevented European governments from rebuilding their shattered cities. The Americans recalled the end of the First World War. Communism had thrived in countries like Russia, Germany and Hungary, wherever there was poverty and despair.

The Americans devised a plan to give massive financial aid to the governments of Europe. It would help them recover from the damage which war had done to their economies. It was first outlined, in June 1947, by a former American wartime commander – General Marshall – now US Secretary of State (Foreign Minister). In other words, the Marshall Plan (page 142) was yet another way in which the Americans could carry out the Truman Doctrine – helping democratic governments counter the spread of communism.

Any country accepting Marshall Aid was expected to be friendly to the United States. The Americans even offered help to Iron Curtain countries as well. Czechoslovakia, governed by a pro-communist Coalition Government, accepted this offer at first – and then withdrew on instructions from Moscow. But Yugoslavia accepted, showing that its leader, President Tito, was independent and not at the beck and call of Stalin. The Russians later provided their own substitute for Marshall Aid when they founded COMECON in January 1949 (COuncil for Mutual ECONomic Assistance).

*Questions*

1 In your own words, say what was meant by **a)** Iron Curtain, **b)** Cold War.

2 Make a list of reasons which help to explain why the USSR and the USA become rivals after 1945.

3 Who was to blame for the Cold War? Was it the fault of: **a)** the United States, **b)** the Soviet Union? Give your reasons.

4 How did the USSR gain control of Eastern Europe by 1948?

## The Berlin Blockade

▶ **What were the causes and the short-term consequences of the crisis over Berlin in 1948?**

**Source A**  Military crossing point separating East and West in Berlin

It had been planned that the occupation zones in Berlin and Germany would be governed jointly by the four occupying powers. By 1948, however, Cold War attitudes held out little hope that Germany would ever be reunited again. Since the Soviet authorities would not allow free access to their zone, the other three Occupying Powers took steps to merge their zones into one. In retaliation, the Soviet authorities put obstacles in their way. The crisis came to a head in June 1948, when the Allies decided to use the same German currency in West Berlin as in the Allied zones of Western Germany. To the Russians, this meant that the Allies were making West Berlin part of Western Germany – even though it was a long way inside communist Eastern Germany. You can see what action they took in the sources.

**Source B**  US Government report, 1948

On June 23, the Soviet authorities suspended all railroad passengers and freight traffic into Berlin, because of alleged 'technical difficulties' on the Berlin-Helmstedt rail line. They also stopped barge traffic on similar grounds. Shortly before midnight on June 23, the Soviet authorities issued orders to the Berlin central electric switch-control station (located in their sector) to disrupt delivery of electric power from Soviet zone and Soviet sector plants to the Western sectors. Shortage of coal was given as a reason for this measure.

Extract from *The Berlin Crisis: A Report*, US Department of State, 1948

**Source C**  From the diary of a US official
▼

28 *June 1948.* Meeting at White House – Berlin Situation. When the specific question was discussed as to what our future policy in Germany was to be – namely, were we to stay in Berlin or not? – the President [*Truman*] interrupted to say that there was no discussion on that point, we were going to stay period. We were in Berlin by terms of an agreement and the Russians had no right to get us out by either direct or indirect pressure.

Extract from *The Forrestal Diaries*, by James Forrestal (US Secretary of the Navy in April 1945), edited by Walter Millis, The Viking Press, 1951

**Source D**  News report in *Time* magazine, July 1948

The incessant roar of the planes filled every ear in the city. It echoed in the hollow, broken houses. It throbbed in the weary ears of Berlin's people who were bitter, afraid, but far from broken. The sound meant one thing: the West was standing its ground and fighting back. At Tempelhof Airport transport planes landed at the daylight rate of one every three minutes.

**Source E**   Supplying Berlin from the air. During the Berlin Airlift food was unloaded straight on to German lorries from Allied cargo planes flying night and day into the city. They supplied the Berliners with everything they needed by air – even heavy raw materials such as coal.

**Source F**   From a Soviet history book published in 1977

This reform [*the new currency*] sparked off a dangerous crisis. The old marks (which were worthless now) poured into the Soviet Occupation Zone. In order to foil the currency speculators [*who made money buying and selling foreign currency*], checks were carried out on passengers arriving from West Germany. Certain restrictions were imposed on transport links between Berlin and the Western zones. Nevertheless, the Soviet side was ready to maintain the supply of food and fuel to the whole of Berlin. Yet every day 380 American transport planes made several flights each into Berlin. All this was simply a propaganda move intended to intensify the cold war.

Extract from *History of the USSR*, translated from the Russian by Ken Russell, Progress Publishers (Moscow),1977

**Source H**   Extract from *Time* magazine: 16 May 1949

Berlin's people had been living mainly on the airlift's dehydrated potatoes, powdered eggs, powdered milk, dried vegetables and occasional cans of meat. This week they would get better food, and more of it. The blockade had shut down much of Berlin's industry, thrown 125,000 out of work. There had been only four hours of electricity a day. Berliners had lighted their homes with candles or gone to bed at sunset. The siege's end meant not only more food, more jobs and more light, but a relatively comfortable winter ahead.

The Berlin Blockade was over. Allied soldiers at all the main crossing points into East Germany, freshened up the road signs and removed weeds from the highway.

**Source G**   Extract from the *New York Times*, Thursday, 12 May 1949

Just as the morning sun rose over the jagged skyline of this broken but defiant city a Soviet zone locomotive chugged wearily into the Charlottenburg Station in the British sector hauling the first train to reach Berlin from the West in 328 days. Arrival of the train completed the relief of the city from the iron vice of the Soviet blockade. At one minute after midnight two jeeps and a convoy of cars, buses and trucks roared out of the city for the western zones.

Questions

1   What reason did President Truman (Source **C**) give to explain the Berlin Blockade?

2   What do the painting (Source **E**) and Sources **B**, **C**, **D**, **G** and **H** tell you about the way in which people in the West viewed the Berlin Airlift?

3   Source **F** is from a Soviet history book published in 1977. How can you tell it is written by a historian from the Soviet side of the Iron Curtain?

4   Use these sources to explain how the Soviet interpretation of what happened during the Berlin Blockade differs from those in the Western sources. Is there any way of knowing which interpretation is correct?

# NATO and the Warsaw Pact

## What were the long-term consequences of the Berlin Crisis?

Source A   Map of NATO in 1949

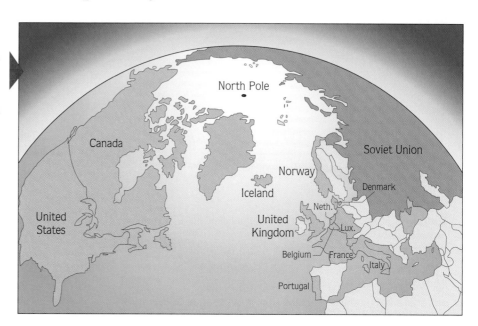

When the Berlin Blockade ended on 12 May 1949, the future course of Europe had changed irrevocably:

- The Western Allies had formed a defensive alliance – NATO.

- Plans for the creation of the German Federal Republic were ready. They came into being eleven days after the lifting of the Blockade.

Both these results had an important 'knock-on' effect. The Russians and their allies regarded the formation of NATO (Source **C**) as a hostile act. It was a threat to their own security. This led, inevitably, to the formation of their own Warsaw Pact alliance (Source **D**) in 1955.

The creation of the Federal Republic made it

possible for Germans in the three Western occupation zones to start rebuilding their country. But it also ensured that Germany would be split in two for forty years. A rival Germany – the German Democratic Republic (East Germany) – came into being on 7 October 1949 – little more than four months after the foundation of its rival the Federal Republic on 23 May 1949.

The North Atlantic Treaty Organisation came into being on 4 April 1949. You can see the principal terms of the Treaty in the panel opposite (Source **C**). It was signed in Washington on 4 April 1949 by Belgium, Canada, Denmark, France, Iceland, Italy, Luxembourg, the Netherlands, Norway, Portugal, the United Kingdom and the United States.  The most significant feature of the Treaty was not so much the fact that it was an alliance of twelve powers – ten in Europe and two in North America – but the fact that it committed the United States, bigger than all the other countries put together, to the defence of Europe.

Since then, NATO has remained strong, despite one or two upsets. In 1952, the Western Allies, despairing of ever coming to an agreement with the Soviet Union, finally made their peace with Western Germany. Germany's schoolchildren were given a day's holiday and the flag of the new German Federal Republic was proudly raised to mark the event. That same year, Greece and Turkey joined NATO as well.

Source B   Cartoon published in the *Daily Express*

150

**Source C**   The North Atlantic Treaty

Article 1: The Parties undertake, as set forth in the Charter of the United Nations, to settle any international disputes by peaceful means in such a manner that international peace and security, and justice, are not endangered, and to refrain in their international relations from the threat or use of force in any manner inconsistent with the purposes of the United Nations.

Article 5: The Parties agree that an armed attack against one or more of them in Europe or North America shall be considered an attack against them all. If such an armed attack occurs, each of them, in the exercise of the right of individual or collective self-defence recognised by Article 51 of the Charter of the United Nations, will assist the Party or Parties so attacked by taking such action as it deems necessary, including the use of armed force.

All measures taken shall immediately be reported to the Security Council and terminated when the Security Council has taken the measures necessary to restore and maintain international peace and security.

## The Warsaw Pact

West Germany also joined NATO in 1955. The idea of a brand new German army so soon after the end of the Second World War became a sore point with the Russians – as you can see from Sources **E** and **F**. As a direct consequence, when the Federal Republic joined NATO on 9 May 1955, it was followed five days later by the signing of the Warsaw Pact (Source **D**).

**Source D**   The Warsaw Treaty of Friendship, Co-operation, and Mutual Assistance

Article 1: The Contracting Parties undertake, in accordance with the Charter of the United Nations Organization, to refrain in their international relations from the threat or use of force, and to settle their international disputes peacefully and in such manner as will not jeopardise international peace and security.

Article 4: In the event of armed attack in Europe on one or more of the parties each in the exercise of its right to individual or collective self defence in accordance with Article 51 of the Charter of the United Nations Organization, shall immediately come to the assistance of the state or states attacked with all such means as it deems necessary, including armed force.

Measures taken shall be reported to the Security Council and discontinued immediately the Security Council adopts the necessary measures to restore and maintain international peace and security.

**Source E**   Soviet cartoon. A fierce dog in a German helmet is restrained by a dog lead made of paper! The caption reads: 'DO NOT FEAR, HE IS ON A CHAIN.' The Russian word on each link in the paper chain means 'guarantee'.

**Source F**   Soviet cartoon of NATO generals goose-stepping

The Warsaw Pact was signed on 14 May 1955 by Albania, Bulgaria, Hungary, East Germany, Poland, Romania, the Soviet Union and Czechoslovakia.

Questions

1  Use Sources **C** and **D** to describe the similarities between the Warsaw Pact and the North Atlantic Treaty.

2  What does the cartoon in Source **B** tell you about Western attitudes to the partition of Germany in 1949?

3  Look at the cartoons in Sources **E** and **F**. Why were they drawn? What do they tell you about Soviet attitudes to NATO and the rearming of Germany?

4  How did the creation of NATO and the Warsaw Pact help or hinder the cause of peace?

5  What were the two main consequences of the Berlin Blockade?

## The Korean War

▶ ### Why was the United Nations involved in a war in Korea

### Why the UN became involved?

On Wednesday, 28 June 1950, Americans woke up to headlines telling them that US armed forces had been ordered to fight in Korea. Korea had been divided in two in 1945 along latitude 38°N (the 38th Parallel). The Republic of Korea in the south was supported by the United States and led by Syngman Rhee. The Korean People's Democratic Republic in the north was Communist and led by Kim Il Sung. Neither part of Korea was happy with the division and both claimed to be the lawful government. The United Nations tried in vain to unite them as the two Koreas built up their armed forces. The UN Commission in Korea warned of the danger of civil war and an uncomfortable peace kept the two sides apart until June 1950 (Source **C**).

**Source B**  Rockets repel a Communist offensive in Korea in 1951

**Source C**  Sunday, 25 June 1950. Report in *Time* magazine

> Just before a grey dawn came up over the peninsula, North Korea's Communist army started to roll south. Past terraced hills, green with newly transplanted rice, rumbled tanks. In the rain-heavy sky roared an occasional fighter plane. Then the heavy artillery started to boom. All along the 38th parallel – the boundary between North and South Korea – the invaders met little resistance.

**Source A**  Front cover of the British magazine *Picture Post* during the Korean War

**Source D**  From US President Truman's Memoirs

> I had time to think aboard the plane. In my generation, this was not the first occasion when the strong had attacked the weak. I remembered how each time that the democracies failed to act it had encouraged the aggressors to keep going ahead. Communism was acting in Korea just as Hitler, Mussolini, and the Japanese had acted ten, fifteen, and twenty years earlier. I felt certain that if South Korea was allowed to fall Communist leaders would be encouraged to invade nations closer to our own shores.
>
> Extract from *Memoirs of Harry S. Truman*, Doubleday, 1956

**Source E**  Headlines in the *Daily Mail*, 26 June 1951

**Source F**  Headlines in the *New York Times*, Wednesday, 28 June 1950

> Truman Orders US Air, Navy Units to Fight in Aid of Korea;
> UN Council Supports Him    The Soviet is Absent
> Council Adopts Plan of US for Armed Force in Korea
> Yugoslavia Casts Lone Dissent – Egypt and India Abstain

**Source G**  Interview with President Truman

*Interviewer*: 'Mr President, everyone is asking in this country, are we or are we not at war?'
*Truman*: 'We are not at war.'
*Interviewer*: 'Would it be correct to call it a police action under the United Nations?'
*Truman*: 'Yes, that is exactly what it amounts to.

**Source H**  *New York Times*, Wednesday, 28 June 1950

HONG KONG. June 27 – The North Korean Government issued a statement today saying that it regarded the cease fire order of the United Nations Security Council illegal because, (1) North Korea was not represented, (2) the Soviet Union and (Communist) China did not participate. The United Nations Charter requires the complete agreement of the five permanent members of the Security Council on questions of substance.

**Source I**  Speech by Soviet Foreign Minister, Andrei Gromyko, quoted in *Time* Magazine

The events now taking place in Korea began on June 25 as the result of an uncalled for attack by the troops of South Korea on the Korean People's Democratic Republic.

**Source J**  Speech by Labour Prime Minister, Clement Attlee, in Parliament

It is being alleged that South Korea attacked North Korea. Anything less likely, in view of the fact that North Korea was heavily armed and South Korea was not, could not possibly be imagined.

Extract from *Report of the Parliamentary Debate in the House of Commons*, 1950

## Course of the war

Over 33,000 Americans were killed and an estimated 3,000,000 Korean civilians died in the war. Apart from South Korea and the USA, 50,000 troops from the UK (Source **A**), France, Canada, Turkey, Greece, Thailand, Australia, NZ, Colombia, Benelux, Ethiopia and South Africa fought there as well, together with medics from India, Italy and Scandinavia.

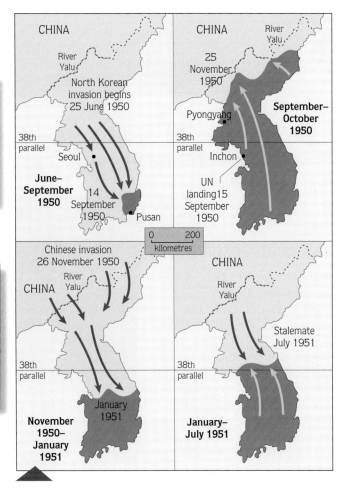

**Source K**  The four main stages of the Korean War. After their initial defeats, UN forces commanded by US General MacArthur crossed the 38th Parallel themselves and advanced rapidly towards the border with China (North Korea's close ally). On 25 November 1950, massive Chinese armies crossed the Yalu River into North Korea and drove the UN forces back once more. After hard fighting, the UN armies eventually held on to a front line on or about the 38th Parallel. Both sides eventually signed an Armistice agreement in July 1953 restoring the original boundary between the two Koreas.

1  Use the sources to explain what caused the Korean War according to **a)** the West, **b)** the Communists, Why did this question matter at the time?

2  Look at Source **D** on page 163. The Soviets would not attend Security Council meetings in July 1950 because Red China (page 186) had not yet been given the seat. This is why only four of the five permanent UN representatives – Britain, France, the USA and Nationalist China – voted for the ceasefire (Source **E**). Were the North Koreans correct, therefore, in saying the UN vote was illegal (Source **H**)?

3  The Korean War has been seen as a triumph and as a failure for the United Nations. What is your verdict? Did it prove that the nations of the world could unite together for the common good?

*Questions*

# After Stalin

**What effect did the death of Stalin have on East-West relations? How and why did the Soviet Union suppress the Hungarian Revolution in 1956?**

## The death of Stalin

Stalin died in 1953. In 1956 his successor, Nikita Khruschev, astounded the world when he denounced Stalin in a speech at the Twentieth Party Congress in Moscow (Source **I** on page 65). Khruschev listed the crimes which Stalin had committed in the 1930s when he purged Russia of many of its top leaders. This denunciation led to de-Stalinization. Many of the labour camps holding political prisoners were broken up. Images of Stalin disappeared from public places, statues were pulled down and cities like Stalingrad and Stalino changed their names. Khruschev put more emphasis on producing consumer goods and raising living standards. He greatly expanded the amount of land under grain in the steppelands of Russia but when his agricultural policies failed, he was removed from office and replaced by Leonid Brezhnev in 1964.

**Source A** Soviet leaders pay their respects to the dead Stalin in 1953

## The Hungarian Rising

Stalin's death and Khruschev's condemnation of Stalin's brutal ways as a dictator had an unforeseen result. They encouraged the Hungarians to seek a more liberal type of Communism. Students and workers demonstrated in the streets of Budapest on 23 October 1956, demanding free elections, greater independence for their country from Moscow and the return of the popular leader Imre Nagy (Source **B**).

**Source B** Demands of demonstrators in Budapest, Tuesday, 23 October 1956

- We demand the immediate evacuation of all Soviet troops.
- The leadership must change.
- Imre Nagy to the Government.

Extract from *Thirteen Days That Shook the Kremlin* by Tibor Meray, translated by Howard L. Katzander, Thames and Hudson, 1958

### NIKITA KHRUSCHEV (1894-1971)

Nikita Khruschev quickly made an impression on the world. He had a cheerful face and a ferocious temper. One minute he was friend, the next enemy. But Khruschev was different from Stalin. He genuinely believed in a policy of peaceful co-existence between East and West. By this he meant a world in which communist and capitalist societies could live in peace, side by side. He told Russians that the danger of nuclear war meant that communism would have to be spread abroad by peaceful means. To prove his point, he visited Britain in 1956 and the United States in 1959. However, his soft words did not stop him taking tough action in Hungary in 1956, in Berlin in 1961, and in Cuba in 1962 (page 156).

Nagy took office as prime minister the next day and had a difficult time trying to control the situation since Soviet forces were already in Budapest and in the Hungarian countryside surrounding the capital (Source **C**). But Nagy went one step too far for Khruschev on 31 October (Source **D**). Soviet forces suppressed the uprising, Nagy was arrested and later executed, and Janos Kadar took his place as leader of Hungary.

**Source C**   Broadcast by Radio Budapest. Wednesday, 24 October 1956

Government organisations have called for help from Soviet troops stationed in Hungary under the terms of the Warsaw Pact. Responding to the Government's appeal, Soviet troops will help in the restoration of order.

*Extract from Thirteen Days That Shook the Kremlin*

**Source D**   Speech by Imre Nagy on Wednesday, 31 October 1956

My dear friends today we have started negotiations for the withdrawal of Soviet troops from our country and for the cancellation of our obligations under the Warsaw Pact. Long live Free Hungary!

*Extract from Thirteen Days That Shook the Kremlin*

**Source E**   Hungarian radio broadcast. Sunday, 4 November 1956

05.20: This is Imre Nagy speaking. Today at dawn, Soviet forces launched an attack against the capital with the obvious purpose of overthrowing the legal Hungarian democratic Government. Our troops are fighting. The Government is at its post.

*Extract from Thirteen Days That Shook the Kremlin*

**Source F**   Headline in the *Daily Mail* on Monday, 5 November 1956

**Daily Mail**   MORNING SPECIAL

A dying nation's last SOS. It reached Vienna from a Hungarian reporter. His full story is in Page 5

good bye we do not forget you    the russians are too near    good bye friends good bye friends , save our souls

BUDAPEST CRUSHED—Red troops storm into Parliament

# The MURDER OF HUNGARY

**Comment** *Nagy marched out at gunpoint*

GET OUT! IKE URGES BULGANIN

Coast defences attacked

**CYPRUS TROOPS BOARD THE**

**Source G**   Soviet delegate at the UN General Assembly. Monday, 3 December 1956

The Fascist rebellion in Hungary has been crushed thanks to the resolute action of the Hungarian people and Soviet armed forces fighting the counter-revolution at the Hungarian Government's request.

**Source H**   The Berlin Wall. The graffiti on the wall reads: 'Halt. Here ends freedom.'

## The Berlin Wall

The crushing of the Hungarian Revolution soured East-West relations and made world leaders wary of Khruschev. The ruthless use of tanks and Soviet armed forces to put down a rebellion of ordinary people hardened attitudes in the West against the Soviet Union. It also had another unforeseen effect. Many Western communists, including leading members of the British Communist Party, handed in their membership cards, disgusted at the Soviet use of force.

In 1960, yet another Cold War confrontation took place when an American, high-flying, U2 spy-plane was shot down over the Soviet Union. Khruschev was furious and the incident brought about the collapse of a summit meeting held in Paris a fortnight later.

The lesson of Hungary was not lost on the other leaders of the Eastern bloc countries. East Germany was losing thousands of skilled workers every year as refugees fled across the border into West Germany in search of a better life. In August 1961 the East Germans (backed by the Russians) closed all the crossing points into East Berlin and erected a wall sealing off the West from the East. A number of East Berliners made daring escapes but many were killed by East German security troops. The Allies protested. American tanks faced their Russian counterparts across the wall but there was nothing they could do. There was nothing further the Russians could do, either, to get the Allies out of Berlin. It only strengthened Allied determination to remain there and created yet another stumbling block in the path of world peace.

1  What was meant by: **a)** peaceful co-existence, **b)** de-Stalinization?

2  What was the significance of: **a)** the shooting down of the U2 spy-plane in 1960, **b)** the erection of the Berlin Wall in 1961, **c)** the student uprising on 23 October 1956?

3  Make a summary of the different viewpoints on the Hungarian Uprising illustrated in Sources **B** to **G**. How and why do they differ?

4  How did the Soviet Union change after the death of Stalin?

*Questions*

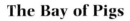

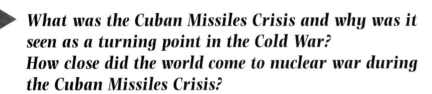

## The Cuban Missiles Crisis

▶ **What was the Cuban Missiles Crisis and why was it seen as a turning point in the Cold War?**
**How close did the world come to nuclear war during the Cuban Missiles Crisis?**

**Source A**  Fidel Castro ▶

### The Bay of Pigs

In January 1959, Fidel Castro, a young, left-wing revolutionary, overthrew President Batista, the corrupt and much-hated dictator of Cuba. Castro brought in many reforms, some of them directed against US-owned businesses in Cuba (only 200 km from Florida). When relations between the USA and Cuba deteriorated, Castro turned to the Soviet Union as an ally. US Intelligence officers, meanwhile, were helping to train 1,500 Cuban supporters of Batista. With

President Kennedy's approval, they landed at Cuba's Bay of Pigs on 17 April 1961, expecting their fellow Cubans to join them in overthrowing Castro. Instead the invaders were overwhelmed and Kennedy was made to look a fool – since any more direct American involvement in the invasion would have been condemned by the world as aggression. Castro made Cuba a communist state in May, so Kennedy banned all US trade with Cuba, depriving Americans of Cuban sugar and Havana cigars. Castro retaliated by stepping up Cuban trade with the Soviet Union. Both he and Khruschev assumed the Cuban rebels in the United States would try again.

### The missiles

Khruschev decided to help Castro. In doing so he took a very grave risk. He sent missiles to Cuba (Source **C**).

**Source C**  By Nikita Khruschev – why I sent missiles to Cuba
▼

> Everyone agreed that America would not leave Cuba alone unless we did something. We had an obligation to do everything in our power to protect Cuba's existence as a Socialist country and as a working example to the other countries of Latin America. During my visit to Bulgaria I had the idea of installing missiles with nuclear warheads in Cuba without letting the United States find out they were there until it was too late to do anything about them. I want to make one thing absolutely clear. We had no desire to start a war. Only a fool would think that we wanted to invade the American continent from Cuba. Our goal was precisely the opposite: we wanted to keep the Americans from invading Cuba.

Extract from *Kruschev Remembers* translated by Strobe Talbot, Little, Brown, 1970

#### JOHN F KENNEDY (1917–1963)

John Fitzgerald Kennedy, a member of one of America's richest families, took office as President in January 1961 appealing to Russia to begin 'anew the quest for peace'. Despite his wealth, Kennedy was a left-wing Democrat like Roosevelt (page 100). He believed passionately in freedom, supported the Black Civil Rights movement (page 190) and tried to make life easier for the poor. Kennedy worked hard for peace but was a determined opponent of Communism. His assassination in 1963 when driving in an open car through the streets of Dallas, Texas, shocked the world.

**Source B**
President
Kennedy ▶

**Source D** Aerial photograph of Soviet missile site in Cuba

CHERRY PICKER

LAUNCH PAD WITH ERECTOR

LAUNCH PAD WITH ERECTOR

MISSILE READY BLDGS

CABLING

FUELING VEHICLES

OXIDIZER VEHICLES

This is why, during the summer of 1962, American spies on Cuba reported seeing Russian cargo ships unloading long cigar-like objects on to lorries. Thousands of Russian engineers were arriving on the island. Why? American experts ignored the obvious answer. The Soviet Union had never stationed missiles in other countries, not even those of the Warsaw Pact. Castro was hot-headed and inexperienced. It was unthinkable that Khruschev would have been stupid enough to place nuclear missiles in his hands – and risk a Third World War. Nonetheless, it was worth making sure. So, on a cloudless day – Sunday 14 October 1962 – two American U2 spy planes were sent to take aerial photographs of the island (Sources **D** and **E**).

**Source E** Report in *Time* magazine, 2 November 1962

As if by magic, thick woods had been torn down, empty fields were clustered with concrete mixing plants, fuel tanks and mess halls. Chillingly clear to the expert eye were some 40 slim, 52-ft. [16 m] medium-range missiles, many of them already angled up on their mobile launchers and pointed at the US mainland.

### Kennedy's options

The news shocked President Kennedy. 'How can you be so sure?' he asked the experts who had analysed the photographs. Convinced they were genuine, he quickly

assembled a group of his most influential colleagues – the Ex Comm committee. What action should he take? Experts told him that when the missiles on Cuba were ready, they could destroy most of America's cities in less than three minutes. Other reconnaissance flights revealed that further missiles were on their way – loaded on the decks of Russian ships bound for Cuba.

We know what happened at the Ex Comm meetings because the discussions were secretly tape-recorded by the President. We can hear them discussing different ways of dealing with the Crisis. There were three main options.

(1) The HAWKS (those who wanted swift military action), such as Dean Acheson (a former Secretary of State), stressed 'the great importance of getting an air strike in with all the benefits of surprise.' The disadvantage? Russian engineers would be killed. World War Three might start at once.

(2) The MODERATES, such as Robert McNamara (Secretary of Defence) wanted to impose a naval blockade as the first step to getting rid of the missiles. They proposed to use the US navy to stop the Soviet ships reaching Cuba. The disadvantage? Kennedy said it might mean 'sinking Russian ships'.

(3) The DOVES (such as Adlai Stevenson, US Ambassador to the United Nations) advised Kennedy to be cautious. He should talk with the Soviet Union and perhaps offer to remove US missiles from Turkey. The disadvantage? The USA would look weak.

1  What proof did the Americans have that the Russians had supplied Cuba with missiles?

2  Is there any reason to doubt Khruschev's explanation of why he sent missiles to Cuba (Source **C**)?

Questions

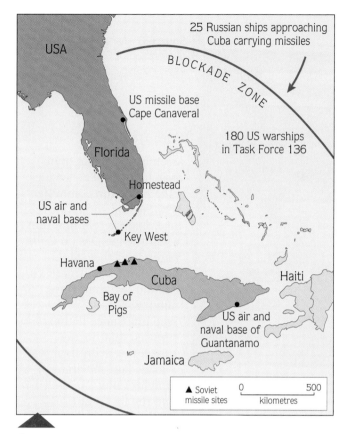

**Source F**  Map of the Cuban Missiles Crisis

Inside the map:
- USA
- 25 Russian ships approaching Cuba carrying missiles
- BLOCKADE ZONE
- US missile base Cape Canaveral
- Florida
- 180 US warships in Task Force 136
- Homestead
- US air and naval bases
- Key West
- Havana
- Cuba
- Haiti
- Bay of Pigs
- US air and naval base of Guantanamo
- Jamaica
- ▲ Soviet missile sites
- 0 ——— 500 kilometres

## The naval blockade

For a week, Ex Comm discussed the options. Meanwhile fresh photographs brought alarming news. The missile sites were nearly ready. At first most of the committee favoured the air strike option, even though they knew this carried the risk of starting a world war. Kennedy, however, was more cautious (Source **G**).

**Source G**  President Kennedy

They, no more than we, can let these things go by without doing something. They can't, after all their statements, permit us to take out their missiles, kill a lot of Russians, and then do nothing. If they don't take action in Cuba, they certainly will in Berlin.

Extract from *The Glory and the Dream* by William Manchester, Michael Joseph, 1975

Kennedy opted instead for a 'measured response'. He would give Khruschev the chance to climb down without admitting defeat. The American navy and airforce would seal off Cuba. All ships would be searched. Any found carrying arms would be sent back to Russia. On Monday evening, 22 October 1962, Kennedy broadcast his decision to the American people (Source **H**).

**Source H**  Headlines in New York papers, 23 October 1962

US IMPOSES ARMS BLOCKADE ON CUBA ON FINDING OFFENSIVE MISSILE SITES; KENNEDY READY FOR SOVIET SHOWDOWN. SHIPS MUST STOP.
OTHER ACTION PLANNED IF BIG ROCKETS ARE NOT DISMANTLED.
ASSERTS RUSSIANS LIED AND PUT HEMISPHERE IN GREAT DANGER.
JFK'S ORDERS: 'SEARCH, AND IF NECESSARY, SINK ANY ARMS SHIP.'

Extract from *The New York Mirror* and *The New York Times*

People throughout the world were dreadfully worried when they heard the news of the President's ultimatum (Sources **I** and **K**). They had seen Khruschev on television, arguing fiercely with British and American politicians, thumping tables, threatening the West – 'We will bury you'. Even the President's closest advisers wondered if they would see another sunset (Source **J**).

**Source I**  Young woman recalling her reaction to the Cuban Crisis

I remember going into a cinema in Sheffield the next evening and wondering 'will I walk out again?'

**Source J**  Dean Rusk, US Secretary of State

I got three or four hours sleep and I remember waking up the next morning and saying to myself, 'Well I'm still here. This is very interesting.' This meant that Mr Khruschev's immediate response had not been to launch nuclear missiles.

Extract from interview recorded in Central Television Production *The Nuclear Age: On the Brink* 1989

It was the start of the gravest crisis since the end of the Second World War. Would Kennedy really sink Russian ships? The alarm would have been much greater had people known that 57 fully-loaded B-52 nuclear bombers were already in the air (to avoid destruction on the ground). As soon as one landed, another took off. In addition, 140 Titan and Atlas missiles were primed and ready for firing. The Russians, too, were on combat alert. Soviet General Gribkov said, 'The slightest spark or false move by either side could have triggered a nuclear catastrophe.'

Demonstrators around the world protested. Some pessimists left a CND demonstration in London and fled to Western Ireland. The theatre critic Kenneth Tynan booked a one-way ticket to Australia. Americans queued up at supermarkets to stock up with supplies. One woman paid on credit because she didn't expect to have to pay for the goods!

**Source K**  Telegram to Kennedy from Bertrand Russell, a British philosopher and CND supporter

YOUR ACTION DESPERATE. NO CONCEIVABLE JUSTIFICATION. END THIS MADNESS.

Extract from *The Glory and the Dream*

**Source M**  Russian ship carrying missiles to Cuba. The evidence was unmistakable even to an untrained eye.

## Kennedy and Khruschev

The two world leaders facing each other across the Atlantic had been acclaimed as peace-makers. Khruschev had denounced Stalin and visited the West. People had begun to talk of a 'thaw' in East–West relations. Now, just when everyone's hopes had been raised, there seemed to be no way out but war. The Russian ships moved closer to Cuba. Kennedy himself was in charge of operations, speaking directly to the naval officers at sea. If US warships were going to open fire, then the President would be directly responsible. The tension in the White House was unbearable (Source **L**).

**Source L**  Robert Kennedy describes his brother as they waited to see what Khruschev would do

I think those few minutes were the time of gravest concern for the President. Was the world on the brink of a holocaust? Was it our error? A mistake? His face seemed drawn, his eyes pained, almost grey. We stared at each other across the table.

Extract from *Thirteen Days* by Robert Kennedy, Signet, 1969

Then came welcome news. Twelve Soviet ships had stopped dead in their tracks. There would be no naval battle. Dean Rusk, recalling a children's game he had played as a boy, said: 'We were eyeball to eyeball and the other side just blinked.' However, the fact that the Soviet ships had turned back did not remove the danger from the missiles already in Cuba.

## Removing the missiles from Cuba

Robert Kennedy talked to the Soviet Ambassador, Anatoly Dobrynin. He told him that his brother would act decisively within the next 48 hours if the Soviets

refused to dismantle the missiles. On Friday, 26 October, Khruschev sent a message to Kennedy saying he would remove the missiles if Kennedy promised not to invade Cuba. But the following day (Saturday, 27 October), Moscow Radio added a new demand. US missiles in Turkey would have to be removed as well (since they were sited close to the Soviet border). That same day, a Soviet ground-to-air missile shot down a U2 spy plane over Cuba, killing the pilot. America's hawks said the President should act at once (Source **N**).

**Source N**  Extract from *The Glory and the Dream*

The Joint Chiefs [*America's top military commanders*] join the Ex Comm meeting. They recommend an air strike Monday, to be followed by an invasion of Cuba. With one exception the Ex Comm believes that there is no other course. The exception is the President. He says: 'We must remind ourselves we are embarking on a very hazardous course.'

Extract from *The Glory and the Dream*

1  Why did Kennedy blockade Cuba? What was he afraid of? What did he mean by a 'measured response'?

2  Which of these sources provides evidence that Kennedy had to restrain the hotheads in his government?

3  Which of the following statements is supported or contradicted by the sources on these pages?

a) 'No conceivable justification' (for the Blockade).

b) 'Your action desperate' (meaning Kennedy).

c) 'Unmistakable' evidence of the presence of Russian missiles.

d) 'World on the brink of nuclear war'.

*Questions*

CASE FILE

## Climbdown or victory?

What happened next is clouded in mystery. According to one report, Kennedy sent his brother Robert to talk in secret with the Soviet Ambassador again. He promised to remove the missiles from Turkey (since they were obsolete anyway) but could not do so at the point of a gun. Khruschev in his memoirs claimed that Kennedy was under great pressure (Source **O**).

**Source O**   By Nikita Khruschev – why I gave way

The climax came when our ambassador in Washington reported that the President's brother, Robert Kennedy, had come to see him on an unofficial visit. 'The President is in a grave situation,' Robert Kennedy said [*to the Ambassador*], 'and he does not know how to get out of it. We are under very severe stress. If the situation continues much longer, the President is not sure that the military will not overthrow him and seize power. The American army could get out of control.' I hadn't overlooked this possibility. We knew that Kennedy was a young President and that the security of the United States was indeed threatened. 'Comrades,' I said, 'we have to look for a dignified way out of this conflict.'

Extract from *Kruschev Remembers* translated by Strobe Talbot, Little, Brown, 1970

It is hard to believe that America's most senior admirals and generals, brought up to believe in democracy, would even have contemplated, let alone staged, a military coup. Whatever the explanation, Kennedy's promises were enough for Khruschev and on Sunday 28 October the crisis was over. The missiles in Cuba would be removed under United Nations supervision (Source **P**).

**Source P**   Moscow Radio announcement

4.0 p.m. Sunday, 28 October. This is Radio Moscow. Premier Khrushchev has sent a message to President Kennedy today. In order to lower the tension threatening world peace, the Soviet Government has ordered the dismantling of the arms in Cuba which have been described as offensive as well as their crating and return to the Soviet Union.

**Source Q**   Nikita Khruschev

## Verdicts on the handling of the Cuban Missiles Crisis

Kennedy paid Khruschev a compliment (Source **R**). It was 'an important contribution to peace', he said. Kennedy kept his side of the bargain as well. Jupiter missiles were removed from Turkey within six months. Khruschev later told a journalist, 'I get nightmares when I think how close we came to nuclear war.'

**Source R**   Extract from *The Glory and the Dream*

The President speaks of how difficult it must have been for Khruschev to back down. He warns that there must be no claims of an American victory. He writes the Soviet premier a careful letter ending: 'I think we should give priority to questions relating to the spread of nuclear weapons and to the great effort for a nuclear test ban.

Extract from *The Glory and the Dream*

**Source S**  Verdict of an American journalist in *Time* magazine, 2 November 1962

Generations to come may well count John Kennedy's resolve as one of the decisive moments of the twentieth century.

**Source T**  Verdicts of some of America's top officers

*Army General* We'd just given Castro too much. And let him off too easy.

*Admiral* We've been had.

*Air Force General* It is the greatest defeat in our history, Mr President. We should invade today.

Quoted in BBC2 *Timewatch Special*, October 1992

**Source U**  Cuban verdict – by Fidel Castro

Simply agreeing to remove the missiles in exchange for a no-invasion pledge made no sense given what the US had done to us before.

Quoted in BBC2 *Timewatch Special*, October 1992

**Source V**  Soviet verdicts

*General:* This was the most humiliating thing for us. The military really resented it.

*Soviet Embassy official in Washington:* It was a humiliation no doubt. And it was well deserved.

*Special Assistant to Khruschev:* It failed in that the missiles were withdrawn. But it did not fail in that there was a commitment not to attack Cuba. And it led to a better climate between the two leaders and the two countries.

Extracts quoted in BBC2 *Timewatch Special*, October 1992

**Source W**  Khruschev's verdict in his memoirs

The Caribbean crisis was a triumph of Soviet foreign policy and a personal triumph in my own career as a statesman and as a member of the collective leadership. We achieved, I would say, a spectacular success without having to fire a single shot.

Extract from *Kruschev Remembers*

## Effects of the Crisis

- It showed Soviet leaders that the President would stand firm if US security was threatened.

- It led to the installation of a telephone link – the hotline – directly linking the White House in Washington with the Kremlin in Moscow.

- It showed the United States that the Russians could be reasonable after all.

- Relations between East and West got better not worse. Russia had refused to start a nuclear war and kept her side of the bargain. Talks on limiting the use of nuclear weapons might be fruitful after all.

- Khruschev's enemies attacked him – either for taking a reckless gamble or because he had climbed down. Two years later, he was deposed.

- Despite their intolerance of Castro and communism, successive American Presidents faithfully kept Kennedy's pledge not to invade Cuba. Castro was still its president over thirty years later.

1  What were the causes and consequences of the Cuban Missiles Crisis?

2  Ask your older friends and relatives what they remember of the Cuban Missiles Crisis. How scared were they of the possibility of a nuclear war? What value is their evidence when compared with the other sources used in this chapter?

3  Write an account saying how close you think the world came to nuclear war during the Cuban Missiles Crisis.

4  Sources **C**, **O** and **W** are from Khruschev's memoirs which were published in the West in 1970. Khruschev denied they were his but many Western experts thought them authentic. What value, if any, is there then in using them to understand the Cuban Missiles Crisis?

5  Look at each of the verdicts (Sources **S** to **W**). For each one, say how and why the people concerned differed in their interpretation of the Cuban Missiles Crisis and the part played by Kennedy and Khruschev in resolving the Crisis.

6  In your own words, say how far you agree that: (**a**) 'Kennedy's resolve was one of the decisive moments of the twentieth century'; (**b**) 'The Caribbean crisis was a triumph of Soviet foreign policy.'

*Questions*

## The United Nations

**Why was the UN set up and what has been its role since 1945? How far has the UN been successful in maintaining world peace?**

### Founding the United Nations

In August 1941, three months before the United States entered the war, Churchill and Roosevelt had a secret meeting where they drew up a document – *The Atlantic Charter* – which set out the sort of world they hoped to see after the war. In particular, they discussed plans to create a world body which would be more effective than the League of Nations. This proposal was followed up at Teheran in 1943 (page 127) when Stalin agreed with Churchill and Roosevelt to set up a United Nations.

Accordingly, delegates from the great powers met at Dumbarton Oaks near Washington, in 1944, to hammer out plans for the new organisation. They agreed it would have a General Assembly (meeting every year) and a smaller Security Council (meeting more regularly) which would consist of the three great powers (the USA, the USSR and the UK) and elected representatives from the other members of the UN.

But there was one point they could not agree on. The Soviet delegate, Andrei Gromyko, insisted that decisions of the three Great Powers on the Security Council must be unanimous. This meant that any one of the three Great Powers could veto a proposal it disliked. Sir Alexander Cadogan (UK) and Edward Stettinius (USA) tried to persuade Gromyko to abandon this requirement (Source **A**) but he refused. Stalin knew only too well that the Soviet Union could be easily out-voted by the West.

**Source A** From Sir Alexander Cadogan's diary

*Thursday, 7 September 1944*. Washington. Ed, Gromyko, and I, lunched together and Ed and I tried to hammer him on the main point – the Great Power Veto. But he was quite wooden on that. Best he could say was that we should 'leave the point open'. I explained to him that this was an illusion. If one 'left it open' one simply wouldn't get a World Organisation.

Extract from *Diaries of Sir Alexander Cadogan* edited by David Dilks, Cassell, 1971

The same issue dominated the San Francisco Conference in May and June 1945 when forty other nations attended and it was agreed that France and China should also become permanent representatives on the Security Council. The smaller countries objected to the veto but there was little they could do. One of the American delegates, however, was very satisfied with the way the conference had gone (Source **B**).

**Source B** By Senator Arthur Vandenberg

May 23, 1945: By hammering it out, we have found an answer which satisfies practically everybody. In my view, that is the great hope for the new League itself. If we do nothing more than create a constant forum where nations must face each other and debate their differences and strive for common ground, we shall have done infinitely much.

Extracts from *The Private Papers of Senator Vandenburg*, Houghton Mifflin, 1952

### Aims and organisation

The UN Charter (Source **C**) was signed by fifty nations on 26 June 1945 and came into being officially on 24 October 1945 – 'United Nations Day'.

**Source C** The UN Charter: Aims

- To maintain international peace and security by acting collectively to deter aggressors and to settle disputes peacefully.

- To develop friendly relations among nations based on respect for the principle of equal rights and self-determination of peoples.

- To achieve international co-operation in solving economic, social, cultural and humanitarian problems.

- To be a centre for harmonising the actions of nations in the attainment of these common ends.

| | |
|---|---|
| **General Assembly**<br>Debates world problems<br>• each member nation has one vote<br>• important decisions need a two-thirds majority | **Security Council**<br>Takes immediate action on behalf of the UN as a whole<br>• 5 permanent members (USSR, USA, UK, France, China) plus 10 elected members (2 years only)<br>• each member has one vote<br>• successful motions need at least 9 YES votes and no NO votes from the 5 permanent members |
| **The Trusteeship Council**<br>In charge of territories under UN control or mandate | |
| **The Economic and Social Council**<br>Oversees matters relating to health, education etc. Supervises the work of the specialised agencies of the UN | **The Secretariat**<br>Runs the UN headed by the UN Secretary General<br><br>**International Court of Justice** |

**UN Agencies**

**FAO** : Food and Agriculture Organisation: improve world farming; increase food production; eliminate famine
**GATT:** General Agreement on Tariffs and Trade: make it easier for goods to be traded between countries
**ILO:** International Labour Organisation: improve working conditions
**IMF:** International Monetary Fund: make it easier to exchange one country's currency for another
**UNESCO:** United Nations Educational Scientific and Cultural Organisation: raise educational standards, promote human rights
**UNICEF:** United Nations Children's Fund: help the world's children
**WHO:** World Health Organisation: raise health standards
**World Bank:** make loans to fund building projects

**Source D**  How the United Nations works

**Source E**  The *New York Times*, 4 November 1956

The Soviet Union early today vetoed a United States resolution proposing Security Council censure of the Russian military attack on Hungary.

## Successes and failures

One of the first major tests of the UN came in 1950 with the war in Korea (page 152). Although several members of the UN (unlike the pre-war League) sent troops to Korea, the bulk of the fighting was done by South Korea herself aided by the United States.

The West saw the Korean War as a simple case of communist aggression. But, as you have seen, the Soviet Union claimed that South Korea attacked first (Source **I** on page 153). In many other cases brought before the UN, both sides have claimed to be the injured party. What is more, the UN has usually been powerless to intervene in disputes where a government has invited in an ally to help them 'keep the peace', such as the use of the Red Army in Hungary in 1956 (Source **G** on page 155). The UN did nothing because the Soviet Union used its veto for the 79th time since 1945 (Source **E**, below).

Although the UK and US delegates argued against the veto at Dumbarton Oaks (Source **A**), both used it, too, when it suited them, such as Britain over Suez in 1956 and the USA over Grenada in 1983. Most of the failures of the UN can be attributed to the unhelpful attitudes adopted by the Great Powers and the inability of most other member countries to see beyond their own regional or power groupings, such as the Communist bloc, the Western Alliance, or the Developing World (Source **F**).

**Source F**  World map showing UN successes and failures

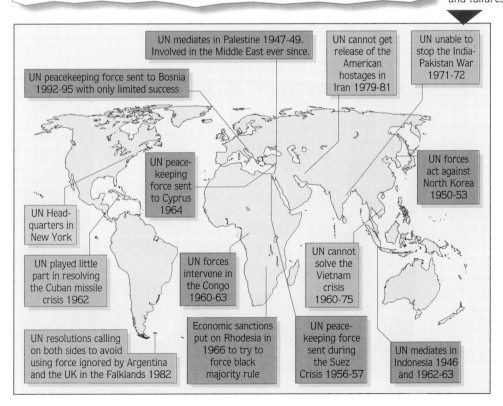

UN mediates in Palestine 1947-49. Involved in the Middle East ever since.

UN cannot get release of the American hostages in Iran 1979-81

UN unable to stop the India-Pakistan War 1971-72

UN peacekeeping force sent to Bosnia 1992-95 with only limited success

UN peace-keeping force sent to Cyprus 1964

UN Head-quarters in New York

UN played little part in resolving the Cuban missile crisis 1962

UN forces intervene in the Congo 1960-63

UN cannot solve the Vietnam crisis 1960-75

UN forces act against North Korea 1950-53

UN resolutions calling on both sides to avoid using force ignored by Argentina and the UK in the Falklands 1982

Economic sanctions put on Rhodesia in 1966 to try to force black majority rule

UN peace-keeping force sent during the Suez Crisis 1956-57

UN mediates in Indonesia 1946 and 1962-63

## Questions

1  Write a short summary explaining how and why the United Nations was set up in 1945.

2  Why did the Soviet Union insist on the right to veto Security Council decisions?

3  To what extent was the United Nations successful in trying to settle disputes in the 1950s?

4  In what ways is the United Nations similar to the League of Nations (page 40)? How is it different?

# 13 Detente: 1963–85

## Arms control and detente

▶ **What attempts at arms control and peaceful co-existence were made before 1985?**

### The arms race

The Russians shocked the West by testing an atom bomb in 1949. When they tested the much more powerful hydrogen bomb in 1953, only a year after the Americans, the post-war arms race began. Both sides spent huge sums developing effective ways of targeting the other. Fast, high-flying bombers were built but could be shot down. By contrast, long distance rockets – intercontinental ballistic missiles – could hit targets on the other side of the world with little risk of interception.

To counter this, early warning systems were developed. Advanced radar stations in the Arctic and in friendly countries were built to flash back news of a missile attack in seconds – giving enough time to launch a counter-attack before the hostile missiles exploded over their targets. Nuclear-powered submarines, such as America's Polaris and Trident submarines, were also built as weapons of retaliation. They could lie submerged and undetected off the coasts of Siberia and North America, equipped with short-range missiles and nuclear warheads targeted at the enemy.

Both sides knew that by launching a missile attack, they would almost certainly destroy their own country as well. Politicians and generals used this knowledge to justify the existence of nuclear weapons as a way of deterring the enemy (Source **B**).

### Campaigning for nuclear disarmament

Ordinary people felt far less secure. The vast increase in the numbers of missiles on both sides caused grave concern throughout the world. Rearmament immediately before 1914 and 1939 had been one of the causes of both world wars. Mistaken confidence on either side – or simply a mistake in identifying a missile attack – could lead to the destruction of the world. CND – the Campaign for Nuclear Disarmament – led protests against nuclear weapons in Britain (page 191). Other groups did the same abroad (Source **C**).

**Source A** Atom bomb explosion

**Source B** An American viewpoint in 1989

West Berlin in 1948 and 1961. Cuba in 1962. Those episodes, scary as they were at the time, should be strangely reassuring. They prove that deterrence works. The very existence of nuclear weapons is like gravity, pulling the superpowers back from the brink during moments of political and military confrontation.

Strobe Talbott in *Time* magazine, 1989. Quoted in *The Time Magazine Compact Almanac CD-ROM*, 1991

**Source C** German anti-nuclear demonstration. The slogan on the poster can be translated as reading: 'The DEAD-certain way to eternal PEACE'. The SS20 was the Soviet equivalent of the American Cruise and Pershing short-range missiles.

**Source D** Arms limitation talks in 1979. Soviet President Leonid Brezhnev (right) shakes hands with US President Jimmy Carter (left)

## Arms limitation talks

By 1958, both superpowers had begun to see that some form of arms control was needed. A half-hearted start was made by ending nuclear tests but these were renewed when East–West relations deteriorated in 1960–1 (page 155). The tension arising from the Cuban Missiles Crisis (page 156) provided the breakthrough. A telephone hotline was installed directly linking the Soviet and American presidents and negotiations began which led to the Test Ban Treaty in 1963 – prohibiting nuclear tests in the atmosphere and under water. Only nuclear tests deep underground were permitted. Five years later, the USSR, USA and UK signed the 1968 Non-Proliferation Treaty to try to stop the spread of atomic weapons to other countries. In 1972, the Soviet Union and the United States signed the Strategic Arms Limitation Treaty (SALT 1) limiting the number of missiles to be held by both sides. A similar treaty – SALT 2 – was signed in 1978 but later suspended by the Americans when the Russians invaded Afghanistan in 1979 (page 172).

## Detente and Ostpolitik

The SALT talks had been made possible because both sides followed a policy of peaceful co-existence. There were frequent summit meetings. US President Nixon visited Moscow in 1972 and 1974 while Soviet President Brezhnev visited Washington in 1973. Denis Healey, Labour Party foreign affairs spokesman, later called it 'a golden age of cooperation between Washington and Moscow'. At the same time, the Americans and Chinese began to bury their differences. Nixon visited Beijing in 1972 to meet Mao Zedong and other Chinese leaders.

Brezhnev's foreign policy was very similar to Khruschev's. He sought detente – a relaxation of the tension between East and West. Both superpowers acknowledged that the other had areas of special interest. The United States claimed a special relationship with Western Europe, the Pacific and North and South America. For his part, Brezhnev was not prepared to see the USSR lose control over Eastern Europe or abandon its interests in the countries which bordered the Soviet Union. This was later called the Brezhnev Doctrine and helps to explain why Brezhnev intervened in Czechoslovakia in 1968 (page 166) and in Afghanistan in 1979 (page 172). Other Western leaders, too, played a part in bringing about detente. The German Social Democrat leader, Willy Brandt, helped to improve relations with East Germany – a policy called *Ostpolitik* ('Eastern Policy').

## Helsinki Human Rights

For much of the 1970s, it looked as if detente could really work and that the superpowers might soon be able to reduce their stocks of arms. Nonetheless, Western leaders were concerned about the lack of basic human rights behind the Iron Curtain. An international conference at Helsinki in 1975, attended by leaders from 35 countries, including the Soviet Union, called on participating nations to respect human rights, such as free speech. But when a group of Soviet dissidents formed the Helsinki Human Rights Group, to monitor Soviet progress on these issues, they were imprisoned by the Russians. This caused a fresh wave of bad feeling between East and West.

*Questions*

1 Draw a time line to show the main developments in the Arms Race between 1945 and 1979.

2 Write a paragraph in your own words using and explaining the following words or phrases: peaceful co-existence; *detente*, *ostpolitik*, arms control, arms limitation talks.

3 Look at Sources **B** and **C**. How do they differ in their assessment of the part nuclear weapons can play in reducing the likelihood of war? What evidence is there that having nuclear weapons acted as a deterrent?

# Czechoslovakia 1968

▶ **Why did the Warsaw Pact countries intervene in Czechoslovakia in 1968 and what were the short- and long-term effects of this action?**

## The Prague Spring

Detente was put to the test in 1968. Alexander Dubcek, newly-appointed Czech leader, had introduced a number of important reforms, including free speech, the abolition of press censorship and greater political freedom. The Czechs called it 'socialism with a human face'. The powers of the secret police were reduced. Travel restrictions were removed. Corruption and bureaucratic delays were exposed on radio and television and in the press. Fresh contact was made with the West, such as trade with West Germany. Nonetheless, the government remained Communist.

The Czechs enjoyed the 'Prague Spring', as it was called, but the growth of freedom in Czechoslovakia and the contacts with the West alarmed the Russians and the leaders of the other Warsaw Pact countries. Over a thousand tanks and 75,000 soldiers were moved to the Czech frontiers. The Warsaw Pact leaders went to a conference in Bratislava (in Slovakia) at the end of July to reason with Dubcek (Source **B**). He insisted on going ahead but reassured them that Czechoslovakia would remain within the Warsaw Pact.

**Source A** Wenceslas Square, Prague. This huge open space in the city centre can hold half a million people. It became a symbol of national resistance in 1968 when demonstrators tried to stop the advance of Russian tanks here.

At first, it looked as if Brezhnev had been convinced. Western politicians were impressed. Detente seemed to be working after all. But Brezhnev was afraid Czechoslovakia might leave the Warsaw Pact after all. What would happen then? Suppose NATO moved in? This would split the Eastern bloc in two and advance NATO's frontier 700 km further to the east so that it bordered the Soviet Union itself.

## The Soviet invasion

On 20–1 August 1968, hundreds of thousands of Soviet troops, backed by units from Bulgaria, East Germany, Hungary and Poland, entered Czechoslovakia and removed Dubcek from office. Soviet and Czech accounts of the reasons for the invasion disagreed with each other (Sources **C** and **D**).

**Source B** Warsaw Pact leaders in Bratislava in 1968. They included: Dubcek (Czechoslovakia – second from right), Kadar (Hungary – extreme left), Zhivkov (Bulgaria – fourth from left), Gomulka (Poland – fourth from right) and Ulbricht (East Germany – third from right)

**Source C**  Czech radio broadcast, 21 August 1968

Yesterday troops of the Soviet Union crossed the frontiers of the Czechoslovak Socialist Republic. This happened without the knowledge of the President of the Republic, the Chairman of the National Assembly, the Premier, or the First Secretary of the Czechoslovak Communist Party Central Committee.

Quoted in *The New York Times*, 21 August, 1968

**Source D**  Soviet press agency statement, 21 August 1968

Tass is authorised to state that Party and Government leaders of the Czechoslovak Socialist Republic have asked the Soviet Union and other allied states to render the fraternal Czechoslovak people urgent assistance, including assistance with armed forces.

Quoted in *The New York Times*, 21 August, 1968

Czechs threw petrol bombs at the Soviet tanks as they rumbled through the streets of Prague. Buildings were set on fire. Protesting crowds massed in Wenceslas Square. Students sat down in the road in front of the Russian tanks, climbed on to them to argue with the Russian drivers, or stood in the way and stared down the barrel of a Soviet gun. 'We don't want to live on our knees,' they shouted. 'We want to know the whole truth'. But there was no armed resistance by the Czech army and less than a hundred people were killed.

The Russians justified the invasion as conforming to the Brezhnev Doctrine – the right to prevent any member leaving the Warsaw Pact. Afterwards there were none of the brutal reprisals seen in 1956 after the Hungarian uprising. But censorship of the media was reimposed and political activities unfavourable to

**Source E**  Czechs demonstrate in Prague against the Soviet invasion in 1968

**Source F**  Square in Prague named after Jan Palach. Jan Palach, a student, set fire to himself in Wenceslas Square in January 1969 to protest against the Soviet invasion. After he died, Czech students replaced an official sign – Red Army Square – commemorating the invasion with one renaming it Jan Palach Square. Although this was soon pulled down by the authorities, the name lived on and became a permanent fixture after 1989 (page 180).

the ruling Communist Party were banned. Dubcek was later released but most of his reforms were abandoned.

## Effects

Brezhnev's action was successful in tightening Communist Party control of the country but the invasion provoked a storm of criticism and as much was lost as was gained.

- President Ceaucescu of Romania refused to send troops to join the invading Warsaw Pact forces and afterwards took an independent line against Moscow.

- Albania did likewise and left the Warsaw Pact for good.

- China criticised the invasion – not because Mao Zedong approved of Dubcek's reforms but because the Soviet Union used force to bring a fellow communist state to heel. What the Soviet Union could do to Czechoslovakia might one day be done to communist China as well.

- Western nations and many Third World countries were appalled. The Czech invasion slowed down the process of detente although it did not bring it to a halt.

1 Look at Source **B**. Use Source **D** on page 165 to locate Brezhnev.

2 Write a letter from Prague dated 23 August 1968 explaining to a friend what has happened.

3 Examine Sources **C** and **D**. In what respect do they contradict each other? Which do you believe to be the correct version of events? Give your reasons.

4 Why did the Warsaw Pact countries invade Czechoslovakia? What were they afraid of? Was it a successful intervention?

5 Compare events in Czechoslovakia in 1968 with those in Hungary in 1956 (page 154). What were the similarities? How do you account for the differences?

*Questions*

## The Vietnam War

**How and why was America involved in the civil war in Vietnam and what were the consequences of her involvement?**

### The domino theory

As you can see from the map (Source **C**), French Indo-China became a battleground between Communist and non-Communist forces after France was forced to withdraw from her former colony of French Indo-China. US advisers, arms and equipment – and later troops – were sent to help the South Vietnamese to the approval of the American press (Source **A**).

**Source A**   Article in *Time* magazine, 24 November 1961

> If the USA cannot or will not save South Vietnam from the Communist assault, no Asian nation can ever again feel safe in putting its faith in the US – and the fall of all of Southeast Asia would only be a matter of time.

Although the Viet Cong were heavily outnumbered and outgunned by US armed forces, they had the advantage of knowing the jungle (Source **B**). This is why they fought as guerrillas, preferring to attack in small groups against isolated targets rather than fight a full scale battle they were sure to lose.

**Source B**   Viet Cong guerrillas – by an American journalist in *Time* magazine, 1961

> Every night furtive little bands of communist guerrillas, dressed in black peasant pyjamas or faded khakis, splash through the marshes of the Mekong Delta or dart silently along jungle paths of South Vietnam, pursuing their intent, murderous missions.

Although the Americans claimed to be defending the free world, the people of South Vietnam were not free to choose their leader. The right-wing dictator Ngo Dinh Diem refused to agree to popular elections (Sources **C** and **D**).

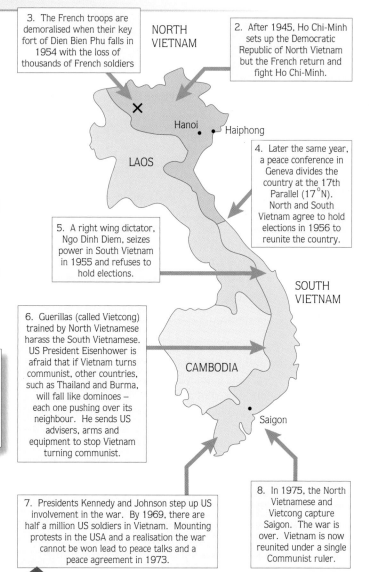

1. French Indo-China occupied by Japanese troops in July 1941 without meeting resistance from neutral France. But a Communist politician from Vietnam, Ho Chi-Minh, leads guerilas against the Japanese.

2. After 1945, Ho Chi-Minh sets up the Democratic Republic of North Vietnam but the French return and fight Ho Chi-Minh.

3. The French troops are demoralised when their key fort of Dien Bien Phu falls in 1954 with the loss of thousands of French soldiers

4. Later the same year, a peace conference in Geneva divides the country at the 17th Parallel (17°N). North and South Vietnam agree to hold elections in 1956 to reunite the country.

5. A right wing dictator, Ngo Dinh Diem, seizes power in South Vietnam in 1955 and refuses to hold elections.

6. Guerillas (called Vietcong) trained by North Vietnamese harass the South Vietnamese. US President Eisenhower is afraid that if Vietnam turns communist, other countries, such as Thailand and Burma, will fall like dominoes – each one pushing over its neighbour. He sends US advisers, arms and equipment to stop Vietnam turning communist.

7. Presidents Kennedy and Johnson step up US involvement in the war. By 1969, there are half a million US soldiers in Vietnam. Mounting protests in the USA and a realisation the war cannot be won lead to peace talks and a peace agreement in 1973.

8. In 1975, the North Vietnamese and Vietcong capture Saigon. The war is over. Vietnam is now reunited under a single Communist ruler.

**Source C**   Map of the Vietnam War

**Source D**   American comment in *Time* magazine, 19 March 1956

> South Vietnam rightly argues that no free election could possibly be allowed in the more populous Communist north, and a rigged one would give the communists a chance to grab the whole country.

Diem was himself killed in a coup in 1963 and succeeded by a hard-line army general called Nguyen Van Thieu.

**Source E** Ho Chi-Minh, the part-Nationalist and part-Communist leader of North Vietnam

## The war escalates

When Lyndon B. Johnson became President of the United States in 1963, he used a greatly exaggerated incident – North Vietnamese torpedo boats firing at a US destroyer in the Gulf of Tongking – to get the approval of Congress 'to take all necessary steps to repel the aggressor'. He widened the conflict, using American command of the air to try to bomb the North Vietnamese cities of Hanoi and Haiphong 'into submission'. But the air raids – like those on London in 1940–1 – only strengthened the determination of the North Vietnamese to resist, despite the horrific damage inflicted on their economy and on their people.

Helicopter gunships attacked Viet Cong positions in the jungle but the Americans often had difficulty locating the enemy since the Viet Cong guerrillas took shelter in villages where the people were sympathetic to their cause. The frustration of the US troops sometimes exploded, as at My Lai in March 1968, when over a hundred Vietnamese men, women and children were shot dead and their homes, farms and animals destroyed. The news horrified people around the world when some of those involved blurted out the truth. An army photographer said he saw a soldier with an automatic rifle shoot 'two small children, maybe four or five years old'. The officer in charge was court-martialled but claimed he had only been obeying orders.

Other tactics used by US forces in Vietnam were much criticised, such as using napalm – jellied petrol – which stuck to its victims, causing horrific burns. A weed killer called Agent Orange was sprayed from the air – as a defoliant – to strip away leaves and undergrowth, leaving the Viet Cong guerrillas without protective cover. Unfortunately, it contained a highly toxic chemical called dioxin which not only poisoned the environment but contaminated US troops as well, later causing cancer and serious skin complaints.

## Protests against the war

In 1968, the Viet Cong launched a major new campaign – the Tet Offensive. As the fighting intensified, hundreds of dead American soldiers were sent back to America each month, many of them conscripts. The war seemed pointless and led to riots and demonstrations. Students taunted Johnson with slogans (Source **F**). Many young men burned or tore up the draft papers ordering them to join the armed forces.

**Source F** Student slogans against the Vietam War

Hey! Hey! LBJ! How many kids did you kill today?
We don't want your war
Draft beer, not boys
Dump Johnson
Eighteen Today, Dead Tomorrow

Opposition to the war was so bitter, it culminated in tragedy when four students, two of them women, were shot dead in an anti-Vietnam demonstration at Kent State University in Ohio in May 1970 (Source **G**). Many others were wounded.

**Source G** News report in *Time* magazine, 18 May 1970

Horrified students flung themselves to the ground, ran for cover behind buildings and parked cars, or just stood stunned. Then screams broke out. 'My God, they're killing us!' one girl cried. They were.

1 Which US President first got the USA involved in Vietnam? What was his main reason for doing so? Write a short account explaining why American soldiers were fighting in Vietnam.

2 Use the sources to explain how the war in Vietnam affected civilians: **a)** in Vietnam, **b)** in the United States.

3 **a)** Design a poster accusing US forces in Vietnam of war crimes. **b)** Write a short press release for the US Army justifying the use of chemical weapons in Vietnam.

4 To what extent is Source **D** a fair or biased comment on the elections which both sides agreed to hold in 1956?

Questions

## Different perceptions of the war

On 27 June 1993, Channel 4 televised a programme in which Julian Pettifer, a former BBC war correspondent, went back to Vietnam to make a reassessment of the war 25 years on. He revealed that during the war, the Viet Cong working well inside South Vietnam had dug a huge network of tunnels, 250 km long, equipped with kitchens, sleeping accommodation and hospitals (Source **I**).

**Source I**   Julian Pettifer on Channel 4, 27 June 1993

The American story was that this was an example of the success of their bombing and shelling campaign. They told me that it showed that the Viet Cong were so demoralised that they were having to take refuge underground. Well I must confess that I bought that version of the story. It was only later when it was discovered how enormous the complex was and how skilfully the Viet Cong used them and how the tunnels actually extended under the American base camp itself, that I started to think for myself and I realised that this was not a sign of how demoralised the Viet Cong had become but how determined they were.

**Source H**   Images of the war in Vietnam were daily screened on television sets in the late 1960s and early 1970s. Many Europeans saw it as a war between Goliath – the USA, with a huge army of unwilling conscripts and sophisticated weapons – and David – Vietnamese peasants fighting a guerrilla war to take control of their homeland against a corrupt, American-backed government. To many Americans, however, it was simply right against wrong, freedom against enslavement, the defenders of the free world preventing the spread of communism in South-East Asia.

## Bringing an end to the war

The mounting opposition to the war, softened up the American government. Lyndon Johnson, target of most of the criticism, told his 'fellow Americans' he would not stand again for US President. At the same time, he said he was curtailing the air raids on North Vietnam to enable peace talks to begin. These made only slow progress. In 1970, the new US President – Richard Nixon – escalated the war still further, hoping to force the North Vietnamese into making serious concessions. North Vietnam was bombed once more and US forces attacked Laos and Cambodia which were being used to send supplies and reinforcements to the Viet Cong. The position in the region was further complicated by a civil war in Cambodia between the communist Khmer Rouge guerrillas backed by North Vietnam and the American-backed right-wing government of Lon Nol.

Peace talks held in Paris eventually led to an agreement negotiated by Nixon's Secretary of State, Dr Henry Kissinger, and by the North Vietnamese spokesman, Le Duc Tho. Both were awarded the Nobel Peace Prize in 1973 when a cease-fire was arranged in South Vietnam. By this time, most of the American troops had already gone. Two years later, the North Vietnamese and Viet Cong armies seized Saigon and occupied the rest of South Vietnam without intervention from the US Government. At the same time the Cambodian capital city of Phnom-Penh fell to the Khmer Rouge.

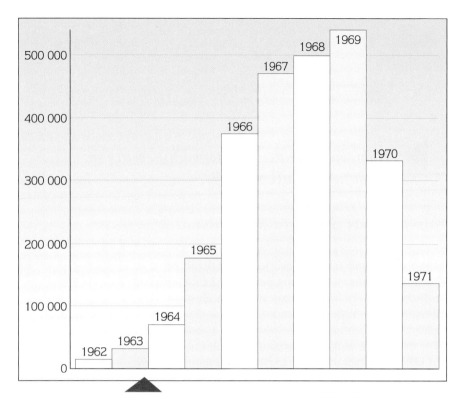

**Source J**  US servicemen in Vietnam 1962–71

## Results of the war

- The loss of the major French colony of Indo-China encouraged other nationalist groups in the French empire to seek independence.

- The Americans were accused of colonialism: supporting an unpopular dictator in order to keep South Vietnam in the pro-Western half of the world.

- The American withdrawal of forces from Vietnam was seen as a defeat.

- Thailand, Burma, Malaysia and other South-East Asian states did not fall to the Communists.

- War broke out later between communist Vietnam and communist Cambodia (later renamed Kampuchea) and later still between communist China and communist Vietnam.

- Nearly 57,000 US soldiers were killed in a war which cost billions of dollars and did untold damage to American prestige and influence throughout the world.

- Hundreds of thousands of American servicemen were permanently scarred. Many suffered recurrent nightmares, recalling the horrors they had seen, suffered or inflicted on the enemy. Many became addicted to drugs during the conflict. Others took to a life of violent crime or failed to adjust to civilian life after the war.

- The war also damaged Vietnam itself: leaving behind thousands of orphans, maimed civilians and former soldiers; scarring the countryside and leaving a badly-damaged environment pitted with unexploded bombs, shells, bullets and mines. Half the country's forests were destroyed as well as much of its farmland.

- The once-prosperous South Vietnamese economy was devastated by the war. Thousands of Vietnamese boat people later tried to flee to the West to escape the misery at home. Many drowned, some were attacked by pirates, the lucky ones survived and were accepted as refugees in the West.

---

**1** Look at Source **J**. In which year was American involvement in Vietnam at its peak? Which US President escalated the war most? Was it Kennedy (1961–3), Johnson (1963–9) or Nixon (1969–74)?

**2** How effective was Eisenhower's Domino Theory (Source **C** on page 168) as a forecast of what would happen in Vietnam if the US forces withdrew?

**3** What were the consequences of American involvement in Vietnam? What did the United States achieve? What did it lose?

**4** Study Source **I**. How and why did Julian Pettifer's interpretation of the Viet Cong tunnels in 1993 differ from the one he was given by the US Army in 1968?

# Soviet intervention in Afghanistan

▶ **How was detente threatened by events in Afghanistan after 1979?**

## Russia sends troops to Afghanistan

Detente came to a sudden halt on Christmas Eve 1979. Communists had seized power in Afghanistan in Central Asia but were having difficulty controlling the country's fiercely independent Muslim tribesmen. Brezhnev sent in Russian troops 'to render urgent political, moral, military and economic assistance'. Shortly after seizing the airport in Kabul, the KGB shot President Hafizullah Amin and installed a communist hard-liner, Babrak Karmal, as his successor.

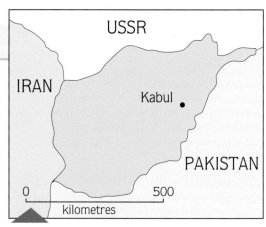

**Source A**  Afghanistan

No one can say what really persuaded the Russians to react as they did. They may have been worried that the fundamentalist Islamic governments of Pakistan and Iran – both anti-communist – would unduly influence their fellow Muslims in Afghanistan and the neighbouring Muslim republics of the Soviet Union, such as Uzbekistan.

## Effects of the Soviet intervention

Relations between East and West were so bad in the period immediately following the Soviet invasion, that people called it the 'Second Cold War' and feared the consequences for detente and the talks aimed at limiting the spread of nuclear weapons (Source **E**).

US President Carter called for a boycott of the 1980 Moscow Olympics and imposed a ban on American grain sales to the Soviet Union. He was worried that the Soviet invasion might lead to Soviet expansion in Central Asia and pose a threat to Middle East oil. Carter made it clear he wouldn't hesitate to send US troops to the region if it was in American interests to do so. In fact, there was little he could do (Source **F**).

**Source B**
Cartoon in the *Daily Telegraph*, 3 January 1980

THE HAMMER & CRESCENT

The rebel tribesmen, hopelessly outgunned, retreated into the mountains and waged an effective guerrilla war which eventually tied down over 100,000 Russian soldiers. To many outside observers, it began to look like a 'Russian Vietnam' (Source **C**). A senior American officer said 'I think it's great. It tickles me to death.' The tribesmen, however, rarely acted together and sometimes fought among themselves.

**Source C**  David Halberstam quoted in *Time* magazine

▼

The Soviets are learning the big Vietnam lesson, that it is easier to go into those countries than it is to get out. They will find out, just as the US did, how amazingly easy it is for a little country to swallow a military machine.

**Source D**  Mujahedeen fighters in Afghanistan

▼

**Source E**   By Denis Healey, leading Labour Foreign Affairs spokesman in the 1980s

When the eighties began, the prospects for world peace seemed worse than at any time since 1945. Brezhnev's invasion of Afghanistan had already led President Carter to break off negotiations with the Soviet Union: he withdrew the SALT II treaty from the Senate, where it was certain to be rejected, and started a massive rearmament programme.

Extract from *The Time of My Life* by Denis Healey, Michael Joseph, 1989

**Source F**   Richard Helms, US diplomat, quoted in *Time* magazine, 7 January 1980

It's no gamble at all. What are we going to do about it? We have no forces there, no bases. What can we do for the time being but remonstrate?

## Star Wars

One unforeseen outcome, however, came about when Carter was succeeded by the right-wing Republican, Ronald Reagan. Reagan called the Soviet Union the 'Evil Empire' and said the USA was developing a Strategic Defence Initiative (SDI) – 'Star Wars' – which would use satellites orbiting the Earth to detect and shoot down hostile missiles targeted at America. The prospect appalled many Western leaders, as well as the Soviets, since it seemed to make the risk of nuclear war more, not less, likely. Denis Healey explained why (Source **G**).

**Source G**   By Denis Healey in *The Time of my Life*

There was a real danger that if Washington ever looked like deploying an effective strategic defence system, Moscow would feel it had no alternative but to get its blow in first, by attacking America's missile bases while they could still do so.

In the end, the Red Army had its work cut out maintaining a grip on Afghanistan. Western aid, channelled through Pakistan, helped the tribesmen to resist. After ten years of hardship and heavy losses – and a substantial thaw in East-West relations (Chapter 14) – the Red Army finally pulled out of Afghanistan on 15 February 1989.

## Afghanistan and Vietnam – a comparison

- Both the USA and the USSR justified their interventions claiming they had been invited in to help the government.
- Afghan and Viet Cong fighters showed little fear of the superpowers despite their superior weapons.
- It was as easy for the Afghan rebels to hide in the mountains as it was for the Viet Cong to take refuge in the jungle.
- The Soviet Union had a common frontier with Afghanistan. Vietnam was thousands of kilometres from the US mainland.
- Many of the Muslim peoples of the Soviet republics, such as Turkmenistan and Uzbekistan, shared the same religion, traditions and heritage as the rebels.
- The Afghan rebels came from different tribal groups, often in dispute with each other. They needed a Ho Chi Minh to help them unite and to lead them to victory.
- Television and press coverage of the war was subject to censorship in the USSR.
- The cost of the war in Afghanistan was as big a drain on the Soviet economy as Vietnam was for the USA.
- Neither the USSR in Afghanistan, nor the USA in Vietnam, could claim victory. Some 16,000 Russian soldiers and 57,000 US servicemen were killed for very little gain. In addition, 1.7 million Vietnamese and over a million Afghans also died and 5 million Afghans fled to Iran and Pakistan to escape the fighting.

*Questions*

1   Look at Source **D**. What advantage did the Afghan rebels have over the Russians?

2   Explain the cartoon (Source **B**).

3   In your own words, what were the consequences of the Soviet intervention in Afghanistan?

4   How similar was Afghanistan to Vietnam? Draw a chart divided like this and write in the points of comparison you think were most significant:

|  | USA in Vietnam | Soviet Union in Afghanistan |
|---|---|---|
| Similarities |  |  |
| Differences |  |  |

5   How had relations between the United States and the Soviet Union changed in 1963–85 compared with 1945–62 (Chapter 12)? Write a short account explaining which elements of these changes could be counted as successes and which as failures.

# 14 Collapse of the Soviet empire: 1985–91

## Solidarity in Poland

▶ **What was the significance of 'Solidarity' in Poland?**

**Source A** Solidarity demonstration in Krakow in June 1983 ▶

## Poland before 1980

Poland with 35 million people was easily the largest of the Iron Curtain countries of eastern Europe. It was also different from the others, not least because many of its people were devout Roman Catholics. In 1956 Khruschev had allowed the Poles to select a liberal communist, Wladyslaw Gomulka (Source **B** on page 166), as leader. He introduced many reforms, including measures which kept most of the land in private hands instead of in collective farms, as in Russia. But Gomulka couldn't stop food prices rising and, after a series of food riots, he resigned in 1970. His successors had little better luck and by the late 1970s there was considerable unrest in Poland.

## Lech Walesa

In 1980 a series of strikes in the Lenin Shipyards in the Polish port of Gdansk (formerly Danzig) led to the formation of a new and independent trade union, which the Polish workers called *Solidarnosícú* (Solidarity). This was an astonishing departure for a communist country, since strikes were usually forbidden. Solidarity, led by a shipyard worker called Lech Walesa, caught the imagination of the Polish people and had the support of the Catholic Church. Strikes spread to many other industries – from coal mines to steel works. There could be no doubting the popular support the movement received.

At first the Polish Government made concessions (including the right to form trade unions). It introduced reforms under a new communist leader Stanislaw Kania. But when these failed

**Source B** General Jaruzelski with Lech Walesa

to stem the growth of Solidarity and the movement to greater freedom, the Polish Communist Party called for sterner measures to deal with the crisis. The Soviet Government may well have had a hand in persuading them to replace Kania with another leader – General Jaruzelski.

## Crackdown

In 1981 the more extreme Solidarity members demanded reforms which called into being the very existence of the Communist Party in Poland. Soviet army manoeuvres near the Polish border worried Western leaders, who thought it might be a prelude to a Soviet invasion of Poland. The West warned Brezhnev that any such move would harm East–West relations, despite Brezhnev's denial that any such move was contemplated.

General Jaruzelski, who was much more a Polish Nationalist than a hard-line communist, was convinced that Poland was under real and imminent threat – from Solidarity threatening revolution – and from Brezhnev if they did. Brezhnev issued an ultimatum: sort out the situation at once or face the possibility of invasion and having Poland's essential raw materials (including oil) cut off. Jaruzelski felt he had no alternative (Source **C**).

**Source C**   General Jaruzelski interviewed by a Western writer

▼

We had to convince our allies that we would not undermine the Warsaw Pact or allow the state to be undermined.

Quoted in *The War That Never Was: The Fall of the Soviet Empire 1985-91* by David Pryce-Jones, Weidenfeld and Nicolson, 1995

Jaruzelski banned Solidarity, ordered the arrest and detention of Lech Walesa and other leaders and declared a national state of emergency. He gave his reasons to the Poles (Source **D**).

**Source D**   General Jaruzelski, December 1981

▼

Our country is on the edge of the abyss. Achievements of many generations, raised from the ashes, are collapsing into ruins. State structures no longer function. New blows are struck each day at our flickering economy.

The secret police arrested nearly 7000 dissidents and killed a number of people including a Catholic priest called Father Jerzy Popieluszko. Most of the internees were later released and the laws relaxed once the new Government felt they had the situation under control. However, the arrests and the ban hit Solidarity hard and forced it into obscurity. For the moment, Jaruzelski and his communist government had won.

Since the suppression of Solidarity in Poland coincided with the Soviet invasion of Afghanistan (page 172), the old atmosphere of mutual distrust and suspicion which had characterised the Cold War returned. When the NATO governments of Western Europe agreed to deploy the American Cruise and Pershing Missiles in 1983, the Russians retaliated by deploying their own medium range missiles in Czechoslovakia and other Warsaw Pact countries.

Six years later, the situation had changed. Brezhnev died in 1982 and was followed by two hard-line successors, Yuri Andropov (who died in 1984) and Konstantin Chernenko (who died in 1985). The new Russian leader in 1985 was Mikhail Gorbachev (page 176), a reformer with ideas much more in keeping with those of Lech Walesa than Jaruzelski and his colleagues. Soon after Gorbachev visited Warsaw in 1988, Jaruzelski initiated a series of Round Table talks with Solidarity which ended in an agreement to lift the ban on the union, allow opposition political parties to be formed and go ahead with free elections. As a result, a non-communist member of Solidarity, Tadeusz Mazowiecki, became Prime Minister of Poland in August 1989, the first non-communist to lead an Iron Curtain country. Just over a year later, Lech Walesa was elected President of Poland by a huge majority.

1   In what ways did Poland differ from the Soviet Union and the other Iron Curtain countries?

2   How and why did General Jaruzelski clamp down on Solidarity in 1981?

3   Write a television address for General Jaruzelski telling the Polish people the real reasons why Solidarity was banned.

4   Use Sources **C** and **D** to explain why the growing influence of Solidarity was seen as a threat to the Soviet Union.

5   Which events do you think Denis Healey must have had in mind when he said: 'When the eighties began, the prospects for world peace seemed worse than at any time since 1945' (Source **E** on page 173). Look back at the period 1945–85. Do you agree with this interpretation?

*Questions*

## Glasnost and Perestroika

> ### How did Gorbachev change the Soviet Union?
> ### How and why did communism collapse in Eastern Europe?

### Mikhail Gorbachev

In 1985, Mikhail Gorbachev was nominated to the post of Secretary General of the Soviet Communist Party by the veteran hard-liner, Andrei Gromyko, who told his colleagues: 'This man has a nice smile but iron teeth.' Gorbachev immediately set out to change the course of Soviet history. He based his plans on *glasnost* (greater openness and toleration of criticism) and *perestroika* (reconstruction, reorganisation and reform).

When Gorbachev became Soviet President in October 1988, he began moves to bring in a new constitution with increased powers for the President and free elections to the Congress of People's Deputies. During this period, he negotiated massive cuts in defence spending with US Presidents Reagan and Bush and attempted to revitalise the Soviet economy – putting more emphasis on providing the people with the food and consumer goods they needed. Increasingly, as you will see on pages 182–5, he faced opposition from hard-liners who thought he was going too far, too fast.

**Source A**  By Denis Healey, leading Labour Foreign Affairs spokesman in the 1980s

In just two years Gorbachev transformed President Reagan and Prime Minister Thatcher from fanatical anti-Soviet crusaders into champions of detente and disarmament.

Extract from *The Time of My Life* by Denis Healey, Michael Joseph, 1989

### Glasnost and perestroika in Eastern Europe

As you can see from the chart opposite, communism collapsed in the Iron Curtain countries of Eastern Europe in 1989. There were several reasons for this. Visits by Gorbachev were greeted with enthusiasm by the people but not by Party leaders. 'People power' – massive, uncontrollable crowds – unsettled Iron Curtain leaders used to mass obedience. Liberals in the Communist Party seeking glasnost and perestroika at home added their weight to the movement for reform.

The key event took place in Hungary in September

### MIKHAIL GORBACHEV (1931–present)

Mikhail Gorbachev was born in Privolnoye, a small farming village in southern Russia, on 2 March 1931. In 1950, he went to study at the Moscow State University where he met Raisa Maximovna Titorenko, a philosophy student, who became his wife in 1954. The young Gorbachev worked for the Communist Party and by the late 1970s had become an important official in his home area, specialising in agriculture. In 1980, he became by far the youngest member of the Politburo (the Soviet Cabinet) at the age of 49. When Brezhnev died in 1982, he had already been earmarked as a future Soviet leader – a position he achieved in 1985.

Gorbachev showed extraordinary skill in getting the Western leaders behind him in his search for world peace (Source **A**). At a summit meeting in November 1985, he and Reagan agreed to work together to reduce their stocks of nuclear weapons. Gorbachev claimed 'the world had become a safer place'. A year later a similar summit ended in stalemate when Gorbachev unsuccessfully tried to get Reagan to drop his 'Star Wars' defence system. In December 1987, they signed an anti-missile treaty together getting rid of medium-range missiles. Finally, on 3 December 1989, Gorbachev and Bush told waiting journalists in Malta that the Cold War was over. By 1991, the ill-advised 'Star Wars' project itself was dead.

when barriers preventing people crossing the frontier into Austria were opened. Thousands of East Germans 'on holiday' in Hungary crossed over to the West. It was followed two months later by the dismantling of the Berlin Wall. The Iron Curtain had fallen, at last.

**Source B**
Fall of a hero – Lenin's head on the ground in East Berlin

# Overview Chart: 1989 The Year of Revolutions

After visits by Mikhail Gorbachev in 1987 and 1988, people in Eastern Europe want *Glasnost* and *Perestroika* in their own countries. Extensive unrest. Hungarian hard-liner, Janos Kadar (Source **B** on page 166), falls in May 1988. Strikes in Poland and Hungary. Demonstrations in Czechoslovakia.

| 1989 | POLAND | HUNGARY | EAST GERMANY | CZECHOSLOVAKIA | BULGARIA | ROMANIA |
|---|---|---|---|---|---|---|
| JANUARY | Crisis talks between Solidarity and the communist Government | Parliament passes laws permitting opposition parties to be formed. | | 19th: Police break up protesters seeking Gorbachev reforms. | | |
| FEBRUARY | | | | | Free trade union like Solidarity formed. | |
| MARCH | . | 15th: Demonstrations for freedom. | | | | |
| APRIL | 17th: Ban lifted on Solidarity; elections to be held in June. | | | | | |
| MAY | | | | 1st: May Day rally broken up by police. | | |
| JUNE | 6th: Solidarity wins most seats in election. | 16th: Remains of Imre Nagy (page 154) given State Funeral. | | | | |
| AUGUST | 24th: Non-communist, Tadeusz Mazowiecki, is made Prime Minister. | | Thousands travel to Hungary hoping to flee to the West. | | | |
| SEPTEMBER | | Barbed wire on Austrian border removed; used by thousands of Germans to flee to the West; free elections agreed. | 4th: Massive protest demonstration broken up by police in Leipzig. | | Demonstrations for freedom. | |
| OCTOBER | | Communist Party changes its name to Social Democrats. 23rd: Non-communist republic comes into being. | Huge protest meetings after Gorbachev visit; Erich Honecker. orders use of force but Egon Krenz refuses. 18th: Krenz takes over from Honecker. | | | |
| NOVEMBER | | | 10th: Hated Berlin Wall comes down on orders of Egon Krenz. | 17th: Police break up demonstration in Prague. Rumour of a dead student sparks off massive protests. 24th: Milos Jakes and other Party officials resign but Communists still rule country. 27th: General strike brings country to a standstill. | 10th: Communist hard-liner, Todor Zhivkov (Source B on page 166) forced out of office. 18th: Massive demonstrations in the capital Sofia by protesters wanting free elections and the sacking of Communist hard-liners. | |
| DECEMBER | | 3rd: Communist Party leadership resigns; free elections to be held next May. | | 10th: Non-communists in the majority in new government. 29th: Vaclav Havel, a former dissident, elected President. | 16th: Reforms approved – including free elections and formation of opposition parties. | 17th: Riots in Timisoara. Ceaucescu orders use of force. Many killed. Riots spread to Bucharest. Government falls. 25th: Ceaucescu and wife Elena executed. |

**Questions**

**1** In which of the East European countries did communism fall first and in which did it fall last?

**2** How did glasnost and perestroika bring down the Iron Curtain and end the Cold War?

**3** What part did Gorbachev play in the collapse of communism in Eastern Europe?

## German reunification

▶ **How and why was Germany reunified in 1990 and what effect did this have?**

**Source A** Demonstrators pack the Alexander Platz in East Berlin in November 1989. 'People-power' played an all-important part in giving East Germans their freedom (see Chart on page 177)

So long as the Iron Curtain remained intact, the East German economy did well. Its people had a higher than average standard of living compared with other Iron Curtain countries. But the people were German by tradition, birth and language. Contact with relatives in the West made it only too clear what they were

**Source B** Pulling down the Berlin Wall

missing in the East, such as freedom to travel, choose a job or find a place in which to live.

Until 1989, this was only a dream – especially when the building of the Berlin Wall in 1961 blocked the only escape route to the West. A wide strip of no-man's land with an electric fence, ferocious dogs and armed soldiers deterred all but the foolhardy from trying to cross the frontier. But when the Hungarian frontier with Austria was opened in September 1989 and the Berlin Wall fell in November (Sources **B** and **C**), there was nothing to stop East Germans crossing over in their thousands. The trickle became a flood, to the alarm of the East and West German governments alike.

**Source C** A MILLION MARCH TO FREEDOM – *The Sunday Times*, 12 November 1989

More than one million Germans from East and West held the world's biggest non-stop party in Berlin yesterday, as their sober leaders tried vainly to dampen the euphoria by warning that a united Germany was not yet on the political agenda. East Berliners poured into West Berlin to celebrate their liberty on free beer and wine, and queues of East German cars stretched back 40 miles from the border. Berlin was a city reborn. The party clogged the streets. Teams were knocking down the wall. Every small piece chipped off was seized as a souvenir. 'I just cannot believe it,' one young man shouted to no-one in particular, 'Are we free, or is this a dream.'

Peter Millar and Richard Ellis in *The Sunday Times* 12 November, 1989

The migration of skilled workers, plus the growing demand for German unity, put pressure on both governments. In March 1990, free elections in East Germany gave the Alliance for Germany Party an easy victory. Talks on sharing the same currency were opened, to try to stem the flow of emigrants. Some Western leaders, such as Britain's Margaret Thatcher, had their doubts about German reunification, fearing the dominance of a unified Germany in Europe. Many

East Germans worried, too (Sources **G** and **H**). Gorbachev shared some of these fears but when NATO changed its strategy, the Russians agreed that reunification could go ahead. On 12 September 1990, the four Allied Powers – the UK, the USA, the USSR and France – signed a treaty bringing an end to the post-war occupation of Germany. Reunification came at last, at midnight, on 3 October 1990 (Sources **D** and **E**).

**Source D**  GERMANY CELEBRATES AS ONE from *The Independent*, 3 October 1990

▼

Berlin was engulfed in a sea of black, red and gold flags last night as a million people converged on the city to celebrate the birth of the new, united Germany. An emotional Chancellor Helmut Kohl hailed it as a 'day of joy for all Germans'. Mr Kohl has been one of the main driving forces behind the unity process which developed an unstoppable momentum after the fall of the Berlin Wall last November and the dramatic collapse of East Germany's former communist regime. The Chancellor nevertheless acknowledged that unity would not have been possible without the full backing of the international community. He warmly thanked the Soviet President, Mikhail Gorbachev, for his part in making German unification possible, and paid a special tribute to the three Western Allies – the United States, Great Britain and France – for protecting the freedom of West Berlin for more than four decades.

**Source E**  By Lothar de Maiziere, the last East German Prime Minister, from *The Independent*, 3 October 1990

▼

We all have reason to be happy and thankful. We are leaving behind a system which called itself democratic but was not democratic. Unity will of course bring many difficulties, but we have the great advantage of having a strong partner on our side.

**Source F**  Message sent to Chancellor Kohl from the Yad Vashem national shrine, Israel, in *The Independent*, 3 October 1990

▼

We are filled with deep anxiety since it was a united Germany, under the Nazi rule, which brought upon the Jewish people the most horrendous tragedy of this century.

**Source G**  An older East German woman interviewed on television in 1990

▼

We haven't been asleep for forty years. We've worked hard, produced things. I don't know what they want. You hear things aren't so good in the West either. OK the shops are full, that's nice, but what about high rents and unemployment, and so on? The gap between rich and poor is much greater than here.

Translation of an interview for *Last Year in Germany*, Channel 4 television programme, 28 October 1991

**Source H**  East German teenager interviewed on television in 1990

▼

We'll be bottom of the heap if Germany's reunified. Only those with the right profession will earn anything. Here you work from 6 am to 4 pm and what do you get? Nothing. With reunification, everyone will be on the street. There are already enough unemployed there.

Translation of an interview for *Last Year in Germany*

**Source I**  An East German woman in West Berlin interviewed on television in 1990

▼

I just can't cope with it – all the free choice of where you work, etc. Over there you had no choice. In catering it was all organised and secure. The state catering service employed you and decided where you worked.

Translation of an interview for *Last Year in Germany*

---

1  Look at Source **A**. Why were communist leaders helpless when faced by crowds of this magnitude?

2  Why did East Germans emigrate to the West?

3  Draw a flow diagram like the one on pages 14–15 to show the key events which led to the reunification of Germany in 1990.

4  Who feared a united Germany: **a)** because of its possible effect on Europe as a whole; **b)** because of Germany's previous record when united, and **c)** because it would mean large-scale unemployment in East Germany?

5  Use the sources to write an account saying how and why people differed in their attitudes to German reunification.

*Questions*

# *The Velvet Revolution, 1989*

▶ **How and why did Czechoslovakia gain its freedom in 1989?**

**Source A** Memorial in Wenceslas Square, Prague, to 'Victims of Communism' ('Obetem Komunismu'). Jan Palach and Jan Zajic set themselves on fire to protest against the Soviet invasion in 1968 (see page 166).

Illegal political groups and underground newspapers kept the spirit of the Prague Spring alive in Czechoslovakia after 1968. About 250 dissidents, the Charter 77 group, signed a document in 1977 re-affirming these beliefs. Their most famous member, the playwright Vaclav Havel, was sent to prison.

Renewed hope of a more liberal government came again in 1987 when Mikhail Gorbachev (see page 176) visited Prague. His visit was not welcomed by the government, but was greeted warmly by the Czechs who lined the streets. When asked what difference there was between 'perestroika' and the Prague Spring, Gorbachev's spokesman said 'nineteen years'. In other words, Gorbachev could see little difference between his ideas and those of Dubcek in 1968.

In January 1989, a crowd of people chanting, 'Gorbachev! Gorbachev!' gathered in Prague's Wenceslas Square to commemorate the twentieth anniversary of the death of Jan Palach (see page 167). Predictably, the Czech security police – the StB – broke up the meeting with great brutality. Yet a similar ceremony on 17 November 1989 was allowed to go ahead. But by this time (page 177), events in Eastern Europe were moving at lightning speed – as you can see from the diary on the right.

**Source B** Alexander Dubcek in Wenceslas Square, 24 November 1989

▼

We have been too long in darkness. Once already we have been in the light, and we want it again. The new Civic Forum is being consolidated with a platform of new democratic reform. Here today, in front of you citizens and workers of Prague, I declare my support for it.

*Diary of the*

**Friday, 17 November 1989**
Thousands of students hold a peaceful demonstration to commemorate Jan Opletal, killed by the Nazis in 1939. Later, they are brutally attacked by the StB after being led up a Prague side street by an undercover police officer posing as a student. Over 500 demonstrators are injured.

**Saturday, 18 November 1989**
Street posters inflame Czechs when they read about the demonstration. Rumours spread that a student called Martin Smid was beaten to death by police. People are outraged. Huge crowds gather in the streets of Prague.

**Sunday, 19 November 1989**
Vaclav Havel helps to found Civic Forum – a group of dissidents set up to co-ordinate the growing opposition to the communist government.

**Monday, 20 November to Wednesday 22 November 1989**
Student banners with slogans, such as, 'Workers, come and join us' and 'Czech nation wake up', are everywhere in the city. Hundreds of thousands of protesters, wearing badges and singing freedom songs, gather in Wenceslas Square. Schools, universities and actors go on strike.

**Tuesday, 21 November 1989**
Members of the Politburo cannot make up their minds what to do. Some, like Milos Jakes, First Secretary, want to use force to restore order. Others say this will only make matters worse and doubt whether the soldiers will obey orders anyway. No one wants to see bloodshed. So they do nothing!

**Thursday 23 November 1989**
For the first time, factory workers join demonstrators in

**Source C** Outside a large factory in Prague

*MIROSLAV STEPAN (addressing workers):* It is inconceivable that in any country fifteen-year-old kids should be deciding when the president should or should not resign, or who should be president. But unfortunately this is what has happened.
*CHANTING WORKERS:* We're not kids! We're not kids! We're not kids! Resign! Resign! Resign!'

Based on news footage from the Channel 4 documentary *Twelve Days in November*, televised on 25 February 1990, and the BBC2 documentary *Czech-mate*, televised on 30 May 1990

The Czech government later tried to find out the truth about 17 November 1989. They discovered that 'Martin Smid' was an undercover StB officer who had faked his own death. Why he did so remains a mystery. Some think there was a conspiracy planned by StB supporters of Gorbachev who assumed that the death of a student would so enrage Czechs that the hardliners would have to give way to the liberals in the communist party.

**Source D** Headlines in *The Independent* daily newspaper in 1989

**A**

# Czech leader quits
## Cheering crowd hail resignation of Jakes and entire Politburo

**B**

# Communist rule ended in Czechoslovakia
## Havel tipped for President as Husak goes and reforming government takes office

**C**

Dubcek addresses Bratislava rally as workers join 500,000 Prague demonstrators

# Czech protests gain momentum

**D**

Party's hold on power crumbling as up to 200,000 march through Prague to demand democracy

# Czechs tell Communists to go

## Velvet Revolution

*Wenceslas Square. Alexander Dubcek, hero of 1968, addresses a huge crowd in Bratislava.*

**Friday, 24 November 1989**
*Over 500,000 people (half the population of Prague) fill Wenceslas Square. They listen to Alexander Dubcek (Source B). People dance for joy when news comes through that Milos Jakes and other party leaders have resigned.*

**Saturday, 25 November 1989**
*Prime Minister Ladislav Adamec meets Vaclav Havel and addresses a vast crowd of a million people at Letenska Plan. Shouts of 'Long live Adamec' turn to boos and whistles when he offers to reform the communist party but seems to ignore demands for 'Freedom', 'Free Speech!' and 'Free Elections!'*

**Monday, 27 November 1989**
*Workers throughout Czechoslovakia join a two-hour general strike called in support of the students. Motorists show their support by waving flags and sounding horns. Miroslav Stepan, Prague party boss, tries to persuade workers not to join the strike (Source C).*

**Tuesday, 28 November 1989**
*Ladislav Adamec bows to pressure. He agrees to form a joint government with Civic Forum but later resigns when Gorbachev fails to back him.*

**Sunday, 10 December 1989**
*Czechoslovakia's first non-communist government in 40 years takes power.*

**Friday, 29 December 1989**
*Vaclav Havel is elected President of a free Czechoslovakia.*

1 Look at Source **D**. Place the four headlines, A, B, C and D, in chronological order. For each one, say which issue of *The Independent* you think it came from: 21, 24, 25 November or 11 December.

2 What mistake did Miroslav Stepan (Source **C**) make when addressing the factory workers? Use the sources and quotations on these pages to describe the feelings most Czechs had about Communism in their country.

3 If there was a conspiracy, when and why did it go wrong?

4 Why did the Czech liberals succeed in 1989 where their predecessors had failed in 1968? Why was it called 'The Velvet Revolution'?

5 What role did Mikhail Gorbachev play in the Czech revolution?

*Questions*

## The Second Russian Revolution: 1991

 **What was the Second Russian Revolution, what were its causes and what were its effects?**

### Opposition to Gorbachev

In 1990, Gorbachev's reforms continued to gather pace and in February, the ruling Communist Party even agreed to give up its leading role in Soviet society to allow other political parties to contest elections. Gorbachev was always the communist, however, seeking to reform the communist party from within. But by the start of 1991 he was under attack from both the left and the right. Old-style, hard-line communists in the government, such as Valentin Pavlov, the Prime Minister, KGB Head Vladimir Kryuchkov and Dmitri Yazov, the Defence Minister, said he had gone too far. Others, such as Boris Yeltsin, leader of the Russian Republic, were equally convinced he had not gone far enough along the road to democracy and a free-market economy like those in the West.

In February 1991, Yeltsin openly attacked Gorbachev and sparked off a massive demonstration which led Gorbachev to call in troops. The risk of a dangerous confrontation evaporated when the Government backed down but it left Yeltsin in a strong position, especially since food shortages had already dented Gorbachev's image as a popular leader. When Siberian coal miners went on strike demanding greater political freedom, it was Yeltsin, not Gorbachev, who persuaded them to go back to work. Attempts by hard-liners to get Gorbachev to resign as Secretary of the Communist Party for his failure to clamp down on the miners were resisted (Source **B**).

**Source A** Like most leaders, Gorbachev wanted colleagues who supported his policies. He got rid of one of the last of the old guard in September 1988 when the Cold War veteran Andrei Gromyko was voted out of his job as Soviet President by the man with the 'nice smile and iron teeth'!

**Source B** Mikhail Gorbachev interviewed for BBC Television in 1991

I couldn't let it [*the Communist Party*] out of my control. It was the most powerful organisation in the country. It touched every aspect of life. If I let it go, there'd be no more perestroika.

Transcript of an interview for *The Second Russian Revolution: Countdown to a Coup*, BBC2 television programme, transmitted 23 November 1991

### The Union Treaty

Matters came to a head in the summer when Gorbachev initiated a conference to resolve the problem of how best to hold the Union of Socialist Soviet Republics together. Boris Yeltsin as leader of the Russian Republic had already given his backing to the Baltic republics of Lithuania, Latvia and Estonia, whose leaders were seeking independence from the Soviet Union. Hard-liners were appalled. 'The Union has to be preserved,' said Anatoly Lukyanov, Speaker of the Soviet Parliament. Although his own ministers expressed dissent as well, Gorbachev let them keep their jobs even though he knew the strength of opposition to the new Union Treaty – an agreement to loosen the ties between the republics and grant them considerable independence. Kryuchkov opposed it, saying: 'Only a single, powerful Soviet Union can protect us.'

**Source C** Mikhail Gorbachev with his wife Raisa

## Gorbachev is arrested.

On 2 August 1991, Gorbachev announced that the Union Treaty would be signed on the 20th of the month – and then went on holiday to the Crimea – a risky thing to do in the circumstances (Source **D**). In his absence, Pavlov, Yazov, Kryuchkov and Vice-President Gennady Yanayev met in secret and agreed to send a high-level delegation to the Crimea, backed by soldiers, to tell Gorbachev to resign. When Gorbachev refused, he and Raisa were placed under house arrest. Their villa was surrounded by troops and all the telephone lines were cut. 'This is treason,' said Gorbachev in a message recorded on the family's video camera.

**Source D** Russian bystander quoted in *The Independent*, 20 August 1991

Gorbachev's an idiot. He should never have gone on holiday. They've done him just like Khruschev.

## The August Coup

On 19 August 1991 (the day before the Union Treaty was due to be signed) Radio Moscow shocked Russians – and the rest of the world – with an announcement saying that Yanayev had replaced Gorbachev 'to prevent society from moving towards a nation-wide

catastrophe'. A state of emergency had been declared and the Coup leaders warned that the laws and constitution of the Soviet Union must be enforced before those of the separate republics took effect. Tanks rolled into the centre of Moscow but the amateurish nature of the Coup soon became apparent when it transpired that they had failed to arrest Yeltsin and other powerful opponents of the regime. A Yeltsin aide said later: 'We quickly decided our only option was to resist.' They were backed by massive crowds of demonstrators who gathered in central Moscow, unmolested by the troops (Sources **E** and **F**).

**Source E** Encounter between a woman and a soldier in Moscow: 19 August 1991 from *The Independent*, 20 August, 1991

'How can you take part in this military coup? 'We won't fire. We haven't even got any bullets. But we wouldn't fire on our own people.

**Source F** Lance Morrow in *Time* magazine, August 1991

Citizens poured into the streets, determined, methodical and astonishingly unafraid. They defied the junta's curfew, built barricades around the Russian Parliament Building, where Boris Yeltsin had organised his resistance. A crowd of Muscovites brought a column of armoured personnel carriers to a halt, stuffing rosebuds and wildflowers into gun barrels. A line of women stood ready to face down troops with a single banner: SOLDIERS: DON'T SHOOT MOTHERS AND SISTERS. Clearly the soldiers had orders not to use force. Tank drivers, even paratroop commanders, defected to the resistance. Miners went on strike.

Standing on a tank in front of The White House (the Russian Parliament building in Moscow), Yeltsin urged Russians to support Gorbachev against his opponents (Source **G**).

**Source G** Boris Yeltsin's appeal to the Russian people

Citizens of Russia. On the night of 18 August 1991, the lawfully-elected President was deposed. Let us be clear. We are dealing with a reactionary, unconstitutional coup. I call on all soldiers. Take no part in this reactionary coup! We call for a general strike.

Transcript from *The Second Russian Revolution: Countdown to a Coup*

## A shock to the world

News of the Coup appalled the world after six worry-free years of glasnost and perestroika (Source **H**).

**Source H** Headlines in *The Independent*, 20 August 1991

# YELTSIN DEFIES COUP 'TERROR'

## We won't fire on our own people

# WORLD REACTS WITH OUTRAGE AND FEAR

## WESTERN STOCK MARKETS TUMBLE

YELTSIN WARNS OF A 'REIGN OF TERROR'

Experts warn of purges, trials and civil war

# OLD ALLIES SHIVER AS 'ICE AGE' POLITICS RETURN

## KOHL WARNS AGAINST FORCE AND 'SPILLING OF BLOOD'

Germans lead scramble to pull out their loans

## SECRET CHINESE GLEE AS MAO'S MAXIM LIVES ON

[Mao said *'political power comes from the barrel of a gun'*]

## The Coup collapses

Although there were one or two clashes between troops and civilian demonstrators, only three people were killed. The Minister of Defence, Dmitri Yazov, insisted: 'We will do everything to ensure force isn't used against civilians.' When Yanayev was seen on television visibly shaking, however, Gorbachev and Yeltsin supporters could sense that the Coup leaders were faltering. A KGB plan to attack the White House collapsed when the officers involved refused to take part. Afterwards, Yazov explained why the Coup had failed (Source **I**).

**Source I** By Marshal Yazov

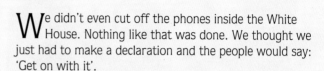

We didn't even cut off the phones inside the White House. Nothing like that was done. We thought we just had to make a declaration and the people would say: 'Get on with it'.

Transcript of his official interrogation for *The Second Russian Revolution: Countdown to a Coup*

Unable to put down the rebellion with force and faced by defiant crowds, the Coup leaders flew back to the Crimea to see Gorbachev. Yeltsin supporters, worried the Coup leaders would assassinate the President, followed them in haste and returned to Moscow in triumph with the Gorbachevs. Meanwhile, the leaders of the Coup were arrested and sent to jail. At least two of the men involved committed suicide.

## The Soviet Union after the Coup

The defeat of the Coup brought little joy to Gorbachev. Instead of reinforcing his authority, the failure of the Coup brought about his downfall. Yeltsin humiliated him in front of the Russian Parliament, pointing out that he had chosen all the Coup leaders himself.

**Source J** Headlines in *The Independent*, 24 August 1991

# POWER SLIPS FROM GORBACHEV
## THE OLD ACT FAILS TO CHARM RUSSIA'S HOSTILE DEPUTIES

The failure of the Coup meant an end to the Union Treaty. The separate republics were no longer prepared to form part of the Soviet Union (Source **K**).

**Source K** Report in *The Independent*, 27 August 1991

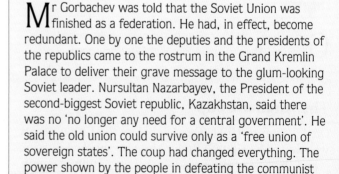

Mr Gorbachev was told that the Soviet Union was finished as a federation. He had, in effect, become redundant. One by one the deputies and the presidents of the republics came to the rostrum in the Grand Kremlin Palace to deliver their grave message to the glum-looking Soviet leader. Nursultan Nazarbayev, the President of the second-biggest Soviet republic, Kazakhstan, said there was no 'no longer any need for a central government'. He said the old union could survive only as a 'free union of sovereign states'. The coup had changed everything. The power shown by the people in defeating the communist old guard had created a new wave of independence-minded republics.

An American journalist called the failure of the Coup a turning point in history (Source **L**).

**Source L** Lance Morrow in *Time* magazine, 2 September 1991

▼

The people of Russia last week purchased their freedom and citizenship. They abolished serfdom in Soviet political life. The event is one of the turning points of world history, proclaiming the end of a totalitarianism that has destroyed so much of the 20th century.

Russia, Ukraine, Belarus, Kazakhstan and seven other republics formed CIS – the Commonwealth of Independent States – in December 1991 to replace the Soviet Union. The three Baltic republics – Estonia, Latvia and Lithuania – and Georgia remained outside the new organisation. Since the old Soviet Union was dead, Gorbachev's position as Soviet President disappeared and he became a private citizen, leaving Yeltsin as President of the Russian Republic with most of the country's nuclear weapons and the bulk of its army – and its problems.

## Tailpiece: 1995

Western experts who had celebrated the end of communism in 1991 got a rude shock when communists and former communists made a dramatic comeback in 1995 (Source **M**). Yeltsin supporters were defeated in Russia and even Lech Walesa was defeated in Poland.

**Source M** By Diane Kunz, history professor at Yale University, *The Sunday Times*, 24 December 1995

▼

Did the fall of the Berlin Wall in November 1989 mark the beginning of a new golden age or the end of one? Six years on, the countries of the former communist bloc have delivered their verdict. Free and democratic elections have brought communists back to power in Poland, Hungary and Bulgaria. They never left Romania, and last weekend saw Gennady Zyuganov lead his communist party to victory in the Russian elections.

▲

**Source N** Wooden Russian dolls
These dolls, bought in Poland in 1995, depict Lenin, Stalin, Brezhnev, Gorbachev and Yeltsin

Questions

1 Why were the communist hard-liners against the Union Treaty proposed by Gorbachev in 1991? What were they afraid of?

2 Use the headlines in Source **H** to describe the effect the Coup first had on Russia and the world.

3 Write a paragraph explaining why the events of August–December 1991 have been called the Second Russian Revolution. How did it differ from the revolutions of 1917 (Chapter 6)?

4 What mistakes did the members of the Coup make in attempting to overthrow Gorbachev?

5 Look at Source **N**. Identify Gorbachev, Brezhnev, Lenin, Stalin and Yeltsin. Each doll fits inside the next largest doll, leaving the largest doll holding all five. In other words, Lenin, Stalin and Brezhnev can all be found in Gorbachev! Is this a fair assessment of Gorbachev and his policies? Is it true of Yeltsin as well?

6 How do Sources **L** and **M** differ in their assessment of the consequences of perestroika and the revolutionary changes it provided behind the Iron Curtain? What are the drawbacks to interpreting recent history?

# 15 World issues: 1945–95

## The emergence of China

 **What were some of the main issues facing the world after the end of the Second World War?**

**Source A** Red Guards reading the thoughts of Chairman Mao. Mao Zedong's 'Thoughts' were published in a 'little red book' which everyone in China carried with them during the Cultural Revolution in the 1960s

### The emergence of China

Mao Zedong's proclamation of a People's Republic in October 1949, signalled to the world the emergence of China as one of the world's most powerful states. Dealing with China became an issue for both the USA and USSR. You can see a brief note of the events which led up to this and the subsequent history of China in Source **B**.

**Source B** Red China: 1945–95

**Source C** The Cultural Revolution by a Chinese official

You can't imagine how exciting it all was. Every morning, you came to your office. You could hardly wait to get there to see what was new, to see what the new posters said. You never knew when you yourself might be attacked. It was a continuous fever. Everyone was swept up in it. Something was happening all the time. It was a wonderful experience. It was the great experience of my life. Now I know what life in China means.

Extract from *To Peking – and Beyond*, by Harrison E. Salisbury, Arrow Books, 1973

**1945–8** *Civil war* between Mao Zedong's communists and Chiang Kaishek's Nationalist government. The communists are more popular with the people. They redistribute land among the peasants in the areas they occupy.

**1949** The Nationalist opposition crumbles. China becomes the People's Republic. The defeated Nationalists escape to Taiwan.

**1950s** Mao follows Stalin in developing heavy industry first – under a Five Year Plan – and reorganising the countryside into collective farms.

**1957** Mao calls for open discussion. 'Let a hundred flowers blossom and a hundred schools of thought compete,' he writes. But the scheme is abandoned when a large number of criticisms are made.

**1958** 'The Great Leap Forward'. Huge communes are formed by merging collective farms. Local communities set up workshops and even build backyard iron furnaces to produce the goods and raw materials China needs.

**1960** Relations with Russia deteriorate when Mao accuses Khruschev of 'revisionism' (failing to adhere to strict communist principles).

**1965–9** *The Cultural Revolution*. Mao rekindles the revolutionary spirit (Source **C**). Young people, organised as Red Guards (Source **A**), denounce 'false communists'. Intellectuals, officials and experts are sent into the fields to

do manual labour 'to get back to Marxist and Maoist fundamentals'.

**1970s** Clashes along the Soviet border. China seeks friendship with the USA.

**1976** Mao Zedong dies. His successors open up China to foreigners and introduce Western ideas.

**1984** Deng Xiaoping leads the new China. Responsibility System introduced – giving peasants the responsibility of planning and cultivating their own plots. Private businesses are encouraged. China begins to develop on Western lines.

**1989** Gorbachev visits China. Demonstrations seeking greater political freedom are brutally put down (Source **D**). The West disapproves.

**1990s** Chinese industry and technology expand at a rapid rate – but China's human rights record is attacked in the West.

**Source D** A lone protester tries to halt the advance of Chinese tanks in June 1989

## The Arab/Israeli Conflict

For almost thirty years, Britain tried to keep the peace in Palestine after it had been put under British control as a League of Nations mandate in 1919 (page 40). In the fifty years since the war, the Middle East has rarely been at peace. You can see a summary of the main events since 1945 in Source **F**.

**Source E** Dutch cartoon from the 1970s. The four Western leaders at the table are Brandt (West Germany), Pompidou (France), Nixon (USA) and Heath (UK)

**Source F** Fifty years in the Middle East: 1945–95

**1945–8** Jewish refugees refused entry by the British because they fear Arab reaction. Jewish terrorist groups try to force Britain to give way.

**1947** Britain places the Palestinian problem in the hands of the UN. Plans to partition the country are rejected by Arabs and Jews alike.

**1948** Britain pulls out of Palestine. The Jewish population declares Israel to be an independent state. Arab armies from neighbouring countries attack at once but are driven back. Arab civilians are killed and half a million others flee from Israeli-held territory to settle in camps which later become the breeding ground for terrorists and the home of the PLO (Palestine Liberation Organisation).

**1950s** Israel welcomes floods of Jewish immigrants and begins to build a modern state.

**1956** *Suez Crisis*. President Nasser of Egypt nationalises the Suez Canal. Britain, France and Israel launch a joint attack and seize the Canal but UN action – backed by both the USA and USSR – forces them to withdraw.

**1960s** Soviet influence grows in the Middle East as Russian experts help to build a dam across the Nile. Russian weapons rearm the Arabs.

**1967** *Six-day War*. Israel, fearing attack, strikes first and captures Egypt's Sinai Desert, West Jordan and Syria's Golan Heights. Arab armies forced to seek a truce.

**1973** *Yom Kippur War*. Arab armies attack Israel on a Jewish Holy Day but are repelled and forced to agree a truce. Arab producers cut off oil supplies to the USA and double oil prices to force the West to put pressure on Israel to withdraw.

**1979** *Camp David peace agreement* between Israel and Egypt. Israel goes back to her pre-1967 boundary with Egypt. Other Arab countries refuse to negotiate. Meanwhile, an Islamic Revolution in Iran leads to the seizure of American hostages in Teheran.

**1980–90** Iraq at war with Iran.

**1990** Iraq invades Kuwait and ignores Western and Arab demands to withdraw.

**1991** Western and Arab armies launch 'Desert Storm' – a war against Iraq which they quickly win.

**1993** Israeli leader Yitzhak Rabin signs historic agreement with PLO leader Yasser Arafat. Agreement also reached with Jordan.

**1995** Yitzhak Rabin is assassinated by a Jewish extremist.

**1** Why has there been almost continuous conflict between Arabs and Israelis since the end of the Second World War?

**2** Look at Source **E**. To which event in Arab/Israeli history does this cartoon refer? Explain the point of the cartoon.

**3** What were the key features of the Cultural Revolution in China? What was Mao Zedong hoping to achieve?

**4** Look at Sources **A** and **D**. Why did the photographers choose these viewpoints to take their photographs? What do they tell you about communist China? What does this evidence tell you about the use of photographs in history?

*Questions*

# Nationalism and independence: India

## Effect of the Second World War

The break-up of the great European empires was one of the most notable effects of the war. There were a number of reasons for this.

(1) The position of the European powers – Britain, France, Belgium, Portugal, Spain, the Netherlands – had been greatly weakened. Japan had shown only too clearly that the European powers were no longer capable of protecting individual colonies against a powerful and determined aggressor.

(2) Many Asian nationalists welcomed the Japanese as liberators. Some even fought with the Japanese against the British.

(3) The defence of the European overseas empires was not a war aim for the Russians or the Americans. When Churchill and Roosevelt signed the Atlantic Charter in 1941, they agreed to 'respect the right of all peoples to choose the form of government under which they wish to live'.

(4) When the UN Charter was signed (Source **C** on page 162), member states agreed that relations between countries should be 'based on respect for the principle of equal rights and self-determination of peoples.'

(5) Allied soldiers, returning to their homes in Africa, Asia and the Caribbean after liberating Europe from Nazi oppression, also had good reason to seek freedom for their own peoples as well (Source **G**).

**Source G**    From a book published in Zimbabwe in 1982

> Men who had fought side by side with European troops, had shared the same hardships and experiences, and had found that bullets did not discriminate between black and white, found it difficult on returning home to understand why they were no longer equals.
>
> Extract from *Zimbabwe Epic*, P. C. Mazicana and I. J. Johnstone, Harare National Archive, 1982

## Independence at last

After the War it was only a matter of time before the colonial peoples of the world sought and gained their independence. Britain's Labour Prime Minister, Clement Attlee (page 140), made his position clear in 1946. 'We do not desire to retain within the Commonwealth and Empire any unwilling peoples,' he said.

Attlee immediately began moves to give India her independence. The main problem was how best to do this. India's Congress Party (mainly but not exclusively Hindu) wanted a single, united India. But the leader of the Muslim League, Mohammed Ali Jinnah, wanted a separate, independent Muslim state to be known as Pakistan (Source **I**).

**Source I**    Jinnah explains why he is against a united India

> Everything pulls us apart. We have no intermarriages. We have not the same calendar. The Hindus consider cows sacred. We, the Muslims, want to eat them. There are only two links between the Muslims and the Hindus: British rule – and the common desire to get rid of it.'
>
> Eve Curie in *Journey Among Warriors*, Heinemann, 1944. Extract from Documents and Descriptions, *edited by R. W. Breach, Oxford, 1966*

Violent clashes between Muslims and Hindus eventually persuaded Earl Mountbatten, the British Viceroy, to urge the Attlee Government to grant independence as soon as possible and to partition (divide) the country in three to accommodate Jinnah. The mainly Muslim communities of the north-west and north-east, 1600 km apart, became West and East Pakistan, respectively, while the rest of the sub-continent remained as India. But the partition line in the Punjab split the Sikh community in two and left millions of Muslims in Hindu India and millions of Hindus in Muslim West Pakistan. It was a recipe for disaster. Hundreds of thousands of people died in the massacres and revenge killings which followed independence. Over 1200 Muslim refugees, for instance, were slaughtered when their train stopped at Amritsar, the Sikh holy city. A train loaded with Sikh refugees was attacked by Muslims. Much of the blame for these appalling atrocities was levelled at the British. They were blamed by some for leaving India too soon, and by others for leaving India too late.

# Racial discrimination: Apartheid in South Africa

**Source J**
Segregation of public conveniences in South Africa

Another important issue of the post-war period has been racial discrimination and segregation – most notably in the United States (page 190) and in South Africa under the apartheid laws. Apartheid – keeping the different racial groups in South Africa apart – meant that only whites were allowed to live in designated areas. Many public facilities, such as hospitals, schools, ambulances, buses and beaches, were segregated for use by Whites Only or Non-Whites (Source **J**). What was even worse, only whites were allowed to vote, so blacks had no legal way of redressing these wrongs (Source **K**).

**Source K** Nelson Mandela in Court in 1962

Why is it that in this courtroom I face a white magistrate, am confronted by a white prosecutor, and escorted into the dock by a white orderly? Can anyone honestly and seriously suggest that in this type of atmosphere the scales of justice are evenly balanced?

Quoted in *Apartheid The Facts*, International Defence and Aid Fund for Southern Africa, 1983

**Source L** The effects of apartheid in 1976

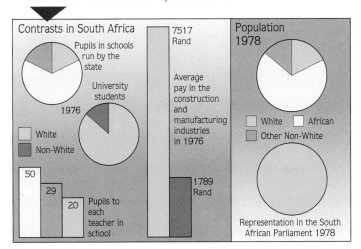

**Source M** Apartheid: 1948–94

**1948** Nationalist Party, dominated by Afrikaaners of Dutch descent, elected to power on a policy of apartheid.
**1949** Mixed marriages between races forbidden by law.
**1952** Chief Luthuli and Nelson Mandela of the ANC (African National Congress) organise peaceful protests against apartheid.
**1959** Government starts a policy of segregating blacks from whites by setting aside special areas – the black homelands (Bantustans) – for peoples of different tribal groups. To enforce this policy, blacks (but not whites) are required to carry pass books confirming their identity.
**1960** Sharpeville massacre – 56 blacks killed and another 162 wounded – when demonstrators protest against the pass laws. The ANC is banned and goes underground.
**1964** Nelson Mandela is sentenced to life imprisonment (Source **K**).
**1976** Afrikaans is made the official language in black schools. Over 100 blacks demonstrating against the new law are killed in riots in Soweto, the black township on the fringe of Johannesburg.
**1980s** Mounting world pressure against apartheid (including a ban on international sport) and increasing violence at home forces white South Africans to have a change of heart.
**1990** Newly-elected President F. W. de Klerk defies Afrikaaner extremists and lifts the ban on the ANC. Nelson Mandela is released from jail. Talks begin between the Government and the ANC.
**1992** White South Africans vote 4 to 1 in favour of reforms which end apartheid. Non-racial elections to be held in 1994.
**1994** Nelson Mandela is elected President of South Africa

Questions

1  What do Sources **J**, **K** and **L** tell you about apartheid?

2  What immediate effect did the achievement of independence have on the people of India? To what extent could this have been avoided?

3  What basic human rights were involved in:
  **a)** Nelson Mandela's statement in 1962 (Source **K**),
  **b)** the decision to abandon apartheid in 1992,
  **c)** granting independence to India in 1947?

**Source N** US troops escort children to a school in Kentucky

## Segregation

Civil rights, such as the right to a fair trial and equal pay for equal work, have been important issues since the war. You saw earlier (page 94), how American blacks were discriminated against in the 1920s and 1930s. Their condition had barely improved after the war. Blacks were anything but equal in the United States. It was worst in the Deep South with its segregated buses, restaurants, theatres, schools and its WHITE and COLOURED signs on drinking fountains, waiting rooms and public lavatories.

Black Americans who had fought to liberate Europe from Nazi oppression resented their treatment in 'the land of the free'. The Civil Rights movement began to agitate for equal rights. In 1954, the most important law court in the USA – the Supreme Court – ruled that segregated schools were unlawful. Some southern states openly defied the Supreme Court ruling but were forced to comply when President Eisenhower sent in the US Army to escort children to school (Source **N**).

## The Civil Rights Movement

When Mrs Rosa Parkes was arrested in 1955 in Montgomery, Alabama – for refusing to give up her seat in a bus to a white man – Martin Luther King, one of the city's Baptist ministers, organised a successful black boycott of the public transport system. It was the start of the Civil Rights Movement. A similar protest in Greensboro, North Carolina, followed the refusal of a restaurant to serve four black students. In August 1963, Luther King reminded a huge crowd of Civil Rights protesters in Washington that America's blacks were discriminated against – and still poor – despite the great wealth of the United States. Yet despite all the difficulties they faced, he still had 'a dream,' he said (Source **O**).

**Source O** Speech by Martin Luther King, 28 August 1963

I have a dream that one day this nation will rise up and live out the true meaning of its creed: 'We hold these truths to be self-evident: that all men are created equal.' I have a dream that my four children will one day live in a nation where they will not be judged by the color of their skin but by the content of their character.

Extract from *The Peaceful Warrior*, by Martin Luther King, Jr, Pocket Books, New York, 1968

Martin Luther King was later awarded the Nobel Peace Prize but died in 1968 after being shot by a white gunman in Memphis, Tennessee.

## Civil Rights legislation

Laws to put right many of these injustices made slow progress through the US Congress. In 1964, segregation was banned at work, and in hotels and shops. In 1965 black voters were protected against discrimination and, in 1968, it was made illegal to discriminate against blacks with regard to renting, selling or buying houses and most types of property. Progress under King's leadership, however, did not come fast enough for many militant black Americans (such as the Black Panthers). 'We want black power now,' they said (Source **P**).

**Source P** By Malcolm X

The black man in this country has been sitting on the hot stove for nearly 400 years. And no matter how fast the brainwashers and the brainwashed think they are helping him advance, it's still too slow for the man whose behind is burning on that hot stove.

Extract from the article 'What Their Cry Means to Me', in *Life* by Gordon Parks, 31 May 1963

There were serious riots in over a hundred American cities in 1965–8 and many people were killed. President Johnson called it 'tragic and shocking' and told the rioters they could not obtain their rights 'through violence.' But the death roll continued: 36 people died in Los Angeles, 26 in Newark and 43 in Detroit. When the black football hero, O. J. Simpson, was on trial in 1995 accused of murdering his white wife, Americans were still divided by colour when asked to assess his guilt.

## The changing role of women

### Women's rights since 1945

The issue of women's rights, as you have seen, has been a recurrent theme in the twentieth century. After an Act of Parliament was passed in 1919 women could no longer be barred from entering the professions or the universities. But it was not until 1928 – when many more women had jobs – that all women over 21 (see page 33) gained the same voting rights as men. The first substantial re-awakening of the women's liberation movement after the war began in the 1960s and 1970s. It was worldwide in its appeal, especially in Europe and America, where it was enriched by the writings of leading feminists, such as Germaine Greer's *The Female Eunuch* and Simone de Beauvoir's *The Second Sex*. The burning issues were equal pay, removal of all forms of sex discrimination and the acceptance of women on equal terms with men (Source **Q**).

**Source R**   Women's group protesting against nuclear missiles in the 1980s

**Source Q**   Women's rights in Britain: landmarks since 1945

**1951** 25% of married women have a job.
**1961** 33% of married women have a job.
**1967** Abortion Act makes it possible for a pregnant woman to terminate her pregnancy legally – provided two qualified doctors certify that her health will suffer otherwise or that the baby may be born with abnormalities. Family Planning Act enables women to obtain contraceptives through the National Health Service, including the pill.
**1969** New Divorce Act makes divorce easier and cheaper to obtain, provided marriage has irretrievably broken down.
**1970** Equal Pay Act guarantees equal pay for equal work.
**1970s** Opponents blame the Abortion, Family Planning and Divorce Acts for 'the growing permissiveness in society and

the breakdown of the traditional family unit'.
**1974** Despite the Equal Pay Act, average women's earnings are only just over half that of men's.
**1975** Sex Discrimination Act makes it illegal to discriminate between men and women, such as in advertisements for jobs, education, employment, the provision of goods and services, selling a house, at work. The Equal Opportunities Commission is given the job of supervising the working of the Equal Pay and Sex Discrimination Acts and bringing offenders to court.
**1985** Women form over 40% of the workforce.
**1986** The Equal Opportunities Commission reports that women still earn less than 75% of the average pay of men.

## Questions

1 Study Source **Q** and the related information on pages 8–9, 30, 32–3, 137. Under headings, such as *Right to Vote*, and *Employment*, write a short account explaining the main ways in which you think opportunities for women have changed in the twentieth century.

2 In what ways were the campaigns for Civil Rights in the USA and Women's Rights in Britain similar? What were the main differences?

3 How far do Sources **O** and **P** help to explain the differences between Martin Luther King's ideas and those of the Black Power movement?

# Index